YALE HISTORICAL PUBLICATIONS

Lewis P. Curtis · Editor

MISCELLANY

L

PUBLISHED UNDER THE DIRECTION OF
THE DEPARTMENT OF HISTORY
FROM THE INCOME OF
THE FREDERICK JOHN KINGSBURY
MEMORIAL FUND

Jesuit and Savage in New France

BY

J. H. KENNEDY

NEW HAVEN

YALE UNIVERSITY PRESS

LONDON · GEOFFREY CUMBERLEGE · OXFORD UNIVERSITY PRESS

1950

For A. H. K.

For when the Gentiles, who have not the law, do by nature those things that are of the law; these having not the law are a law to themselves:

Who shew the work of the law written in their hearts, their conscience bearing witness to them, and their thoughts between themselves accusing, or also defending one another . . .

Romans 2:14, 15

PREFACE

EUROPE imported the idea of the savage from North America almost as soon as she imported fish and furs. If the first commodity had no cash value, it was nonetheless real. In colonial times the reciprocal bonds uniting the two continents were not solely economic. In a modest measure America began early to repay Europe for her gifts of the mind and the spirit. The savage was translated to Europe chiefly by the agents of the Counter Reformation. He assumed his most vital significance in France, at the time the intellectual center of the continent. In that country the *philosophes* of the eighteenth century wove the idea of the savage into the fabric of western culture. Although these men fought against the past, they were its heirs. However much they revolted against the old forms, they could not escape the substantive ideas that filled them; they recast that substance into their own new forms. Thus did they adapt the idea of the savage. Insofar as this book illuminates a debt of Bourbon France to Indian America and of freethinking reformers to men of orthodoxy, its tendency may be called revisionist. But primarily it investigates the growth of the idea of the savage from the physical reality in New France.

I am as heavily and variously indebted to others—while as personally responsible—as was Father Charlevoix, who borrowed more from his contemporaries and predecessors than perhaps any other observer. Like him I make my literary acknowledgments in their proper place. But here more abiding if less tangible debts should be stated; they cannot be repaid. The late John M. S. Allison started in me an interest in the subject and guided its growth through the germinal stages of a dissertation. The suggestions of Mr. Geoffroy Atkinson have helped immensely to delimit the subject as it now stands. Messrs Hajo Holborn, Leonard Krieger, Andrew R. Morehouse, Henri Peyre, and the Reverend Francis X. Talbot, S.J., have generously read the manuscript and criticized it fruitfully and acutely. Finally—lavish, to an extent that they alone know, of their time and all virtues but especially patience—Lewis P. Curtis, the editor of this series, and my wife, Hattie Wise Kennedy, have rendered me services difficult to count or measure.

J.H.K.

October, 1949

CONTENTS

INTRODUCTION: *ACADIA*

ON THE "holy day of Pentecost," May 22, 1611, a weather-worn ship, the *Grâce de Dieu*, dropped anchor in the harbor of Port Royal, a fortified French post in Acadia, on the coast of North America. She had set sail from her home port four months earlier, put in first at the Isle of Wight, and thence dared the wintry Atlantic. There her "sworn foe" the west wind had buffeted her south to the Azores and north among the icebergs and released her to the easterlies, which carried her over the Grand Banks of Newfoundland to drop her at the northeastern tip of the Acadian peninsula. The *Grâce de Dieu* hugged the shore southward, turned into the Baye Françoise, as the Bay of Fundy was then known, and reached the still waters of her destination. Port Royal, one day to be seized by the English and renamed Annapolis, commanded the bay and aspired to rule the mainland opposite as far south as Cape Cod. Founded by the adventurous Sieur de Poutrincourt in 1604, the community had struggled meanly for existence in the stony wilderness and had just survived another hard winter. Its wretched citizens, at the sight of a sail, yelled, danced, and wept for joy.[1]

The ship brought them new life—cheese, brandy, seed for spring planting, warm cloaks, gunpowder, and other goods equally precious. The crew had news from families and friends, from the seaports, and from Paris, where the great king's death had unleashed grief, turmoil, and new intrigues. The ship also brought two passengers: Pierre Biard and Ennémond Massé, Jesuit priests who had come as missionaries to the infant outpost. Their arrival this day at Port Royal betokened an interest in America that ranged far beyond the visible hills and forests.

In 1608 King Henry IV had resolved to send missionary priests to Acadia to assist the traders and explorers to establish French rule there. At his suggestion Father Pierre Coton, his Jesuit confessor, had enlisted the Society of Jesus in the project; and Coton

---

1. Pierre Biard, "Lettre au R. P. Christophe Baltazar, Provincial de France, à Paris," *The Jesuit Relations and Allied Documents,* ed. Reuben G. Thwaites (73 vols., Cleveland, 1896–1901), I, 144–152, 158–160. The Thwaites series will be cited hereafter as *Jesuit Relations.*

selected Biard to take charge of the new mission.[2] This priest burned with zeal; he had a quick tongue and, to judge by his literary remains, broad knowledge. From Lyon, where he had taught theology, Biard proceeded to Bordeaux in search of passage to the new world; but the Huguenot merchants and sailors engaged in the Atlantic traffic boycotted him. In 1610 Coton detailed Massé, whose oxlike qualities of patience and fortitude complemented Biard's fiery nature, to join him, and the two journeyed together to Dieppe. In the meantime the exasperated confessor had obtained the patronage of the Marquise de Guercheville, a lady-in-waiting to the queen mother; she bought the *Grâce de Dieu* and negotiated with the son of Poutrincourt to convey the fathers to Acadia.[3] When her agents had completed arrangements for the voyage, the Jesuits came down from their nearby retreat at Eu to the port and boarded the vessel for their momentous journey.

Once ashore, quickly forgetting past hazards, the missionaries turned to examine the landscape and the "condition of Christianity." Like others before him, Biard called the land New France, "a twin with ours, subject to the same influences, lying in the same latitude, situated in the same climate; a vast land, and so to speak, infinite"; in fact nothing lay "between Guyenne and these said countries but our western sea, at its narrowest eight hundred or more leagues wide, and one thousand at the widest." Three chief regions comprised New France. To the north, along the shores of the great river and the Gulf of St. Lawrence, lay Canada; Acadia flanked Canada on the south; while across the Baye Françoise from Acadia and "still farther down" stretched the indeterminate region of Norumbega. But the name Canada, despite its original reference, was in Biard's time already used to designate loosely all French North America in the Laurentian basin and along the Atlantic; such license, which the French permitted themselves, will also be used in these pages. In all the land Biard saw only wilderness and endless forest, except for the rare meadows that lakes and rivers created by overflowing their banks. The ocean had cut into every

2. Joseph Jouvency, "Canadicae missionis relatio ab anno 1611 usque ad annum 1613," *Jesuit Relations*, I, 207–211; cf. Biard, "Relation de la Nouvelle France," *Jesuit Relations*, III, 160. Hereafter a "Relation" or a "Relatio" located in *Jesuit Relations* will be cited with volume and page number only.

3. Biard, "Lettre au T. –R. P. Claude Aquaviva, Général de la Compagnie de Jésus, à Rome," *Jesuit Relations*, I, 126–137; "Lettre au R. P. Christophe Baltazar," *Jesuit Relations*, I, 140–144; "Relation de la Nouvelle France," III, 162–176.

reach of shore and carved out rocky headlands and islands.[4] In the wilderness behind the sea lived the savages who soon monopolized the attention of the missionaries.

When Biard and Massé first celebrated mass at Port Royal, they noticed with great pleasure that a few Indians were in attendance. Now Poutrincourt had not neglected the religious needs of his colony. If in 1610 he had managed to sail from France without taking the Jesuits aboard, nevertheless he had made a concession to the wishes of Henry IV by bringing over a secular priest, one Jessé Fleché of Langres. In that year Fleché converted one hundred and forty Indians of the local Micmac tribe under the leadership of Membertou, who was baptized Henry out of reciprocal political courtesy.[5] No doubt Poutrincourt represented baptism to the Micmacs as a symbol of alliance, in order to insure the most peaceful living conditions possible for his colonists.[6] In any case, the conversions had remained superficial and unfathomed. Straightway Biard and Massé set out to instruct Membertou; they readily won his friendship. As proof of his love for them, if not his comprehension of their teachings, the chief promised to have the rest of his tribe baptized or make war on them.[7] Confiding in God and encouraged by Membertou, the Jesuits ventured to build their first mission at St. John, across the Baye Françoise from Port Royal.

The Micmacs lived a nomadic life fishing and trapping in Acadia, on the shores of the Gulf of St. Lawrence, and on Cape Breton Isle. Their hunting lands verged on those of their cousins, the Etchemins, who roamed the seacoast from the head of the Baye Françoise south to Mount Desert Island, and traded with the Armouchiquois tribes of New England. Away to the northwest limitless forests sheltered other tribes friendly to the Micmacs and Etchemins. Near the sea the population was sparse. But the Etchemins often ventured inland; and from their base at St. John,[8] Biard and Massé intended to accompany them to make quick contacts with many tribes.

Yet Poutrincourt had never manifested a very warm regard for

4. "Relation de la Nouvelle France," III, 32, 39–67; "Relatio rerum gestarum in Nova-Francica missione, annis 1613 & 1614," II, 199.

5. Marc Lescarbot, "Relation dernière de ce qui s'est passé au voyage du Sieur Poutrincourt en la Nouvelle France depuis 20. mois ença," II, 154–161.

6. Cf. Pierre Biard, "Missio Canadensis," *Jesuit Relations*, II, 89.

7. M. Bertrand, "Lettre missive touchant la conversion et baptême du grand sagamos de la Nouvelle France," *Jesuit Relations*, I, 121.

8. Biard, "Lettre au R. P. Christophe Baltazar," *Jesuit Relations*, I, 179.

the Jesuits. When he quarreled with Mme. de Guercheville over the ownership of the *Grâce de Dieu* and its cargo, his tenuous support of them turned to ill-concealed hostility. Consequently the fathers worried about their sea-borne supply line and, postponing their trips into the interior, clung to the seacoast. Here they learned the Indian tongues and ways. While Massé walked along forest paths from village to village in Acadia, making friends and preaching when it was practical, Biard, planning for the future, coasted along the shore with Poutrincourt or his son. By 1613 Poutrincourt had almost completely broken with Mme. de Guercheville, who now determined to erect a new Catholic colony at St. Sauveur (near the present site of Bangor, Maine). For that purpose she sent out a ship with soldiers, supplies, and two more Jesuits as reinforcements for Biard. The ship picked up Biard and Massé in Acadia and sailed south to Mount Desert Island. There the English freebooter Argall surprised the French, killing one Jesuit, dispersing their Indian followers, and capturing the rest, ship and all.[9] Thus was the first Jesuit mission in New France brought to a rude end.

Yet the sequence to this missionary episode bore such rich fruit that it cannot be deemed a failure. Biard was spirited off to Virginia and restored to France in 1614 after a sojourn in England. He spent his last years teaching in the colleges of his order and died in 1622, after a tour of duty as chaplain with the French fighting Mansfeld.[10] But during those years he did not forget New France and published the *Relation de la Nouvelle France* (1616) and *Relatio rerum gestarum* (1618) as the stories of his experiences. In both books he argued cogently for a resumption of his interrupted work. As for Massé, Argall sent him directly to Europe on the French ship captured at Mount Desert Island. He resided at the Jesuit college of La Flèche for ten years, where he inspired many young priests with tales of the rude wilderness. In 1625 he went out again to New France, only to be expelled by the English three years later and to return once more to La Flèche. In 1634 he went back a third time to his work and labored humbly among the Indians until his death twelve years later.

The adventures of Biard and Massé augured the history of the missions in New France from 1611 to 1763. In France commercial interests proved indifferent to religion itself (although the Hu-

9. Biard, "Relatio rerum gestarum," II, 247–275.
10. Jouvency, "Canadicae missionis relatio," I, 197–201.

guenots bitterly opposed a Jesuit embarkation), and only the wealth and influence of Mme. de Guercheville enabled the Jesuits to set forth. In New France the missionaries quickly fell into competition with other priests, bickered with the secular rulers, and sought to attach both colonists and natives to their own side. As a result, New France did not attain the invigorating harmony it needed so urgently. The English alone derived the benefits and in the end drove the French out; for Poutrincourt, bankrupt and wanting friends at court, soon relinquished Port Royal. The same elements that figured in the episode of 1608–14 appeared again in the events of 1625–29 and the final catastrophe of 1754–63.

I

THE PRELUDE TO THE ACADIAN MISSION

THE arrival at Port Royal in 1611 of Jesuit priests under royal patronage signified a momentous stage in the evolution of both Catholicism and France. In 1575 who would have thought that Henry of Navarre might one day try to substantiate old French claims to America? Or send missionaries there— much less the notoriously ultramontane Jesuits? The answers to such questions lie in the progress of the Society of Jesus and the development of French royal interest in North America.

When Martin Luther hammered at the already dilapidated structure of medieval Europe, it certainly seemed as though the Catholic church would collapse. Indeed, the church had not only built a large part of the structure and furnished its fine, rich ornament; she had then gone to sleep and, by tolerating the decline of morality, faith, and theological speculation, seemed herself to connive at its destruction. The promise of the thirteenth century remained unrealized. The kings had wrested vast powers from the distracted papacy, and the dogma itself left many men unsatisfied. Already, before the seamless garment of Christendom was rent, it had been worn very thin. But the church did not collapse. Menaced by a formidable array of enemies, faithful Catholics rallied to the Chair of Peter and began the hard task of reformation. The church, although at first timid and often reluctant or torn with internal dissension, nevertheless purified her clergy, consolidated her hierarchy, and restated her doctrines. That much accomplished, she confronted the larger problem of reviving Catholicism among the people, of winning back their allegiance. While the constitutional phase of the Counter Reformation came to a close with the final decrees of the Council of Trent in 1563, the propagation of the reforms lasted well down into the seventeenth century. To insure the maximum effect for their efforts the popes enlisted every available person in every possible field of activity. They found indispensable aid among the regular orders and congregations, many of which now sprang up as if ready-made for the new burdens, as older orders had in the past. Chief among the new groups were the Jesuits, today inseparably associated with the Counter Reformation.

As Monod has observed, the Society of Jesus did not originate in the mind of Ignatius Loyola as an instrument of reform.[1] The founders of the order had vowed simply to serve God for the salvation of souls, and in his bull of institution Pope Paul III refrained from limiting their activities. He admonished them to nourish souls in Christian life and doctrine, to propagate the faith by preaching, ministering, and teaching, and to console the faithful by hearing confession—a broad mandate, susceptible of free interpretation, subject solely to a special vow of obedience to the pope.[2] At its birth in 1540, then, the order received no direction consecrating it to a specific mission. But the pope had already issued a call for a general council; Rome, which Ignatius made his headquarters, bristled with projects of reform. At Trent, where the council assembled five years later, three Jesuits occupied places of eminence and, under the distant but prudent eye of Ignatius, guided the course of the discussions. The council owed much of its final success to the determination, continuity, and intelligence imparted to it by the Jesuits. But the church did not derive the sole profit from their work; they too, conversely, found their true mission. Now they bent their hitherto diffused efforts toward a harmonious implementation of the program for Counter Reformation that the council had legislated.

Because it remained within the old Catholic framework, the Counter Reformation could not effect such radical changes as were permissible to the Protestants, who reverted freely to the primitive church. On the other hand, the very urgency of reform demanded drastic innovations and posed to Catholics the question of how far they could proceed without damaging the framework. The Jesuits saw the paradox that novelty-in-orthodoxy presented and strove to evolve a compromise that would adapt the dogmatic and ecclesiastical conservatism of the church to the new conditions of European life. They might well have taken for their mission the motto of St. Augustine, "unity in necessity, freedom

1. Gabriel Monod, "La Place de la Société de Jésus dans l'histoire de la réforme," *Séances et travaux,* Institut de France, Académie des sciences morales et politiques, CLXXII (1909), 617–618.
2. *Bullarum diplomatum et privilegiorum sanctorum Romanorum pontificum Taurensis editio* (27 vols., Augusta Taurinorum 1857–94), VI, 304.

in doubt, charity in all." They dreaded novelty. But they had to face it, for they undertook to reform popular morality. As a result, they were often if unjustly accused of heretical innovation.

Working inside the Tridentine framework, then, the Jesuits executed the papal mandate. Their competence, proved at Trent and elsewhere in the early years, soon disarmed the suspicions that many rulers had at first entertained about the seven Spanish founders of the order. Their abilities in classroom and pulpit as quickly won over large sections of the Catholic middle classes. Yet even within Catholic ranks their compromises and evident ultramontanism never vanquished all opposition; for as they presented their own interpretations of dogma and promoted their own schools and missions, they invaded the domain of older organizations. Bitter rivalries broke out, and the consequent threat to Catholic solidarity was often ominous.

The most serious menace loomed over dogmatic questions, which the Jesuits tackled eagerly since they underlay a reform of popular morality. It was in this field that the Protestants had dealt the most telling blows at the church; but just here the conservative Catholic theologians took their firmest stand. The Council of Trent had labored long over the doctrines of justification, grace, and free will. On these subjects the Jesuits had already begun to develop new ideas, but at Trent the church needed unification above everything else, and they refrained from stating their views explicitly. They relied upon ambiguities or omissions in the final decrees to permit a canonical formulation of their theories later.

The problem was, of course, the old one of reconciling divine omnipotence with human freedom. In general terms the Jesuit theologians modified the Thomistic doctrine of grace by compromise that attributed to God, the source of grace, a middle knowledge (*scientia media*) of things that might occur under any possible or probable circumstances, between the knowledge of present or future existing things and the knowledge of things simply possible. Then they confirmed human freedom. They placed the responsibility for accepting grace that was efficacious (i.e., to salvation) squarely on man's cooperation with God, albeit preceded by sanctifying grace. The key to salvation, then, lay in human congruity with grace—not, as the Dominicans had always interpreted St. Thomas, in the infallible nature of efficacious grace. To the Dominicans the Jesuit theory, called congruism, derogated from the majesty of God; in addition they said that such a reliance upon man rather than upon grace for salvation was semi-Pelagian and thus heretical. The Dominicans also felt that the Jesuits, in their efforts to make theology more accessible to human nature and less rigid in precept and to mold a faith better suited to human frailty and worldly considerations, were relaxing moral standards. Much of what the Dominicans said was true. Yet the church scrutinized congruism minutely and did not find it semi-Pelagian. Furthermore, congruism seemed a very effective weapon to promote the Counter Reformation.

After the Council of Trent forty years of controversy were necessary for a final definition of congruism. At Louvain the theologian Baius, also striving to humanize the scholastic doctrine, overshot the orthodox position by calling grace a natural attribute of man, not a divine gift. The Jesuits sprang to defend the canons of Trent; but they used congruist and not traditional arguments. Though Baius was condemned for heresy, he persisted; the Louvain quarrel ended only with his death in 1589. In the meantime the Dominicans sniped at congruism and regarded the Louvain dispute as simply a bicker between two heretical splinter groups of the theological left. In 1589 the publication of the *Concordia*, by the Jesuit Molina, shifted the focus of controversy to Spain, where the Dominicans immediately launched a full frontal attack.[3] Although all Jesuits did not agree with Molina, his book embodied the most complete system of congruism, and they found themselves forced to defend Molinism for the sake of the entire order. The book, while purporting to comment on some questions in the *Summa theologica* of St. Thomas, so abounded in reinterpretations and qualifications that it seemed to verge on heresy. The Dominicans sustained the assault for eighteen years and transformed it from a dispute before the faculty at Salamanca to a formal investigation before the Roman Curia in which the Catholic monarchs took vital interest. In 1607, alarmed at the threat of a new schism over the matter, Pope Paul V ruled that the issues raised did not pertain to dogma but simply to interpretation, and so put an end to it.[4] He postponed a final judgment, which has never yet been rendered. The Jesuits regarded his decision as a victory: they had given congruism an exhaustive exposition, and

3. Luis de Molina, *Concordia liberi arbitrii cum gratiae donis, divina praescientia, providentia, praedestinatione et reprobatione* (Olyssipone, 1588–89).

4. Cf. Jean Antoine Gazaignes, *Annales de la Société des Soi-disans Jésuites* (5 vols., Paris, 1764–71), I, 695–823.

no part of it had been branded as heretical. Thereafter, it is true, they refrained from teaching the entire system of Molina and contented themselves with the safer, because less subtle, congruism of Bellarmine. Nevertheless, they did not discard Molinism utterly but turned many of its ideas to good use. The extreme position of the *Concordia* sharpened definitions, clarified distinctions, and illustrated how far interpretation of the canons of Trent could safely go. By 1607 the Baianist and Molinist controversies had made Catholic intellectuals acutely aware of the qualities and capacities of grace and nature. The Dominicans had predicted truly: henceforth, within the limits of orthodoxy, theologians took the nature of God more and more for granted and emphasized the problems of man, in his present and future states. Theology became more comprehensible and more practical.

The tendency to humanize Catholic principles showed up even more clearly in Jesuit pedagogy. Before the Reformation the church had not profited by the rebirth of interest in classical learning in order to modernize her educational theory; the medieval curriculum continued to dominate the schools, with a few exceptions like the Collège de France and the schools of the Rhenish brotherhoods. To convey orthodox doctrine to the people and thus consolidate the Catholic reform, a revision in education was obviously necessary. Under the papal bull of 1540, which directed them to propagate the faith by teaching, the Jesuits undertook to become "the schoolmasters of Europe."

Conceived at the University of Paris, naturally the order always demanded a high scholastic standard of its members. From the beginning, therefore, Ignatius had envisaged building colleges in which to train new members. He saw his followers as "rather a small group of . . . gifted, trained university men, of whom St. Francis Xavier was a perfect example; men of executive ability, bound by no petty cares, much less the daily routine of the classroom." [5] But the complaints of that same St. Francis and other progressive Catholics that the current system of education was inadequate soon led Ignatius to broaden the educational mission of the order. In a letter to Phillip II, written in 1556, the year of his death, he revealed his final views:

The entire good of Christianity and of all society depends on a good education of the young; soft as wax, receiving most easily the imprint

5. William J. McGucken, *The Jesuits and Education* (Milwaukee, 1932), p. 6.

of the form that is desired. . . . Thus among other offices which [the order] exercises, not the least of its duties is to maintain colleges where not only its own members but also those outside receive gratuitously from it, along with the knowledge necessary to a good Christian, the humane sciences, from the rudiments of grammar to the highest branches of study, more or less, according to the resources that the different colleges offer.[6]

All of the principles that this letter mentioned were later embodied in the *Institutes*, or by-laws of the order, and finally codified in the *Ratio studiorum* (1599) as two generations of experience and deliberation had tempered them.[7]

Aiming to promote learning and virtue, the Jesuits based their curriculum on a study of Christian principles, of Latin, Greek, and Hebrew. They did not dethrone theology; rather they raised secular studies to an equal eminence. The times suggested the wisdom of such a policy, for the Jesuits recognized the desirability of training all talents as well as the expediency of offering to the rising middle class what had previously been an aristocratic and clerical monopoly. But their studies, while offered in great variety, nevertheless remained essentially verbal; the Jesuits made their most original contributions to pedagogy in their policy of admission and in techniques of instruction.

Aside from the underlying moral principles, Latin dominated the subject matter. The emphasis on Latin provides the key to their compromise: as the sacramental and canonical language of the church, the vehicle of both classical and Renaissance scholarship, and the common tongue of medieval Christendom, Latin represented the blend of learning and virtue that the Jesuits so ardently desired to achieve. In addition, the Roman rhetoricians and orators were the best examples of that eloquence in writing and speaking "purely, properly, abundantly, and elegantly," which a Jesuit priest needed for a propagation of Catholic principles.[8] Finally, the incorporation of the classics in Catholic education undermined the accusation that the church was antihumanistic. With justice the Jesuits maintained that many pagans, so far as their unenlightened natural virtue permitted, had pre-

6. Quoted in François de Dainville, *La Naissance de l'humanisme moderne* (Paris, 1940), p. 37.

7. Edward A. Fitzpatrick, *St. Ignatius and the Ratio Studiorum* (New York, 1933), includes an English translation of the *Ratio Studiorum*.

8. *Epistolae P. Hieronymi Nadal* (4 vols., Matriti, 1898–1905), IV, 653–658.

pared men for the good life, and insisted that such useful writings could not be ignored. Thus Cicero, followed by Quintilian, Ovid (edited, of course), and Seneca, speedily relegated St. Thomas, Peter Lombard, and even Pliny, to the more special courses in philosophy and theology where the Jesuits thought they belonged. And once again conservative Catholics, especially the Dominicans, blamed the Jesuits for making a modernist compromise tantamount to irreligious practice.

Some of the criticism launched against Jesuit education sprang not from differences in theory but, unfortunately, from the selfish concern that older organizations felt for their entrenched positions. Since the Jesuit teaching was orthodox, erudite, and free, it rapidly gained popularity among all classes. In France, as a pertinent example, they opened their first college at Billom in 1556; in 1618, when they finally achieved legal recognition in the kingdom, they were conducting forty-eight colleges; and by 1729 they had one hundred and thirteen. Pupils overflowed their classrooms; their college administrations were generally hard pressed for adequate funds and faculties. The order strove valiantly to comply with popular demands for their services and gladly accepted foundations from wealthy individuals or municipalities when personnel was available to man a new college. But few of their institutions in France—notably the royal college at La Flèche, Clermont in Paris, and Pont-à-Mousson, patronized by the Guises —could give the full curriculum of thirteen years that the *Ratio studiorum* stipulated. On the other hand relatively few pupils desired to go beyond the six years of the elementary cycle of letters. As a result, the finished products of the system consisted chiefly of clerics and scholars. Nevertheless, the Jesuit colleges served a much broader function than training teachers and preachers. They also raised the general level of culture in Catholic countries and enabled the adherents of the old faith to keep abreast of the new knowledge.

However accessible to Catholic laymen congruism and the *Ratio studiorum* made Catholic principles in theory, in practice the Jesuits were still unable to reach the people without consent of the secular governments. In countries where papal bulls received full accreditation simply upon their promulgation, the Jesuits gained admission as of 1540. After the Council of Trent the Society of Jesus expanded in most Catholic countries with comparative ease. But some monarchs, supported by national churches, had wrested from the papacy the right to register and thus implicitly to reject bulls and other decrees of the popes. Such was true in France; there the Jesuits found admission difficult. The Concordat of Bologna had granted the right of registration to the monarchy, whence it devolved to the *parlements* of the land; the latter, extremely jealous of their powers, generally resisted the king. Also, the concordat had intesified national feeling in the church, and as long as Spanish-born priests dominated the Society of Jesus it was suspected of a treasonous allegiance to the Habsburgs. The spread of Calvinism among the parliamentary nobility further reinforced nationalistic opposition to papal decrees. The scholastics of the University of Paris, moreover, persisted in their antique ways and dreaded the rivalry of the Catholic humanists. In a word, the Jesuits were not welcome in France—ultramontane to the Gallicans, papists to the Huguenots, Spanish agents to patriots, and radicals to the schoolmen.

Nevertheless, France had to be preserved for the church. If Francis I was blind to the danger of Calvinism, Henry II and Catherine de Medicis were not. They feared for both faith and crown, saw the necessity of strong rule and Catholic reform, and meant to use Jesuit aid to accomplish their ends. Twice Henry II requested the parlement of Paris to register Paul III's bull of 1540, but in vain; he succeeded merely in uniting the parlement, the Bishop of Paris, and the university against him. These three based their opposition on the argument that the Jesuits would undermine the security of the state. In reply the royal party accused these groups of themselves seeking to undermine the security of the state and looked to the Jesuits and foreign rulers for support of their policy of strengthening the monarchy.

Yet in actual fact, beside the power of Spain or even of Lorraine, the Jesuits figured very small in the ambitious and subtle calculations of Henry's widow—a fact they neither ignored nor resented. Now the pawns of the monarchy, they intended, once the political aims were achieved, to convert the royal power into a fit weapon for their own ultimate aim, the complete counterreform of France. Accordingly, the Jesuits took such crumbs as fell to them, and were grateful. In 1562 the parlement allowed them to hold classes in Paris, and they immediately opened the college of Clermont. Two years later the university grudgingly extended its privileges to Clermont. In 1580 the parlement ruled that they could teach throughout its whole jurisdiction, which amounted approximately to half of France. Civil war again broke out in 1585, and the Jesuits barred their doors and kept off the streets; but they did not surrender gains they had so hardly won.

The accession of Henry IV seemed to forebode repression for the Jesuits, if not their expulsion from France. But they had already proved their usefulness to the monarchy, and the astute Bourbon realized he could not afford to throw away such a valuable ally. Except for banishing the Jesuits from the diocese of Paris (1595–1603) under public pressure, the king sponsored them with great energy. For them he pried open the parliamentary jurisdictions of Guyenne, Languedoc, and Burgundy. Twice he pleaded their cause before the pope in the controversy over Molinism, hinting that a judgment against the Jesuits might provoke a French schism. In 1603 he publicly sealed the Bourbon-Jesuit alliance: overruling the bishop and the university, he brought the fathers back to Paris; he appointed Pierre Coton as his confessor and hence his closest confidant; and he generously endowed them with a college at La Flèche in his patrimony of Vendôme. Now indeed it was a small matter that the Paris parlement refused to register the papal bull. By 1607, when Paul V finally shelved the controversy over Molinism, the Society of Jesus found itself firmly entrenched in France. And as long as the Jesuits remained there they never left the side of the descendants of Henry IV.

Using the plans that his effete cousins had but sketched out before him, Henry IV laid the foundations not only of orthodoxy and absolutism but also of wealth and empire. In pursuit of the latter two he came upon New France, as his predecessors had. There, as at home, he sought to associate any partners who would advance his enterprise, including, of course, the Jesuits.

In the past the interest of the French kings in America had been fitful. Francis I, alone of all his house, took serious steps to establish French power there, and his efforts remained always subordinate to the capricious conduct of his anti-Habsburg policy. By 1504 Normans, Bretons, and Basques had already ousted the Portuguese fishermen from the Grand Banks and built lean-to huts and drying frames for their nets in the rocky coves of Newfoundland. In 1524, on the basis of Verrazano's explorations, Francis I laid claim to the coast from Newfoundland to Cape Hatteras. But he did nothing more for ten years. Then, during a lull in his wars with Charles V, the king dispatched Jacques Cartier to Newfoundland. In envious emulation of his Habsburg rival, Francis expected to win imperial domains and golden riches in America and perhaps find a passage to the Indies; there is no evidence that he dreamt of colonizing. Cartier's first voyage disappointed his king: he found no gold and no western passage. But he circumnavigated Newfoundland, proving its insularity; he planted the cross on the Gaspé promontory, inside the Gulf of St. Lawrence; and—not least important—he brought back to the poetastering Italianized court at Fontainebleau two American savages.

Cartier immediately set out again, and this time he wintered on the St. Lawrence, returning only to procure men and supplies for a permanent colony. By this time his royal master had resumed his wars, and Cartier found himself detained in Europe to serve against the Spanish fleet. In the meantime he was committing his experiences to paper and formulating the first French arguments for empire, which echoed the renewed religious conscience of the time. Cartier observed in the opening pages of his *Bref récit et succincte narration* (Paris, 1545) that the holy faith had been sown first in the Holy Land, which lay in Asia, to the east. With the passage of time this faith spread to France, and now it should follow the course of the sun to the western lands. Then, addressing the court more directly, Cartier pointed out that as the king of Spain had spread the gospel to Spanish America, so should the French in other unknown and infidel regions. Next he described the Indians, and concluded that "by what we have seen and been able to understand of these people it seems to me that they should be easy to tame—with the benevolence of God in His holy compassion." [9]

But the evocation of the crusades and the appeal to dynastic rivalry were well calculated to start a vigorous response in the cavalier king. Moreover, the simplicity of the two Indians he had seen impressed him strongly; in the conversion of their people he hoped to win rich rewards: a harvest of souls, consequent papal favor, empire, and perhaps untold natural wealth. Accordingly, in 1540—the same year in which Paul III was instituting the Society of Jesus in Rome—Francis I commissioned Cartier to undertake another voyage, this time with religious conversion as the main impulse. The king explained his actions thus:

As for the desire of learning and having acquaintance of several countries which are called inhabited and others possessed by savage people

9. *Bref récit et succincte narration de la navigation faite en 1535 et 1536* (Paris, 1863), p. 3–5, 32 a.

living without knowledge of God and without the use of reason, we have for a long time at great cost and outlay sent to discover these said lands many good pilots and others our subjects of good sense, learning, and experience, who from these countries have led diverse men whom we have held for a long time in our kingdom, making them to be instructed in the love and fear of God and of the sacred law and Christian doctrine, in the intention of having them taken back to the said lands in company of a goodly number of our subjects of good will in order more easily to induce the other peoples of those lands to believe in our sacred faith.

And Francis expressed his will to create a permanent colony of Frenchmen, living among the natives "in order to attain better our announced intention and to do something pleasing to God our creator and redeemer and which may be to the augmentation of his holy and sacred name and of our mother Holy Catholic Church of whom we are called and named first son." [10] For the moment the king was in earnest. He named the Sieur de Roberval viceroy and lieutenant general in Canada and lord of Norumbega, granted him a handsome subsidy, and made Cartier his pilot.[11] But soon afterward Europe diverted Francis again and America vanished from his plans. Forgotten almost before it was launched, the expedition sailed west, wintered drearily on the St. Lawrence, and returned home in defeat before the cruel weather and the barren land. In disgust Cartier retired to his farm; yet he sallied out once more, in 1543, to rescue the miserable remnants of the colony. At this point the first phase of the development of New France drew to a close. Francis I had put forth claims of shadowy legality and made some effort to confirm them by possession; but the claims remained tenuous. Also, along with Cartier, he had given to imperialism the motivation of religious as well as economic and territorial conquest—a combination that characterized French policy in Canada until 1760.

For fifty years after Francis I died it seemed as if the monarchy had forgotten New France. Occasionally Huguenot gentlemen fled across the Atlantic with their families to found colonies of refuge; but always a lack of funds, poor organization, or Catholic

10. *Edits, ordonnances royaux, déclarations et arrêts du conseil d'état du roi concernant le Canada* (3 vols., Québec, 1854–56), I, 3, 5–6; cited hereafter as *Edits concernant le Canada.*

11. Raphael Bellamare, "Vice-rois et lieutenants généraux des rois de France en Amérique," *Mémoires de la Société Historique de Montréal,* II (1859), 99.

enmity ruined them. The fishermen who cast their nets in the waters of the Grand Banks every year were more successful, yet they were not colonists. By 1578 at least one hundred and fifty vessels plied Canadian waters annually, and many of these trafficked with the Indians as far south as the Potomac River. But of imperial expansion the distracted widow of Henry II could not even dream. The kingdom was too turbulent and too poor. Thus, when the Marquis de la Roche obtained the trade monopoly in New France in 1578, the grant remained a dead letter.

La Roche had hoped to trade cheap gauds and weapons to the Indians in exchange for furs. With the accession of Henry IV and the pacification of France, such a commerce seemed possible and profitable. Anxious to encourage healthy economic activity, the king appointed La Roche viceroy and lieutenant general in 1598, and reaffirmed his trade monopoly. The royal letters patent bespoke the desire to carry on the tradition of Francis I, "for this holy work and the aggrandizement of the Catholic faith"; but religious enthusiasm seemed secondary to territorial conquest and mercantile gain.[12] Yet no aspect of the project should be overlooked; 1598 was also the year of the Edict of Nantes and of the first French representation in favor of the Molinists at Rome. To colonize and trade the new viceroy set forth. He landed his colonists (so carefully selected from the jails of Rouen) on the sand bar called Sable Isle, one hundred miles off Acadia, intending to reconnoiter a site for the new colony. But adverse winds blew him to Europe, and left the would-be colonists stranded. (Not until five years had passed did the miserable survivors reach home.) La Roche was ruined. In his wake the Sieur de Monts stepped forth to wrest wealth and glory from the ocean and the forest.

In 1603 the king transferred La Roche's titles and monopoly to Monts, who mounted a large expedition financed by some merchants of La Rochelle. Among his officers there shipped Samuel de Champlain, who had originally fired Monts's enthusiasm for Canada, and Jean de Biencourt, Sieur de Poutrincourt, whom Biard and Massé were to meet later at Port Royal. All of the gentleman-adventurers except Monts were Catholic, and on their account a priest sailed with the company. But the royal patents did not emphasize spiritual considerations, still less mention missionary

---

12. *Edits concernant le Canada,* III, 8.

activity. The primary motive of all concerned, whether at court
or in the countinghouses of La Rochelle, was profit. But like La
Roche and Roberval, Monts failed too. Nevertheless, his efforts
finally opened New France for permanent exploitation.

In 1604 Monts invested Poutrincourt with the command of
Port Royal and three years later granted him free and full title
to the post. Poutrincourt busily built a stockade and some crude
cabins and soon brought over his family, a few colonists, and Father
Fleché. But, as Father Biard observed, his dogged persistence
brought him merely heartbreak and bankruptcy. Poutrincourt,
to be sure, might have succeeded, since, unlike his predecessors,
he did not battle the hostile American elements unaided. The king
offered him ample resources and the cooperation of the Jesuit missionaries. But he fatally spurned such assistance when he avoided
the two priests in 1610, and thereby wrote his own doom.

In the last years of his reign Henry IV was groping toward
a fixed colonial policy. While his rule was as personal as that of
Francis I, he heeded the needs of the kingdom, not the whims of
his own person. Hence he championed the Jesuits on frequent
occasions, although he never trusted them entirely. In addition,
the general stimulation of commerce and industry encouraged the
king to venture into new fields of economic activity. For religious,
political, and economic reasons, then, Henry revived royal interest in New France. He had invested money in the ventures of La
Roche and Monts and lost it. In consequence, he was scarcely in
a mood to send more good money after bad. On the other hand, he
could not abandon New France completely; therefore he determined to bring the vast territory more firmly under royal control.

The overtures of the king to Coton for a Jesuit mission in Acadia
represented the first step in the execution of his policy. In view
of Henry's record of largess to the order, Father Jouvency has
praised the king as "ever more solicitous for religion than for
commerce," and not entirely without reason.[13] But it is difficult to
credit Henry IV with such single-minded zeal for souls. While
the memory of his ancestor Louis IX may have heated his crusading blood more than it did that of Francis I, he was nevertheless
more akin to the latter by circumstance and interest: a modern
king, he wanted easy conquests for profit and political prestige.
Yet in any light the promise of New France shone brightly. Henry's
dual course was best summed up by Parkman, when he wrote that

13. "Canadicae missionis relatio," I, 206.

"policy and commerce . . . built their hopes on the priests." [14]
Like the Counter Reformation church, he too, within the compass
of his domain, sought to enthrone authority, unity, harmony,
and prosperity. New France provided him with another lien on the
loyalty of those religious and commercial groups most apt to abet
his purpose.

In May, 1610, the assassin's knife struck down Henry IV and
dealt a cruel blow to the monarchy and to the nation. A child of
eight succeeded the prudent monarch; direction of the state fell
to the boy's mother, Marie de Medicis, the arbitrary and embittered wife of Henry's politic middle age. Nevertheless, Father
Coton still retained control over the royal conscience. The Jesuits
embalmed King Henry's heart on the altar at La Flèche and ma-
neuvered to secure full legal recognition in all France. Finally
they sped Biard and Massé on their way to Acadia.

After she had bought the *Grâce de Dieu* and arranged for the
son of Poutrincourt to carry the Jesuits to America, the Marquise
de Guercheville purchased from Monts all his rights to New France,
including the viceroyalty, and held them for the benefit of the
Society of Jesus. Thus, from Hatteras to the St. Lawrence, America lay at the disposal of the Jesuits—except only Port Royal,
whose lord was a doubtful friend. But the Jesuit empire was as
unreal as it was pretentious, as Captain Argall from Virginia
proved in 1613.

In spite of the collapse of Mme. de Guercheville's plans, their
scope gave some hint of the eminence to which the Jesuits had
arrived in France—such an eminence that the stimulus given under
Henry IV could continue of its own momentum after he was dead.
The Acadian mission of 1611 constituted a bold full statement
of the alliance of the French monarchy and the Society of Jesus.

14. Francis Parkman, *Jesuits in North America in the Seventeenth Century*
(Boston, 1912), p. 131.

II

CANADA, 1608–1629

AS THE *Grâce de Dieu* bearing Biard and Massé finally cleared the fogs and ice floes of the Newfoundland Banks in May, 1611, it hailed another vessel bound to the northwest. That ship was carrying Samuel Champlain to Quebec, the trading post he had founded three years earlier on the banks of the St. Lawrence. In 1613, when the English dispersed the Jesuit mission and expelled Poutrincourt, the banner of France still floated over Canada at Quebec. There Champlain won a permanent foothold for the French and laid firm foundations for the future. Ever afterward Quebec remained the nerve center of New France.

Champlain owed his success in some measure to his predecessors, particularly to Henry IV for pacifying France and reviving seaborne commerce, but chiefly to his own character and experience. He was not simply an explorer like Cartier or a gallant mending his fortune like Poutrincourt or a greedy profiteer like the common run of traders or yet a devout but distant patron of religion like Mme. de Guercheville. He combined curiosity, bravery, a desire for gain, and humanity in a personality that reason tempered and fortitude invincibly sustained; and his accomplishments dramatized his versatility. Born probably in 1567, Champlain grew up in Brouage, a seaport just south of La Rochelle. The son of a fishing captain, he soon knew the men and soundings of French coastal waters. But he did not take up a life at sea immediately; first he served in the armies of Henry IV during the civil wars. Then in 1598, thrown out of work by the Peace of Vervins, he went to sea; but already soldiering had enlarged his capacities for leadership. Champlain first crossed the Atlantic in 1599 in a Spanish expedition to the Caribbean; there he conceived the passion for America that absorbed the rest of his long and adventurous career. On his return to Europe he signed on a French merchant ship destined for Acadia. He first entered northern American waters in 1603 and seemed immediately to divine the glorious prospects of New France.

Champlain's reports on his return from that first Canadian voyage whetted the appetites of the Sieur de Monts and his backers, who had just obtained from the king a monopoly on the Canadian trade. Champlain eagerly accepted the post of chief navigator and pilot in the expedition of Monts, and from 1604 to 1607 he explored every inlet and cape of the Atlantic coast from the Gaspé Peninsula to Cape Cod. Then he came to the conclusion that the St. Lawrence, being closer to the fur country than the Atlantic littoral, promised a higher profit for his employers. Accordingly, in 1608 he sailed up the broad estuary of the river to the advance post of sailors and traders at Tadoussac. There he transferred his men and supplies to vessels of shallower draft and pushed on until he sighted a spot on the northern bank where the shore line offered congenial harborage, while the cliff that towered behind it seemed a likely site for a lookout and a fort. Landing, he started to erect a palisade, dwellings, and a storehouse. He called the place Quebec after its Indian name. There the explorer hoped to set up a depot for the fur traffic as it funneled downstream from the trapping lands in the west, as well as a base for further exploration and in time a permanent settlement.

No sooner had the French appeared at Quebec than the Indians flocked to them, to trade or simply to beg for food. Eagerly Champlain began to barter with them; but he was not content simply to take their wares and dismiss them. Seeing the hunger and misery of the Indians and realizing that a sustained commerce with them depended upon their well-being, he soon conceived the desire to improve their condition. Something more than commercial interest dictated his attitude: his natural human sympathies were also aroused, along with an active religious faith, to which the idea of converting the heathens appealed. He discovered, too, that friendly relations with the Indians depended on the military aid he could give them. Thus very early his experiences led him to consider the Indians as much more than mere purveyors of the precious pelts. Chiefly as a result of his astuteness and humanity the French developed a policy toward the Indians that always remained far wiser and kinder than that of their European rivals. What Parkman wrote was quite true, that while "Spanish civilization crushed the Indian; English civilization scorned and neglected him; French civilization embraced and cherished him." [1]

The explorer's eagerness to trade made the Indians friendly.

1. *Jesuits in North America in the Seventeenth Century*, p. 131.

His manly sincerity increased their trust. Soon they were acting as his guides, porters, and interpreters. Moreover, his armor and gunpowder as well as the storied might of the great lord of France led the local Algonquin tribe to seek to win his military alliance. This tribe and its friends the Hurons controlled the trade routes west; therefore Champlain felt obliged to accept their diplomatic overtures, and in 1609 he sealed his alliance in blood forever. That summer he joined his new friends in a war party that went up the St. Lawrence by canoe and turned up the present Richelieu River to the lake now called Champlain; on its shores he helped the Indians defeat their bitter enemies the Iroquois. Thereupon he returned to Quebec to supervise the fur trade, see to the entrenching of his palisade, and lay out a garden. In the meantime he made plans for the future of New France.

A man of hard business sense, Champlain also had spacious vision. He yearned to push west, tap the very source of the fur trade, scour the land for precious metals, perhaps find the passage to China, and simply see. Even as he looked at the green wilderness that fringed the St. Lawrence, he dreamed of thriving French villages there, encircled by farms and peopled with artisans, shopkeepers, and traders. But for fulfillment all his hopes depended on the native tribes: they knew the country as no Frenchman ever could; they ultimately held the balance between war and peace that would determine the issue of all his efforts. Some of the Indians had befriended Champlain; circumstances made them, not the French, masters of any such friendship. He had to win over the Indians entirely, and not by harquebuses and chicane but through peaceful persuasion. To convince them of French friendship many common bonds of sympathy had to be developed; therefore the French had to know the Indians long and well. Who were these people, then, who held the key to the future of New France?

In 1609 the redskins ruled the bulk of North America. They made modest demands upon the continent's riches, and the woods and streams bore merely transitory marks of their swift passage. At that time Santa Fé and Quebec represented the high crests of European invasion; between them the sole permanent European settlement in the wilderness was St. Augustine in Florida. Except in Mexico, where a higher culture allowed the white men an easy conquest, barbarism and tribal anarchy rebuffed them at the edges of the continent.

At the time of their widest dispersion the men from the St.

Lawrence were to encounter many different tribes, which ethnologists have classified according to linguistic principles into three large groups: Algonquian, Iroquois, and Sioux. Of these the Algonquians were the most populous; the Iroquois were the most dynamic; and the Sioux, while occupying the largest continental area, as a rule remained on the western fringes of the French advance.

The Algonquians occupied, generally, the territory between the Atlantic and the Mississippi, north to the latitude of James Bay and south to that of Cape Hatteras. They surrounded the Iroquois, who had driven them out of New York long before 1609. The Micmacs and Etchemins, among whom Biard and Massé were soon to spend two frustrating years, belonged to the Abenaki family of Algonquians. The Abenakis controlled Norumbega and Acadia until around 1650, when the Armouchiquois tribes of New England were pushed northward and began to assert their domination. North of the St. Lawrence Champlain already knew the Algonquins, a tribe that gave its name to the entire linguistic group. One historian of the missions, later characterized the Algonquins as "the bourgeois of the Indians"; middlemen between the French and the western trappers, they earned esteem for their honesty in trading and their intelligence and fortitude as guides in the dense Canadian forests.[2] Seminomadic, the Algonquins pitched their rude huts where they found beavers in abundance, and then moved off when the valuable beasts became scarce or when famine threatened. Improvident, they rarely abandoned their wandering completely, and when they did they made poor farmers.

Related Algonquian peoples, designated collectively as the Montagnais, also lived around Quebec. Later the Montagnais retreated out of reach of the Iroquois, northeast to the safer region of the Saguenay. There they wandered in miserable exile, "the villagers and paupers of the Indians," sometimes coming down to Tadoussac to meet the French. The Ottawas, another Algonquian tribe, were living along the river to which they gave their name when Champlain first met them in 1615. Later these "good friends to France"[3] drifted further west, to settle finally around Lake Huron. The Ottawas belonged to the Ojibway (or Chippewa) family of

2. Gabriel Sagard-Théodat, *Histoire du Canada et voyages que les Frères Mineurs Recollects y ont faicts* (4 vols., Paris, 1866), I, 367.

3. Sieur de Diéreville, *Relation of the Voyage to Port Royal in Acadia or New France*, trans. Mrs. Clarence Webster (Toronto, 1933), p. 187.

Algonquians. The Ojibway family also included the Miamis, Maskoutens, Illinois, Kickabous, and Crees, whom Champlain never saw. Together they occupied the territory of the Old Northwest. Other separate Algonquian tribes were the Missassagnes and Nicariagas, who roamed over southern Michigan and northern Indiana; the Nipissings, whom Champlain encountered at the lake of that name and who later moved out to the regions north of Lake Superior; and the Foxes, whom Cadillac was to find near Detroit around 1700.

Beyond the Algonquians, as far west as the Rocky Mountains, ranged the great group of the Sioux. Of them the French from the St. Lawrence were to meet only the Winnebagoes, the Assiniboins, and the Mandans. The Winnebagoes dwelt around Green Bay and were thus hemmed in by Ojibways, with whom they formed a military alliance against the other Sioux tribes. The Assiniboins and the mysterious Mandans lived around the Lake of the Woods, and no Frenchman knew them until the second quarter of the eighteenth century.

In the midst of the Algonquians, south of Lake Ontario, the five strongest Iroquois tribes had already entrenched themselves by 1609. Ruling the wooded lakes and hills that stretched from the Niagara River to the Hudson, the Senecas, Cayugas, Onondagas, Oneidas, and Mohawks composed the Iroquois confederation, a unique example of intertribal government among northern Americans. Unlike the Algonquin or Ojibway leagues that functioned solely in time of war, the Iroquois association remained continually in effect. Under the leadership of the semilegendary Hiawatha the five tribes had confederated around 1450, to present a common front of resistance to the external pressure of the Algonquians. The Iroquois had achieved permanent peace among themselves; but as long as outsiders menaced them in the possession of their lands, they waged war relentlessly. Confederation lent their attacks a force far out of proportion to their numbers, which were never great. As Europeans, from Quebec to Virginia, pressed on into the continent after 1609, the Iroquois grew steadily more belligerent. "The first military power of North America," [4] they subjugated the adjacent regions almost at will, from the Connecticut River to Lake Michigan and from the Ottawa to the

4. Camille de Rochemonteix, *Les Jésuites et la Nouvelle France au XVIIe siècle* (3 vols., Paris, 1895–96), II, 12.

Carolinas. They exacted tribute here, alliance or an acknowledgment of submission there; but they did not hesitate to wipe out or disperse tribes that stubbornly thwarted more peaceful overtures. Sometimes, also, they adopted whole tribes or the survivors of tribes they had crushed, to replenish their own numbers.

The Iroquois rivalry with the Huron-Algonquin alliance had already become traditional when Champlain committed French arms in 1609. Ever afterward the Iroquois remained hostile to the French, until the English progress in New York seemed to present a greater threat and drove some of the five tribes back to the French. But in the meantime, throughout the seventeenth century, their warfare frequently diverted the course of French progress in Canada. Occasionally the Iroquois left the French in peace for a long time; but only because more urgent pressure from the east, south, or west demanded immediate attention. Then they found it expedient to secure their northern marches by a "peace." They did not always attack the French themselves; sometimes, instead, they moved against their Indian allies. Thus in 1650 the Iroquois wiped out their own kin the Neutrals and thereby seized control of the western bank of the Niagara River and the northern shore of Lake Erie. At the same time they destroyed the Hurons, whose lands bordered the Neutrals on the north. Five years later the Senecas clinched the Iroquois hold on Lake Erie by subduing the Eries, a related tribe that lived south of the lake. By 1665 the Iroquois reigned supreme over all their neighbors. When the French later loosened their hold on lands north of the Great Lakes, the Iroquois recouped such losses by conquering the Missassagnes and Nicariagas in Michigan, and consequently reached a position threatening Mackinac, then the chief French outpost in the west.

The Hurons, although they led the Algonquin league against the Iroquois in 1609, nevertheless belonged to the Iroquois group. If they were indeed the Indians whom Cartier had met at the site of Montreal in 1535, then by 1609 they had fled west to the lovely meadows and open woodlands lying between Lake Simcoe and Georgian Bay. Here Champlain found them in 1615, living a more sedentary life than most of their neighbors, farming and trapping. Even more important than their agriculture for French traders was their advantageous position athwart the fur route from the west to the St. Lawrence. Sagard called the Hurons "the aristocrats of the Indians": they carried themselves like noblemen and loved war and hunting.[5] Like the traders, but from far different motives, the missionaries also pinned extravagant hopes on the Hurons. Their riches and farming had brought them a higher culture than most tribes enjoyed, and they appeared to be more amenable to baptism. Perhaps their very good fortune rendered them easier victims to their ruder cousins. At any rate, after the Iroquois ravages of 1648–51 the Hurons vanished as a tribe, and their remnant survived solely on French charity.

On his maps Champlain located the tribes whose homelands he knew and guessed at those of whom he had no direct knowledge. On random occasions—at night, when stormbound, or aboard ship when crossing the Atlantic—the explorer wrote down his observations of the Indians and their lands. Later he drew upon such notes for books and for interviews with his patrons to support the policies that he advocated for New France. In Champlain's mind those policies had to implement the three aims—exploratory, commercial, and religious—that had initially drawn the French to America.

Throughout his entire twenty-five years in Quebec Champlain fought for his vision of empire on two fronts. In New France he struggled to harness the passions of the Indians and the ambitions and errors of his fellow Frenchmen. In France he faced the problems of retaining his trading rights granted by the crown, justifying his continued efforts in the face of meager profits and procuring further subsidy outside the narrow circle of seaport merchants. Abetted by the loyal Monts Champlain lost little time in suing for a broader measure of support at the court of Henry IV. Only the central government, he knew, could check the rapacity of individual traders who wanted nothing from Canada but a quick, easy profit and who recklessly debauched the natives to get it. If the country could be exploited without antagonizing the Indians, then a far greater profit than they now imagined would fall to the merchants, like ripe fruit in a well-tended orchard. Moreover, the monarchy stood to gain hugely from a more direct control of Canada; hitherto the king's piecemeal grants had brought him neither money nor glory.

Henry IV had of course already laid the foundations for a colonial policy with regard to New France when he proposed the Acadian mission of the Jesuits. But he had continued to issue trad-

5. *Loc. cit.*

ing patents to many petitioners, and the fierce competition that resulted had not only led to chaos but cut deep into the profits of Champlain and Monts as well. Despite one positive step a comprehensive royal policy simply did not exist at the time of the king's assassination; if he had cherished any such large scheme it vanished at his death. The ensuing confusion of the regency discouraged Champlain, when he next returned to France. But he did not give up all hope. Instead, he turned to Marie de Medicis, despite her ineptness and limited intelligence, for she remained the center of the government. She had devoutly followed the advice of Father Coton concerning the position of the Society of Jesus in France; she had lent her patronage to Mme. de Guercheville in the cause of the Acadian mission. It could be hoped, therefore, that she would also assist other projects regarding New France, for the sake of her black-robed favorites, if for no other reason.

By 1612 Champlain had persuaded the queen mother to grant, and Charles de Bourbon, Comte de Soissons to accept, the dignity of lieutenant general and governor of New France. The appointment transferred the supreme control of Canadian matters from the hands of merchants like Monts (among whom, incidentally, Huguenots predominated) to the court aristocracy, over which a strong ruler could wield a much easier check. Immediately Soissons delegated the actual direction of New France to Champlain, in a commission that the explorer himself probably helped to draft. As lieutenant of the governor he received broad powers and was encouraged to discover gold, other valuable metals, and the Northwest Passage. But the commission was especially notable for its emphasis upon a policy of exploitation that was explicitly monarchical and Catholic. Champlain was directed to

establish, extend, and make known the name, power, and authority of His Majesty, and to the latter to subject, subdue, and make obey all the peoples of the said land and the adjacent; and by means of this and all other licit means to call them, have them instructed, provoke and move them to the knowledge and service of God and by the light of the Catholic faith and religion, apostolic and Roman, there to establish in the exercise and profession of it, to maintain, guard, and conserve the said places under the obedience and authority of His said Majesty.[6]

6. *Edits concernant le Canada*, III, 11.

Undoubtedly in 1612 such language envisaged an eventual liaison with the Jesuits then working in Acadia.

Emboldened by a first token of royal support, Champlain now published *Les Voyages du Sieur de Champlain xaintongeois* (Paris, 1613) to publicize his past experiences and his hopes for the future. He dedicated the book to Marie de Medicis, whose continued patronage he sought for the sake of the salvation of the pagan natives. His constant desire, he confessed, to make the lily of France and the Catholic religion flourish side by side in New France had motivated his navigations and explorations. A true explorer, he admitted to an extreme fondness for entering unknown regions. Yet he yearned to see the rivers, lakes, and people of the land not simply for the barren satisfaction of curiosity but primarily to lead those people to God.[7] Just as Cartier's appeal to the glory of the crusades had fired Francis I for at least a moment, so did Champlain's religiosity melt the heart of the pious Florentine princess who ruled France.

In later books Champlain continued to exploit the devotion of the royal family. Not that he was insincere: indeed, as he grew older, his faith deepened perceptibly. But he worked every available argument for the sake of New France. He wrote in 1619 that he prized the glory of Louis XIII second only to the glory of God, Whose standard the lilies of France followed in the west as in the east. He felt certain that His Majesty approved of such sentiments and would, accordingly, out of his bounteous charity advance the great work that the missionaries (now once again in the field) could perform among the miserable, godless natives. Thus would the king reap his most sublime reward: "The conversion of one infidel is worth more than the conquest of a kingdom"; victories in battle counted for nothing as against the laurels to be won in the missions. Later Champlain called upon the French nobility to assist him in planting the faith. If they failed him, he warned, they would some day answer to God for the loss of a multitude of souls. He felt confident that if the missionaries received the funds they needed, they could persuade the Indians to settle down permanently. Then it would be but a simple task to lead them to a knowledge of God; then also, since New France would have become self-supporting, the mother country would have discharged her obligation. But, Champlain added in final

7. *Les Voyages du Sieur de Champlain xaintongeois, capitaine ordinaire pour le roy en la marine* (Québec, 1870), p. v–vi.

admonition, while French civilization still struggled to take root
in the new land, French greed must be suppressed: already the
rapacious were alienating the natives and thus injuring the prospects of peaceful growth.[8] Whatever response such appeals as
this elicited may be traced largely to the successful progress of
the ideas of the Counter Reformation.

Amid the intrigues of a fearfully distracted royal court, Champlain soon learned that he had won nothing more than a bare
recognition of his aims. The patronage of Soissons and his successors remained theoretical; they themselves gave Champlain
little material assistance. Quite the contrary, for princes of the
blood grasped as hungrily after money as the merchants of La
Rochelle or St. Mâlo. Yet Champlain consoled himself that he
now commanded a direct line of communication with persons at the
ultimate source of power; he relied upon more practical persons
for the tangible means by which to win his goal. At court Soissons
performed the function of liaison admirably; but he died in 1613.
His nephew, Henri de Bourbon, Prince de Condé, succeeded him
and, continuing the policy of Soissons, kept Champlain as his
chief agent. In 1619 Condé, after languishing in prison for four
years, sold the title to his brother-in-law, the Duc de Montmorency,
who held it under the same conditions until 1625. Then Henri,
Duc de Ventadour, a nephew of Montmorency, purchased the
dignity and held it until Cardinal Richelieu abolished it two years
later. Ventadour, a man of great wealth and piety—he proved
the latter by separating from his wife and his titles to enter the
church—also retained Champlain, and his patent resembled that
of Soissons in the powers it conferred and in its emphasis upon
missionary activity.[9] Between 1612 and 1627, then, the governors
of New France came from the highest aristocracy; they were passive; and they were Champlain's. When necessary, he could invoke
their authority to shield his position.

While winning influential partisans at court to check the merchants and further his own broad schemes, Champlain nevertheless still asked these same merchants to finance the commercial
aspect of his enterprises. As he shuttled through St. Mâlo and

8. *Voyages et descouvertes faites en la Nouvelle France, depuis l'année 1615
jusques à la fin de l'année 1618* (Québec, 1870), p. iii–iv, 87–89; *Les Voyages de la
Nouvelle France occidentale dicte Canada faits par le Sr. de Champlain* (Québec,
1870), p. 4, 8–9.
9. *Edits concernant le Canada*, III, 13.

Honfleur on his regular trips between Paris and Quebec, Champlain spread out his balance sheets on the counters and tavern tables, showed off his pelts as he unloaded them, explained away his losses, painted glowing pictures of the future of Canada. Usually he won adequate if grudging support. In 1613 he and Monts organized some merchants of Rouen, La Rochelle, and St. Mâlo, and a few noblemen (including Condé) into the Company of Associates, for purposes of trade and colonization. Many associates were Huguenots, but they rejected the missionary motives of Champlain as feebly as he spurned their money. Six years later the new governor Montmorency patronized the formation of the Huguenot trading firm of de Caen, which soon absorbed many members of Champlain's older Company of Associates. The two groups virtually monopolized Canadian trade until 1627, when Richelieu revoked their privileges. In all the commercial operations Champlain played an important role, not merely as the real ruler of Canada but also as an investor, a trader, and the chief agent of the Company of Associates.

Simultaneously with his quest for political and economic aid, Champlain also looked for suitable missionaries to carry out his religious intentions. He found them in the Recollet fathers. The Recollets were a reformed order of Franciscans, akin to the Cordeliers or Friars Minor who had already achieved great missionary success in Spanish America, but distinct from the latter in that their organization was exclusively French. With the approval of the pope they eagerly consented to go to Quebec. Undoubtedly Louis XIII looked on their venture with similar favor, for although he did not issue them a formal patent, the sketch of one remains, which hints of his attitude. The royal intent was couched in the following terms:

Since we be filled with an extreme desire to maintain and to conserve for ourselves the said title of Most Christian as the rich finial to our crown, and with which we hope that all our actions will prosper, wishing not only to imitate in everything possible our predecessors but even to surpass them, in the desire to establish the said Catholic faith and this to have proclaimed in lands distant, barbarous, and strange where the holy name of God is not invoked. . . .[10]

In 1615, two years after the Jesuits were so abruptly driven out of Canada, Champlain brought four Recollet friars to Quebec.

10. Quoted in Narcisse E. Dionne, *Samuel Champlain* (2 vols., Québec, 1891–1912), I, 409–412.

When Father Denis Jamet, the chief of the band, celebrated the
first mass on the banks of the St. Lawrence, the last great element
of the French enterprise had found its permanent orientation.
Henceforth the term New France meant to politicians, explorers,
traders, and priests alike, Canada first of all and then Acadia and
Norumbega.

The Recollets touched Canadian soil in a much more buoyant
mood than had the Jesuits in 1611. For the latter, three years
of idling in the ports and intriguing at court had staled antic-
ipation, which a foul passage had turned to determination and
Poutrincourt's equivocal reception to apprehension. In contrast,
the Franciscans embarked quickly, crossed the Atlantic in one
calm, sunny month, and basked in general approbation both at
home and in the colony. On their arrival the Recollets turned
to their tasks with jubilant vigor. Two of the four remained in
Quebec to build a chapel, minister to the needs of the French
traders, and visit the nearby Algonquin villages. A third, Father
Joseph Le Caron, set off immediately for the country of the Hurons
whither Father Jamet, Champlain, and a mixed party of French
and Indians followed him a few days later.

The joyous boldness with which Le Caron darted up the St.
Lawrence in a frail canoe, trusting his unknown red-skinned escort,
became habitual for scores of later missionaries. Unarmed and
alone among strangers, they braved the wild terrain and the fickle
Indian temper with little heed for personal safety or comfort.
They were free even though their freedom sometimes brought
death or torture. During much of the seventeenth century the
missionaries took part in the Canadian venture as full and equal
partners—a status they owed principally to the wisdom of Champlain. As a result they could preach and baptize among the natives
without the distracting accompaniment of muskets, trade pacts,
or political threats. When soldiers, traders, or government agents
crossed their paths, the missionaries quarreled with them as frequently as they cooperated or invoked their help. Cooperation,
when it occurred, arose out of events; by accident rather than by
a purposeful policy that subordinated religion to mundane interests. In fact, the quarrels merely underlined the independence
of the religious groups, and as they became more frequent and
intense, they indicated the rate at which the varied interests
in Canada were coalescing to realize the comprehensive imperial
design. Yet pending that realization the missionaries could act
freely. Therefore they could truly represent themselves to the

Indians as simple religious, with no other aim but conversion. Able, as Le Caron was, to give their trust wholeheartedly, the priests won the trust of the tribes; the Indians received the missionaries more cordially, since they saw in the process of Christianization no ulterior threat to their lands or power. Consequently the priests enjoyed a high prestige among the Indians, which the latter (somewhat unreasonably) transferred to all other Frenchmen. Thus the French as a group surpassed other Europeans in the harmony of their relations with the Indians and, through the clearer eyes of their missionaries, gained a more intimate knowledge of the savage.

In spite of zeal, freedom, official encouragement, and a cordial welcome from the natives, Father Le Caron accomplished pitifully little. He wintered among the Hurons, numbed by the cold and baffled by their language. He saw the savage beauty of the wilderness, the rich Huron farm lands, and many of the curious rites his hosts practiced. But he made not even one adult convert. In the spring he came down to Quebec. Le Caron's experience demonstrated what his brothers at the trading post were perhaps already thinking and what became more evident the longer the Recollets remained in New France: the strict monastic poverty, the discipline of contemplation, and the limited numbers of their order did not provide the best basis for missionary work in a far-flung land peopled by barbarians. But whatever the Recollets thought, zeal steadied their determination, and their efforts did not flag.

In the summer of 1616 Le Caron and Jamet went back to France with Champlain. Jamet remained until 1620 to recruit money and men, and dispatched Le Caron in 1617 with two new brothers for the missions. Thereafter, until 1622, one Recollet usually returned to France each year, leaving an average of four to manage the missions. They tried to overcome their small number by the fury of their faith: they built chapels of ease at landings, nailed crucifixes to trees at trail crossings, paddled up and down the St. Lawrence, confessing the French and visiting outlying Indian villages. Constantly they asked questions, explained, and admonished. Two of them ordinarily stayed in Quebec, the center of activity. One went downstream to Tadoussac, almost as busy a place as Quebec in early summer, and often another visited Three Rivers, a favorite Indian rendezvous above Quebec. In 1619 the priest at Tadoussac ventured out around the Gaspé to Acadia, where he tried to reclaim for Christianity the Micmacs whom Biard and Massé had already baptized.

By 1622 the number of Recollets had risen to eight, and they felt able to renew the effort in the west, so suddenly dropped after Le Caron's disappointment. Father Poulin set off for the Nipissings but reached them only after a harrowing captivity among the Iroquois. The next year Father Viel and Brother Sagard landed at Quebec, and Le Caron snatched them away to the Hurons, where Poulin eventually joined them. In 1624, their ranks swelled still further, the Recollets were conducting the three stations on the St. Lawrence on a permanent basis and anticipating a steady expansion; the mission seemed well established. But they were too sanguine. That very year they gave up the Acadian post. The next year Father Jamet died, another missionary was drowned, the Huron mission again collapsed, and at least two Recollets returned to France. In addition, they had run out of money.

Scenting the possibility of disaster in 1624, the Recollets had then sent Father Piat to France to cast about for auxiliaries. The Jesuits, who had gained immense prestige since 1613 and finally won legal recognition in 1618, seemed the obvious choice. Piat applied to Ventadour, the new governor, through his Jesuit confessor, and Ventadour consented to finance a Jesuit mission. In 1625 six eager Jesuits set sail for Quebec, under the nominal leadership of Charles Lallemant (1587–1674), who later became one of the ablest champions of the Canadian missions. In the band traveled Ennémond Massé, glad to go back to the work he deemed so glorious. But it was the third priest who furnished the main strength of the group: Jean de Brébeuf (1593–1649), the son of a noble Norman family, a doughty man of great intelligence and piety. Brébeuf was destined to become one of the sturdiest props of the Jesuit mission in New France.

The advent of the Jesuits seemed to presage a more strenuous missionary effort and proportionately more conversions. But the great influx of Huguenot traders under the aegis of de Caen, just when Richelieu began to exert pressure on the Huguenots at home, had already been making for bitter feelings among the French for some time; the quarrels that broke out damaged the prestige of the French with the Indians. The latter became more wary of dealing with traders, and when the priests themselves bickered with the Huguenots, as sometimes happened, the missions suffered. Champlain strove to reduce the chaos, but in vain; it mounted still. Although ructions among the laymen crippled their work, the Jesuits and Recollets continued their activities side by side in Quebec, Three Rivers, and Tadoussac. They did not all remain on the St. Lawrence: in 1626 Father Brébeuf, after a winter among the Montagnais, went out to the Hurons with a Recollet and another Jesuit. He spent three years in the west, learning Huron and observing manners and customs; but for the moment his eloquence had as little effect as Le Caron's, although he laid the groundwork for a rich harvest of Huron souls in later years. His Recollet companion worked with Brébeuf except for the winter of 1626, when he trekked south to try his eloquence on the Neutrals.

In the meantime, back in Quebec the squabbles of the French factions were jeopardizing the very bases of French rule. Suddenly, in 1627, Cardinal Richelieu brought the dissension to a halt by assuming complete control of Canadian affairs. He first abolished the office of governor; then he purchased from the Marquise de Guercheville the remnants of her claim to Acadia and Norumbega, and canceled the privileges of all traders. He himself assumed supreme authority over New France, re-created a commercial monopoly for the territory, and vested the monopoly in a new company, the Company of New France, or of the Hundred Associates.

In the charter that he issued to the Company of New France Louis XIII stated that he was continuing the colonial policy of his father: counting on divine assistance he intended to lead the natives to a knowledge of the true God, civilize them, and instruct them in the true faith. He declared that the spread of Christianity, the civilization of the natives, and the establishment of royal authority depended each upon the other and together constituted the triune aim of the company. (Thus the ideas of Samuel Champlain passed into official policy.) To insure the real fulfillment of his design the king directed further that New France be henceforth populated exclusively by French Catholics; whether of American or European birth made no difference.

More specifically, the charter obligated the Hundred Associates to send between two and three hundred men of all vocations to New France every year for fifteen years and maintain them for three years after their arrival. The company also undertook to support three priests for fifteen years in each community founded. Each associate was to contribute one thousand livres, and the crown two hundred thousand, to a working fund that would finance the settlement and maintenance. In return the king granted the company two warships, fully armed and equipped, and all New France —from Florida to the Arctic Circle, and Newfoundland to Lake Superior with all therein contained—in perpetuity. The associates could create seignories at discretion; to be valid these needed a simple confirmation by the crown. Until 1643 they received all profits from trade, commerce, and the produce of the soil, except for the fishing of cod and whale, which was declared free to all French subjects.[11]

Through the instrumentality of the company the cardinal completed the partial and tentative efforts of his predecessors and laid down an unambiguous, comprehensive policy for the government of New France. If, as Biard had alleged, Henry IV had said about the new land to Poutrincourt, "Go, I plan the edifice; my son will build it," [12] Richelieu acted now to make that prophecy come true. On the one hand he established a central control, which the crown wielded as much through its financial interest as through the maintenance of the associates and Catholic priests as its agents. On the other hand, he so embraced the varied interests of the French—whether in conversion, conquest, commerce, or simple exploration—that no one entering New France henceforth could escape a jurisdiction or lack a patronage that was at once French, royal, and orthodox. Moreover, he included the Indians: they were, of course, to become French by law and Catholic by religion. In fact, the government later ordered that no legal distinctions were to be made between Catholic Indians and Catholic whites.[13]

Now it remained for Champlain, who as the royal representative at Quebec survived the reorganization, to enforce the new regulations. But for the moment he could not. In the next two years the Iroquois again attacked along the Ottawa and forced the missionaries to abandon the Hurons a second time and withdrew to Quebec. In that village turmoil had broken loose upon the king's declaration of war on the Huguenots. In 1629 the English, allied with the latter, once again took advantage of internal French quarrels: they took Quebec and Port Royal and carried the Jesuits

11. *Collection de manuscrits contenant lettres, mémoires, et autres documents historiques relatifs à la Nouvelle France* (4 vols., Québec, 1883–85), I, 62–68; cited hereafter as *Collection de manuscrits.*

12. "Lettre au R. P. Christophe Baltazar," *Jesuit Relations*, I, 180.

13. *Collection de manuscrits*, I, 70.

—among them Father Massé—and Recollets captive to England. But the English had already made peace with the French before the conquest, and they had to surrender both lands and prisoners. In the end the English incursion helped Richelieu: now he could root the Huguenots out of New France with more color of justification.

A greater obstacle than the English, which finally ruined the Company of New France, was the huge cost of protecting its monopoly and of importing colonists. After the first fifteen years passed, the associates gladly gave over their fur monopoly to the citizens of Quebec, who assumed in exchange the debts the company had contracted in the village. By 1651 the associates estimated they had poured over twelve hundred thousand livres into the missions alone—certainly a long-term investment.[14] In 1663 the company relinquished its charter and seignorial rights to the crown, and New France reverted to the status of a royal colony. Yet despite its financial failure, the company played a large role in working toward the triune aim that the king had enunciated in his charter. Champlain and his able successors consolidated royal authority. Fur and fish yielded much wealth to many investors and brought honest livings to thousands more. Colonists, making the beginnings of a new community life, reproduced many features of the life of old France. The missionaries recorded an increasing number of conversions each year. Even the Indian tribes became somewhat more settled and bade fair to become civilized.

If events along the St. Lawrence from 1608 to 1629 paralleled in many respects the Acadian adventure of 1611–13, nevertheless striking differences between the two episodes stand out. The personality of Champlain, deeper and more versatile than Poutrincourt, accounted for much of the relative success of the Laurentian enterprise. But also Catholic piety walked abroad again in France, owing especially to the work of the Jesuits; and capital came out of hiding, seeking ever greater opportunities for its use. Indeed, many of the true benefits of Henry IV's reign appeared only after his death, despite the political weaknesses of the regency. Thus Richelieu was able to consolidate the interests of the separate groups that had entered Acadia each with only its own limited

14. Ms. les Associés de la Compagnie de la Nouvelle France, "Lettre au T.-R.P. Général de la Compagnie de Jésus," *Jesuit Relations*, XXXVI, 69.

objective in view into an integral policy when he created the Company of New France in 1627. The Acadian adventure together with the first years on the St. Lawrence prepared the way for the great burst of energy after 1632.

III

THE MISSIONS IN NEW FRANCE, 1632–1763

THE account of missionary activity in New France may be divided arbitrarily into three periods. Before 1632 the priests tried in vain to secure a permanent foothold. The period from 1632 to 1685–90 was marked by a vigorous expansion, radiating in all directions from the axis of the St. Lawrence. After 1690 the impulse to expand subsided; the missionaries concentrated on strengthening the posts they had already established. Inevitably the conduct of American affairs at the Louvre or Versailles affected the missions as well as the other institutions in Canada. But Paris lay thousands of miles away; furthermore, the missionaries never acted solely as agents of the monarchy. In the last analysis, therefore, the destiny of the missions depended upon the local and immediate conditions that prevailed in New France itself.

When the French landed at Quebec in 1632 the Jesuits assumed undisputed control of the missions. Had Richelieu consulted simply his own wishes, he undoubtedly would not have chosen members of the Society of Jesus to purvey French Catholicism overseas; for while he relished their orthodoxy and pedagogy as means of stimulating loyalty to throne and altar among the French laity he always suspected their ultramontane tendencies and kept an anxious watch over their influence at court. The cardinal had first offered the Canadian mission to the order of his trusted Father Joseph, the Capuchins, whom he undoubtedly preferred. But those monks declined the offer and recommended the Jesuits or Recollets in their place. The Recollets had already demonstrated their inability to surmount the obstacles that Canada presented; *faute de mieux*, then, the cardinal sent out the Jesuits for their third attempt.

Two former Huguenots—living symbols of the progress of the Counter Reformation—led the expedition that recovered New France from the English. The merchant de Caen represented His Most Christian Majesty and ruled Quebec for a year, in the absence

of Champlain, whom business detained in France. At de Caen's side
stood Paul le Jeune, the energetic new superior of the Jesuit mission. Father Le Jeune (1591–1664) had probably been converted
to Catholicism shortly before 1613, when he entered the Jesuit
order. He had been studying at La Flèche when Father Massé lived
there after his first capture by the English, and heard the priest
tell of his experiences in America, which filled younger men with
curiosity and zeal for the missionary life. Later Le Jeune had
taught rhetoric and theology in several colleges in France. Just
before he sailed for New France he had governed the Jesuit residence at Dieppe, where he must have heard sailors and traders
talk almost daily about the Banks, Tadoussac, or the savages. Now
in 1632 he left his classrooms and oratories for a drafty house
on the St. Lawrence. For seven years he was to direct the mission, and his good sense and diligence left it firmly established.
In addition to his ability as an organizer, Le Jeune also brought
initiative and imagination to his task; the Relations that he sent
back to France contained a mass of information about the Indians
at once keenly perceptive, salted with learning, and suffused with
kindliness and aspiration. He brought another priest to Quebec
with him, and soon three more Jesuits had joined them. Immediately
the little band repaired the chapel that the English had let fall to
pieces and busied themselves with plans for a new and greater
mission.

From 1632 to 1657, except for some Recollets in Acadia (1630–
33) and a few Capuchins farther south, the Jesuits monopolized
religious activity in New France. After 1657 they met growing
competition from other missionary groups, a diocesan organization, and royal officials. Such encroachments on their domain the
Jesuits loudly deplored. But they had only themselves to thank:
they and leaders like Champlain had cleared the way for others,
whose presence became necessary to settle New France completely.
In the meantime the Jesuits had a free hand to carry out the religious task that Louis XIII had prescribed in his charter to the
Company of New France. The international organization of their
order and the prestige they now enjoyed in France allowed them
to tap sources of manpower and funds that had been unknown
to the Recollets. In 1625 Charles Lallemant had already discarded
the inching, piecemeal plan of Biard and Massé. Now Le Jeune,
expanding the ambitious scheme that the Recollets had begun,
regarded the evangelization of the country as one large problem.

Quebec naturally remained the headquarters of the mission. Here the Jesuits stored their modest supplies of sacramental wines, chalices, and clothing; here men fresh from home were briefed before proceeding to outlying posts; here Le Jeune and later superiors received the orders of the provincial in Paris and compiled their reports to him; here too the missionaries retired for rest and spiritual refreshment among their fellows after wearisome solitude in the wilderness. When Le Jeune and his followers had finished their first task of patching up the old chapel they built themselves a residence; for the superior knew that reinforcements would come to Quebec in a steady stream, and they had to be housed. In fact, during his administration an average of five Jesuits came over each year, while only six returned to France and one died. Next, these former rhetoricians and prefects of studies rushed to put up a college; they fondly assumed that the Americans would flock to it for the fruits of European culture. In addition, Le Jeune founded a seminary to provide New France with native-born, home-trained priests. But the seminary did not survive beyond 1641, when the college absorbed it. As the village of Quebec burst its first walls the Jesuit holdings also grew, enriched by contributions of land and money from generous patrons. In time their frame structures gave way to more permanent edifices of stone and plaster, which were proof against destruction until the English bombarded the city in 1759.

As in the days of the Recollets, Tadoussac and Three Rivers still flanked Quebec as advance posts. In 1634 Le Jeune assigned Father Jacques Buteux (1599–1652), who had already met Massé at La Flèche, to resume the work of the Recollets at Tadoussac. Buteux's eloquence and sympathy rapidly built up a thriving mission for the Montagnais. Soon the priest considered founding a post up the Saguenay, whither those unhappy exiles were already fleeing. In 1634 also Father Julien Perrault (1598–1647), very probably another of Massé's audience at La Flèche, moved out from Tadoussac to Cape Breton Isle. Others set up at St. Charles on the Gulf of St. Lawrence.

Like Tadoussac for the east, Three Rivers served as a bridgehead for the west: thence the missionaries could go by canoe south on the Richelieu to Lake Champlain and the Iroquois, or west up the St. Lawrence to Lake Ontario or the Ottawa River. At first the missionaries preferred the northern route, where earlier missionaries and traders had already blazed a trail. The stalwart

Brébeuf himself returned to Canada in 1633 in company with Massé and forthwith gained permission to go back to his Hurons. This time he met with success and built his first chapel at Ihonatiria. Soon four or five priests were out there working with him, tramping from one village to another, which they hopefully christened Ste. Marie or St. Louis or St. Ignace, before they baptized many of the inhabitants.

By 1635 Le Jeune proudly reported the existence of seven mission posts, including two at Quebec.[1] Two years later he supervised the foundation of St. Joseph, four miles above Quebec, as a refuge and mission for the southern Montagnais. Soon St. Joseph changed its name to Sillery in honor of a generous patron whose largess touched off a flood of donations from home.

Barthélémy Vimont (1594–1667), who had visited Quebec briefly in 1629 and had also known Massé at La Flèche, succeeded Le Jeune as superior in 1639; under him the missions showed their first substantial results. In 1640 Vimont reported that twelve hundred Indians had received baptism and as a result were living more settled lives than ever before.[2] These first fruits spurred the missionaries to spread out in all directions. A whole string of priests left Tadoussac for the Saguenay and Lake St. John and ventured across the Laurentian watershed toward Hudson Bay and Labrador. In 1646 the doughty Gabriel Druillettes (1610–81) crossed the St. Lawrence at Tadoussac and set up a mission deep in Abenaki country (near the Kennebec and not far from an English trading post), which he maintained for eleven years. Tadoussac itself became more important, owing to a heavy influx of Montagnais, who did not trust the palisade of Sillery to shield them from Iroquois ferocity.

Above Quebec, too, the Jesuit efforts intensified. In the middle of the St. Lawrence, at the mouth of the Ottawa, stood the island of Montreal, a natural site for the defense of the lower St. Lawrence and the fur traffic against Iroquois raids. Intending to "found a strong colony" there, two of the Hundred Associates purchased the island from the Company of New France in 1641. The associates acted under the guidance of Charles Lallemant, then procurator of the Canadian missions in Paris. Lallemant had returned to Quebec as Champlain's confessor in 1634; but being

---

1. "Relation de ce qui s'est passé en la Nouvelle France en l'année 1635," VII, 263.
2. "Relation . . . 1640," XVIII, 119.

temperamentally unsuited for field work, when Champlain died the following year he went back to France. There his administrative talents found full scope. The Montreal transaction represented but one of his great accomplishments for the missions.

The associates turned over most of the island to the Society of Notre Dame, a charitable organization created by Jean Jacques Olier, the pastor of St. Sulpice in Paris. Olier hoped to found a mission for his priests at Montreal. But at the time he did not have adequate means at his disposal. For the present he followed Lallemant's lead and concurred heartily when the two associates granted the Jesuits a parcel of land "in order to instruct the savage people of those places in the knowledge of God and to attract them to a civil life." [3] Accordingly the Jesuits became the first resident clergy of the new settlement in 1642. Two years later the crown, in the name of the young Louis XIV, added its approbation to the new community "in order to contribute to the general welfare of New France and the conversion of the savages, and since the royal power is established by God on earth only to procure there before everything else the amplification of His glory." [4] Thus, far more than Quebec, may Montreal be said to have sprung from apostolic motives.

Beyond Montreal, Brébeuf and his colleagues labored among the Hurons. By 1640 they had erected five chapels, were reaching about twelve thousand people, and had baptized more than one thousand. [5] The mission seemed to be making tremendous progress. But the French never made the route westward from Montreal entirely safe. Supplies reached the missionaries with great difficulty. The Hurons always dreaded to go down the Ottawa without a priest as the representative of France; in 1644 it took the company of three priests to induce them to hazard meeting an Iroquois war party on the perilous journey. With each year the Iroquois grew bolder. In 1648 they wiped out many villages, martyred one missionary, and scattered the Hurons. The Jesuits reassembled the frightened people only by the most strenuous eloquence and bravery. The next year the Iroquois renewed their assault. They burned the villages and chapels, killed Brébeuf and three of his companions, and captured most of the surviving Hurons. The

3. *Edits concernant le Canada,* I, 20.
4. *Ibid.,* p. 25.
5. "Relation ⸱ . . 1640," XIX, 127; cf. "Lettre du P. Hierosme Lalemant de la Compagnie de Jésus à Monseigneur l'Eminentissime Cardinal Duc de Richelieu," *Jesuit Relations,* XVII, 218–225.

mission collapsed. The pitiful remnant of Hurons who escaped the slaughter fled to their Ottawa neighbors or straggled eastward to a shelter the missionaries prepared for them on the island of Orléans below Quebec. To the immense loss of priests, traders, and soldiers, the Huron tribe had ceased to exist.

The Huron disaster forced the Jesuits to undertake the long-deferred task of converting the Iroquois themselves. In 1643 Vimont cursed the Iroquois scourge as the chief obstacle to Huron conversion and civilization.[6] Already Father Isaac Jogues, whom they first captured in 1642, had tried to bring them to Christianity but with no success. Four years later Jogues returned to the Iroquois, determined to baptize them even at the risk of his own life. He won the crown of martyrdom, but he made no converts. The next years proved only too tragically the truth of Vimont's earlier apprehensions. Finally circumstances favored the priests. In 1653 the Iroquois fell out with the Dutch, the Eries menaced them from the west, and the Susquehanna Algonquins pressed them from the south. They signed a treaty with the French and allowed a mission to be set up among the Onondagas. At one time six priests worked in Iroquois territory. But the Iroquois regarded their peace treaty lightly, and as soon as they had subdued the Eries and Susquehannas they again turned on the French. By 1658 the missionaries, who in five years had baptized very few savages, were living in constant dread of being tortured or left to starve in the forests, and they fled for their lives. Almost immediately war broke out.

Other events beside the Iroquois attacks now came fast to check the continued expansion of the Jesuits. In 1657 Father Druillettes returned to Quebec and left the Abenakis without a pastor. That same year the Jesuits yielded up their charge over Montreal to the Sulpician priests, who had at last acquired the resources necessary for a mission of their own. The Jesuits had already fought bitterly with the Society of Notre Dame over jurisdiction in the village; now they sulkily withdrew to their seignory nearby and watched the new arrivals reap the harvest they had sown. Six years later the Society relinquished its seignorial rights over Montreal to the Sulpicians, who remained lords of the island until 1854.

In 1658 François Xavier de Laval de Montmorency received from the pope the titular see of Petraea and the dignity of vicar apostolic of New France; the following year he reached Quebec,

6. "Relation . . . 1642 & 1643," XXIV, 101.

with a clear mandate to create a diocesan organization for Canada. The Jesuits and the Hundred Associates had been agitating for a bishop of Quebec for some time; the latter had proposed Charles Lallemant, while Anne of Austria had nominated Paul le Jeune. But in the face of determined opposition from the Sulpicians and the archbishop of Rouen (who had always asserted a claim to jurisdiction over New France), the general of the order had ruled out all Jesuit candidates. As a compromise the Jesuits and the court accepted Laval, a member of the great family of Montmorency and a former student of the Jesuits at La Flèche and Clermont.

As vicar apostolic, Laval nullified the unsubstantial claims of the archbishop of Rouen. He also curtailed the activities of the Jesuits as he transformed their missions into parishes manned by his own secular priests. In addition, he stripped the Jesuit provincial in Paris of his claim to alone represent the true religious interests of New France. Yet if Laval's presence deprived the Jesuits of much of their freedom, he did not intend to oust them from their proper missionary functions. In fact he interceded for them often, with governors, Sulpicians, and the crown, and remained a staunch friend of the order until he died in 1708 under their roof. Nevertheless, despite his friendship, Laval was intruding. In 1663, imitating the Jesuits, he founded a seminary in Quebec to train his own clergy. The purpose of the new seminary was "the conversion of the savages and the spiritual instruction of the French colonists." [7] The first function, at least, the Jesuits thought belonged to themselves alone. When the pope created the see of Quebec in 1674, the Jesuits could anticipate being even more closely confined to their own residences, college, and missions.

Indeed, by 1660 the disputes of the Jesuits with traders and settlers as well as the incompetence of the Company of New France made a thorough reform of the government of the colony urgent. Laval embodied only one element of change. In 1663 the company gave up its charter; whereupon Louis XIV made Quebec a province and installed a royal governor and an intendant. He also revived the viceroyalty, as a venal sinecure for court favorites. Although the new government promised greater protection for the colony it centralized control in the hands of fewer men. As a result the Jesuits lost much of their unofficial influence with both colonists and Indians. The nature of their function reverted to the rigid spirituality that had been originally intended; gradually they lost

7. *Edits concernant le Canada*, I, 33–35.

that freedom—often abused, it is true—to go beyond strictly religious matters which had so mightily reinforced their preaching in the past.

While rivals for authority undermined their versatile mastery of Canadian affairs, the Jesuits moved nonetheless farther afield in their quest for souls. For a few years after 1659 the war with the Iroquois cramped their efforts. But then they worked in the old posts along the St. Lawrence, from Three Rivers to St. Charles, trying to teach their settled neophytes French faith and French customs. In 1660 Father René Ménard (1605–61) braved the Iroquois and the portages of the Ottawa River to pioneer in the far west. Ménard, who had also known Massé back at La Flèche, had once worked with the Hurons and spent two years (1656–58) among the Iroquois. Now in his canoe he explored Lake Huron and Lake Michigan, making friends with new tribes, reconnoitering for future missions, and reporting his discoveries back to Quebec. Ménard died on his journey, but he had prepared the way for the far-western missions. Three years later Father Claude Allouez (1622–89), who had served his Canadian apprenticeship at Three Rivers, came west, where he remained preaching to the Ottawa tribes for the rest of his life. Allouez and his comrades explored Lake Superior in the next few years and ventured inland up the Illinois River. In 1670 they established the mission of St. Ignace at the mouth of Lake Michigan and soon revived the old mission to the Nipissings, Sault Ste. Marie, at the eastern end of Lake Superior. St. Ignace, very favorably situated, became the meeting place of the Ottawas and their refuge from the wrath of the Sioux. With the construction of Fort Mackinac by the military, the area's economic and strategic importance grew. Like Huronia thirty years before, St. Ignace now loomed as the western capital of the Jesuits and teemed with piety and optimism. Until 1763 a network of care and devotion radiated from this spot over the vast forests and watery highways of the west.

The French forces crushed the last vestige of Iroquois resistance in 1667, and the Jesuits straightway followed the soldiers into the Iroquois villages. For twenty years they preached and baptized among all five tribes. But the Iroquois remained surly allies and stubborn pagans; they treated the priests as hostages and their converts as traitors. As a haven for the Christian Iroquois the Jesuits built the mission of Caughnawaga, across the St. Lawrence from Montreal. In 1668 the Sulpicians also entered the Iroquois field and established a mission at Kenté on Lake Ontario. These two posts held most of Iroquois Christendom. When the English replaced the Dutch in New York, they again stirred up the five tribes against the French, even using English Jesuits to compete with their French brethren. As a result, the French abandoned their permanent posts in the Iroquois homeland by 1687; their later activities in New York consisted of flying visits from the French forts on the shores of Lake Ontario.

East of Quebec, smallpox and Iroquois still hounded the Montagnais. In 1670 they left their villages around Tadoussac and fled up the Saguenay, across Lake St. John, over the Laurentian divide, and down onto the boggy flatlands that bordered James Bay. The Jesuits followed them, in canoes and afoot, founding the mission of Chicoutimi in their passage. The following year Father François de Crépieul (1638–1702) erected a mission on the pestiferous shore of the northern sea, which he served for many years with patient devotion.

At this very time another event interrupted the second wave of Jesuit missionary expansion to cut still deeper into their activities: the Recollets returned. As enthusiastic and poor as ever the Franciscans set to work immediately. They reappeared in 1673 in Acadia, which the Jesuits had abandoned for greater gains in the west. With their headquarters at Port Royal, they worked so effectively that by the end of the century the Indians were all declared Christian and the country reconstituted into parishes. In 1673 they also assumed the charge of the Iroquois mission at Kenté, which the Sulpicians gave up in favor of a station nearer Montreal. Unfortunately (perhaps under the stress of poverty) the Recollets soon fell into alliance with the governor, Frontenac, who disliked the Jesuits and their ally Laval. Frontenac used the Recollets to counterbalance Jesuit influence throughout New France and installed them in any post from which he could drive the Jesuits.

Around 1680 Jesuit interest in the Abenakis, which had lapsed since Druillettes vanished from their midst, revived. Earlier they had tried to settle some of the Abenakis at Sillery, whither they had come either voluntarily or under pressure from the Armouchiquois on the south. But Sillery lay too far from their homeland. The missionaries gave up that post to the military in 1685 and retraced Druillettes' path up the Chaudière River as far as the falls of St. Francis de Sales, where they built a mission. But they went no farther south at this time; instead, they turned more and more to the western lakes.

In the west, not simply the purposeful wanderings of Father Allouez but even more the daring of Robert Cavelier de la Salle stimulated a rapid growth. La Salle, born in Rouen around 1640, was educated by the Jesuits and had tentatively entered their order. When he took that step he signed over his rights of inheritance to them; later, when he decided to withdraw from the order, he found that he could not recover his property. Embittered and impoverished, La Salle set out to make his fortune in New France. Soon he allied with Frontenac for trade and exploration on the Great Lakes. Tales of the Mississippi River soon fired the curiosity of the two men, and in 1674 La Salle went to France to enlist royal support for a great expedition to discover the Northwest Passage. Since Champlain's day interest in the passage had flagged. Now the English had entered Hudson Bay, and the French court, piqued into wariness, revived its old interest. In 1672 Colbert had stressed the value of finding the storied route for the prosperity of New France.[8] Hence La Salle's overtures found a ready audience at court. Ennobled and basking in the patronage of the Prince de Conti and of Colbert's son, the Marquis de Seignelay, he returned to America in 1678.

La Salle did not find the Northwest Passage. But his first two voyages on the Mississippi opened up glorious prospects for an inland empire, which he promptly christened Louisiana. In Quebec Frontenac's successor opposed the projects of La Salle, who consequently had to go back to France to plead his case. Then the explorer wrote that, while he wished to glorify the king by his conquests and gain the riches of Louisiana, it was primarily the desire to spread the gospel that motivated his enterprise.[9] His argument won over Louis XIV completely: that most Tridentine of monarchs also wished, as he wrote in his patent to La Salle, "to subject to our dominion divers savage tribes and to convey to them the light of the faith and of the gospel." [10] With promises of generous assistance the king conferred upon La Salle the grandiloquent title of

8. Edmund B. O'Callaghan, ed., *Documents Relative to the Colonial History of the State of New York* (15 vols., Albany, 1853–87), IX, 89.

9. Gabriel Gravier, *Découvertes et établissements de Cavelier de la Salle* (Paris, 1870), p. 229–230, 392–393, 364–365.

10. O'Callaghan, ed., *Documents Relative to the Colonial History of the State of New York*, IX, 225.

viceroy of North America. Thus the task of consummating the grand design of Champlain fell to La Salle.

But La Salle was neither so lucky nor so astute as Champlain— nor so free in his actions. The new viceroy left France in 1686 and steered for the mouth of the Mississippi. In the Caribbean he fell ill of fever, his men quarreled among themselves, and some deserted him. Finally La Salle reached the mainland in 1687, but he had misjudged his course and landed several miles west of the river. Still dwindling, his party struggled northeastward through the dense scrub; mutinous dissension was mounting. One night, in the heart of his Louisiana, the viceroy of North America met death at the hands of two treacherous followers.

The murder of La Salle hurt French interests in North America immeasurably. He had barely begun his work; he left Louisiana as unknown as Champlain would have left New France had he died in 1614. The viceroyalty was an empty title, but La Salle's energy and ambition might have given it substance; perhaps he alone could have opened the Mississippi Valley to trade and settlement and French Catholic rule. But now, as the reign of Louis XIV entered its last dark years, he who might have carried on without aid from home was dead. No man of comparable ability or vision succeeded La Salle. But even if such a successor had appeared he would have found the unity of French command in America incurably vitiated. By aligning with Frontenac and the Recollets against the Jesuits and Laval, La Salle had made Louisiana the gage of faction. Henceforth French power in America split: it followed the currents of the two great rivers it aspired to subjugate. The cleavage between New Orleans and Quebec never healed.

Just as La Salle's death crippled imperial plans, so did it impede the progress of the missions. By 1687 tribal wars, English pressure, and internecine French rivalries had combined to cut down drastically the independence of the missionaries and to increase the power that the bishop, governor, and intendant wielded over their activities. Specifically, the Recollets felt La Salle's loss most keenly. He had helped them win a foothold among the Illinois, notably at Crèvecoeur; they had anticipated from him the gift of the entire mission field of Louisiana as their own. But now they abandoned Crèvecoeur and ceased to reconnoiter Louisiana. By 1700 the Recollets had virtually disappeared from the west. They could not compete with the wealthier and more numerous Jesuits, who now reaped the rich harvest of the earlier labors of Ménard and Allouez.

Even for the Jesuits the murder of La Salle was by no means an unmixed blessing. For a vital decade after 1687 they regarded the Mississippi as a diversion and confined their activities to the St. Lawrence watershed. Later they realized they had missed their opportunity to keep their missions unified; for when soldiers and trappers did follow up La Salle's plans, they approached the country from the south, and New Orleans became the center of missionary activity. The Jesuits in Louisiana rarely communicated with Quebec.

Again the missionary division between the two regions accentuated the fundamental weakness in the strategy of the French that the destruction of the Hurons had created. Since 1650 the area west of Montreal, which the Hurons had formerly occupied or policed, lay desolate. The French had preferred the line Ontario-Niagara-Erie over the Ottawa River and its difficult portages as a route to the west. But the southern route lay far more exposed to the forays of the Iroquois. La Salle's ventures in the fur trade, coinciding with French domination of the Iroquois, had stimulated traffic on the Great Lakes and thus furnished some protection for the missions, whether Recollet or Jesuit. But after 1687, along with hostile English expansion from the south and the intensified struggle for Hudson Bay, tribal warfare rose to new heights. The lake route was constantly under fire; and the French found the northern route, little used for three decades, an impracticable alternative. Border captains like Tonti and Cadillac could secure great stretches of lake shore temporarily and hold such single strong points as Venango or Detroit permanently. But after 1700 they could not dominate the region between Niagara and the Mississippi firmly enough to have their position acknowledged. Accordingly, the nature of westward expansion changed in the eighteenth century. Instead of founding new missions the Jesuits kept up their old ones and served as garrison chaplains or with parties of exploration. No longer did they act as emissaries to new tribes; they restricted their independent activity to their own posts. Unlike the ill-starred Recollets or the timorous Sulpicians, they refused to fall back on the St. Lawrence as the principal theater of their endeavors.

The tendency to consolidate old positions became apparent soon after 1687. The Jesuit success at St. Francis de Sales encouraged a secular priest from Laval's seminary to set up a second mission at Nanransouock in 1688. The following year the Recollets built a chapel at Medoctec on the St. John River. Three years later the Sulpicians invited the Jesuits back to their residence in Montreal, and henceforth the two groups shared the religious burdens of that town. At Three Rivers the governor, out of his wish to see the work of conversion prosper, granted the Jesuits more land in 1699. In the same year a Jesuit priest accompanied the Sieur d'Iberville to the Mississippi in the first great attempt to exploit La Salle's discoveries. But finding a secular already among the Natchez Indians, the priest withdrew (1702); Jesuits did not reappear in Louisiana until 1722. Yet the order did not everywhere give way to others. In 1700 they succeeded to the Recollet post at Medoctec, where they remained until the English drove them out eight years later. They also took over the Nanransouock mission in 1703 and stayed for twenty-one years.

By 1710 French missions still dotted the waterways of New France from the Illinois to the St. John, yet the majority of them clustered between Montreal and Tadoussac. In that year, according to Father Jouvency, the Jesuits maintained nineteen posts and several peripatetic missions. Discounting the Iroquois missions (which had vanished entirely by 1708), Nipiskouit among the Abenakis (which was deserted in 1692), and Baiogula (the secular post among the Natchez), Jouvency's list was correct, if a bit optimistic. On the St. Lawrence he counted missions at Seven Isles, St. Charles, Tadoussac, the island of Orléans, Lorette, Three Rivers, and Caughnawaga, as well as residences at Montreal and Quebec, and the college in the latter town. Up the Saguenay stood the post at Chicoutimi; far to the south St. Francis de Sales and Nanransouock were thriving. A wooded and watery desolation separated the eastern stations from those in the west—Sault Ste. Marie on Lake Superior; St. Ignace and St. Joseph on Lake Michigan; St. Francis Xavier on Green Bay; and Immaculate Conception on the Illinois River. Between and somewhat to the south stood the lone mission among the Miamis, the Holy Guardian Angel. Jouvency also mentioned several missions on the Mississippi, Ottawa missions, and, hopefully, "*in silvis missiones.*" [11] By contrast the disposition of the Recollets and Sulpicians emphasized the daring of the Jesuits. Almost all the Franciscans had been absorbed into the diocesan clergy. The Sulpicians huddled close to their island of Montreal. After giving up the post at Kenté they had built another Iroquois refuge, La Montagne, which they aban-

11. "Canadicae missionis relatio," I, 218–224, 236.

doned in 1704 for a more favorable site called St. Louis. They conducted no other missions. In 1710 the Jesuits remained the chief apostles to the Indians, as they had hoped in 1610.

But the general attitude of the French toward Canada had changed mightily in the hundred years since the arrival of Father Biard. Hope had given way to grim determination, apostolic schemes to sectarian rivalries, and imperial visions to bivouacs and bushbeating. The enthusiasm that La Salle had kindled in Louis XIV died quickly. Concern over the Stuart restoration, the Spanish heritage, and orthodoxy monopolized the king's declining energies. As Europe massed against him, his ministers regarded New France more and more narrowly in its strategic aspects. Gradually the country fell under the jurisdiction of the Ministry of Marine; from a colonial enterprise it became a base of operations against the English. The new attitude, which persisted down to 1763, was foreshadowed in a document of 1700, which stated in part that "it is to the interest, glory, and piety of His Majesty to *preserve Canada*; it is the chief and oldest of our American colonies, which has cost His Majesty and his subjects many millions to establish." [12]

At no time did the crown directly curtail the progress of the missions. Yet by 1710 its ironhanded will had fallen heavily upon New France; she lay subject to the same slow, cumbersome, wasteful rule as home provinces like Languedoc or Normandy. Such a regime, even with the finest officials, could not govern the uncharted wastes, much less defend the thousands of miles of ill-defined boundaries. Along with other Canadian institutions the missions suffered grievously from the evils of a centralization that distance rendered utterly inefficient. But the missions had further and more immediate causes for suffering. The piety of the seventeenth century, which had brought scores of brilliant young men, seignories, and abundant funds to the missions, was dying. Religious devotion lost ground rapidly after 1685 (its official apogee) to libertinism or philosophic rationalism on the one hand, to bigoted enthusiasm on the other. Naturally the resources of the Jesuits and Sulpicians declined; the overseas missions were the first to feel the pinch. Therefore retrenchment became a necessity, dictated not simply by policy and external pressure but also by internal deficiencies.

After the Treaty of Utrecht had stripped New France of New-

12. *Collection de manuscrits,* II, 341; italics mine.

foundland, Acadia, and Hudson Bay, the royal officials in Quebec at last realized how seriously the St. Lawrence was menaced. But at home the bureaucrats could not yet grasp the urgency of first crushing the Indians who were revolting against French domination, before attacking the English. Hence they never made adequate provision to defend the vital frontier that ran from Montreal to the Mississippi. Nor, despite their valiant determination and ingenuity, could the Canadians alone stand off the English and their Indian allies, much less crush them.

In the face of mounting difficulties the missionaries faithfully worked on. In 1721, north of the junction of the Ottawa and the St. Lawrence, the Sulpicians founded a great mission, the Lake of the Two Mountains, to which they later transferred the inhabitants of St. Louis. At Nanransouock, now deep in English territory, the heroic Sébastien Rasles struggled against the English Protestant divines for the souls of the Abenakis. Rasles's presence loomed as a political threat to the English, who finally had him killed (1724) and thus extinguished the last permanent French mission in New England. The Jesuits continued to preach at St. Francis de Sales to the north. They also intensified their vigilance in the west, ranging out from Detroit and other forts and adding more priests to those far-flung missions. But they founded no more missions. In 1738 lack of funds forced them to turn away all the Indian charity pupils at the Quebec college. In 1749 the Sulpicians founded the last mission under the French regime, La Présentation, on the south bank of the St. Lawrence a hundred miles above Montreal, as a brave défi to the enemy in New York.

On the eve of the Seven Years' War at least one Recollet, eleven Sulpicians, and thiry-eight Jesuit priests remained in New France.[13] In the final struggle the priests and brothers, regular and secular, gave themselves entirely to the ungrateful cause of France. They negotiated with Christian savages, told raiding parties of short cuts, fords, or portages, said mass in beleaguered palisades, marched through the woods with the troops, and blessed the dying on the field of battle. They matched the ardor of the colonists in the futile defense of their country. But they could not overcome lethargy and corruption in the high command, or

13. "Catalogus personarum et officiorum provinciae Franciae Societatis Jesu. Exeunte anno 1756. Missiones Americae Septentrionalis in Nova Francia," *Jesuit Relations*, LXX, 81–89.

the superior supplies and strategy of the enemy. Quebec fell to the English in 1759, and the next year the surrender of Montreal completed the French rout. The rulers of New France, their ineptness proved, vanished. But the colonists remained, with the culture they had engrafted on Canadian soil; and with them, their priests.

The Capitulation of Canada (September 8, 1760) guaranteed to the French Canadians "the free exercise of the Catholic religion," which the Treaty of Paris confirmed. In addition, the Capitulation preserved the missionaries in their functions and in the complete control of their property.[14] On the other hand, despite such provisions English rule automatically barred the immigration of more priests from France and deprived the Jesuits and Sulpicians of the safeguards of French law for their property. Because the Sulpicians not only were secular priests but also owned the island of Montreal, they remained virtually unmolested by the English. The Jesuits, in different circumstances, did not fare so well.

Ironically, the English conquest saved the Jesuits, at least temporarily, from a more drastic fate. In 1761 the parlement of Paris finally wrung from a reluctant Louis XV the suppression of the Society of Jesus throughout the French realm. The ban did not affect Canada, then supine beneath the English conquerors; but it did Louisiana, which the French yielded to Spain only in 1762: two years later the Spanish expelled the thirteen fathers there. In 1763 twenty-one Jesuit missionaries still worked in Canada. But they received no more recruits, except one refugee from France, a native of Quebec; furthermore the English made feeble attempts to reinstate them in their properties in Quebec, which they had confiscated when that city fell. The conquerors intended to let the order die of old age rather than antagonize the people by harrying their pastors from the land. In fact, by 1773 death had cut the number of Jesuits to eleven.

In that year Pope Clement XIV accelerated the process of extinction by suppressing the Society of Jesus throughout the world. Immediately the English crown, declaring the order dissolved, laid claim to its property in Canada. At the same time (1774) they strove to offset the popular reaction to such a legal but inequitable step by removing the penalties of the Test for Canada. Supported by the bishop of Quebec the Jesuits postponed

14. Quoted in Camille de Rochemonteix, *Les Jésuites et la Nouvelle France au XVIIIᵉ siècle* (2 vols., Paris, 1906), II, 193–194.

compliance with the English demand for sixteen years. In the meantime their operations ceased one by one. The college of Quebec, its buildings ruined in the bombardment of 1759, became a simple primary school in 1768 and closed its doors altogether in 1776. The old missionaries died at their posts: in this fashion the Illinois mission lapsed in 1777 and Tadoussac in 1782. Thereafter four old men gave up all pretext of being missionaries and concentrated every effort on keeping their property from falling into Protestant hands. At last, in 1790, the superior consented to

renounce purely, simply, voluntarily, and in good faith all property and possession of the said gifts and concessions hitherto made to them, and cede and transfer the property and possession of them to the Canadian citizens, in whose behalf they have been made, in order that under the direction and authority and with the approbation of Monseigneur François Xavier Hubert, most illustrious and reverend bishop of Quebec, and of the bishops his successors, provision may be made for the instruction of the savages of Canada and of the young Canadians.[15]

Even in their last futile gestures the Jesuits insisted upon the nature of their original mission as Biard and Le Jeune had conceived it. A grant couched in such terms and dedicated to such an aim as instruction the English could not refuse. Henceforth the Jesuits had nothing to do; simple pensioners, they lived out their time performing charity, nostalgic for the inspired days of the past. The last of them died in 1800, and with him Canada lost the living reminder of that teeming Jesuit band who for almost two centuries had fought infidelity and barbarism on her soil.

Yet the history of the missions had already come to an end with the collapse of New France itself. For the third time, in 1763, the French had failed in the task that Cartier, Champlain, and La Salle had marked out, that Henry IV, Richelieu, and Colbert had ordained. The arena of their final failure had been continental —not confined to the Acadian coast as in 1613 or to the Laurentian Valley as in 1629. In proportion the elements and causes of disaster had multiplied and grown larger; although while rendered more complex by the laminations of time they had remained essentially the same. On the other hand, just as the earlier episodes had produced lasting results for Canada, so did the later in incalcu-

15. "Lettre du Révérend Père de Glapion à Mr. Ls. Germain, fils," *Jesuit Relations*, LXXI, 100–102.

lably higher magnitude. French rule was not simply "a story which would have been a history if faults of constitution and the bigotry and folly of rulers had not dwarfed it to an episode," as Parkman has alleged. In spite of his denunciation of the ideal of material progress, Parkman's ultimate criterion was pragmatic. The churchmen in particular marked Canada indelibly, as that historian himself admitted, even as he deplored that the Canadians "have imposed upon themselves a weight of ecclesiastical tutelage that finds few equals in the most Catholic countries of Europe." [16] True, the French did not achieve their triune aim of conversion, civilization, and the establishment of royal authority; the rot at the core of the Bourbon monarchy finally sapped its vitality. But out of the wreck of 1763 the colonists and priests salvaged a French Canadian civilization; what they have built upon it is today both vital and manifest. The missionaries brought innumerable thousands of Indians to a "knowledge of God" and a more settled condition of life. The Jesuits in particular, as the most active of the groups, nourished souls and propagated the faith in the full spirit of their papal mandate of 1540. As they sired Canadian Catholicism, so their spirit has survived down to the present, whether among the métis of the Ontario bush or the bourgeois of the pavements of Vancouver or Quebec.

Yet the Gallic ways that permeate Canada from Annapolis (where they started) to Fort Macpherson do not represent the sole abiding results of French dominion. Others came to light not in America but in Europe; for them the missionaries stand more singly responsible. The church, revivified by the Counter Reformation, had sent her missionaries out to win converts; led by the Jesuits, in tune with the main currents of European thought, she had rendered her dogma and morality more human. That humanization sustained the missionaries in their labors. Simultaneously, the missions in such barbarous lands as New France fed the process of humanization still further by the very means they used: they studied to know the heathens before they tried to baptize them. The observed facts that the Canadian missionaries, of whom the Jesuits were the most articulate and numerous, poured into Europe gave substance to theories concerning one of the most troublesome problems of the dawning Age of Reason: the nature of man as a moral being. The savage—either as an object of charity or humanitarianism, as a cipher for political or economic

16. *Montcalm and Wolfe* (Boston, 1912), II, 427.

theorists, as a literary cliché, or simply as an interesting member of a strange culture—assumed a species of reality. Of his many interpreters, especially the Jesuits of New France made the savage manifest to Europe.

IV

OFFICIAL MEANS AND ENDS OF THE MISSIONS

WHEN a Jesuit priest received orders from his provincial to proceed to the Canadian missions, he set out obediently for his port of embarkation. As his ship dropped the headlands of France astern and moved over the ocean to the bleak wilderness ahead, he found many hours for reflection midway between the old world and the new. If he reviewed his past or conjured up images of the future, he certainly took stock of himself and of how he was equipped to meet the tasks that lay before him. His material possessions were miserably few; except for his breviary, which he always kept at hand on board ship, they lay tied in a bundle on his bunk. He might also have had charge of larger packages, now stowed below, destined for the superior at Quebec, Yet these things alone could not sustain him. To supplement his material poverty he could draw upon the store of spiritual, moral, and rational riches that had nourished him up to the present moment and upon which his ultimate success as a missionary would depend.

Two general aspects of his calling determined the attitudes of the Jesuit missionary. In public he appeared as a French Jesuit and hence subject to God, his general, and his king. Accordingly, he strove to carry out the wishes of his three masters and worked always toward the corporate goal of the mission in Canada: the conversion of the heathens. But each missionary also led a private life, which was influenced by his training and spiritual experiences.

The missionaries all recognized the invisible guidance of God. As Father Le Jeune wrote, "there is neither chance nor accident with God, His bounty and justice harmonize well with His providence." [1] Whatever their own natural resources, ultimately they depended upon the four "wings" of "grace, love, fear of God, and zeal for souls," which He lent them. [2] Some priests were content,

---

1. "Relation . . . 1640," XVIII, 214.
2. François de Crépieul, S.J., quoted in Thomas A. Hughes, *History of the Society of Jesus in North America* (3 vols., London, 1907–17), II, 261.

in reporting their activities, to submit the bare number of their conversions without comment. Others, like Father Du Jaunay, hymned their gains in triumphant humility: "Jesus, our bountiful King, has made use of me, all unworthy as I am, to enroll in His service, and I hope for ever, one Indian family." [3]

Yet, while the Jesuits relied on divine assistance in their corporate task, they knew He also expected them to labor for Him. Dedicated to the Counter Reformation, their order conceived of their work as a world-wide assault upon heterodoxy, whether European Protestantism or a more exotic paganism. In the early years Le Jeune compared Canada to England, where also his order hoped to establish residences soon.[4] Later, when the priests had had to abandon their Iroquois posts, the superior at Quebec drew a similar comparison: in the hostile forests, "that captive church is a replica of what happened in the hidden church of England, where our fathers disguised themselves as peddlars, to carry on a precious traffic for eternity." [5] It did not matter to the Jesuits where they were sent as long as they could fight the enemies of their church.

Zeal for souls similarly motivated the Recollet friars and the Sulpician followers of Jean Jacques Olier. No less did it appeal to lay exponents of a revived Catholicism. Legitimately allied with mundane considerations, conversion justified trade, exploration, and conquest. Champlain best personified the honest blend of spiritual and material motives; but before him Cartier had already preached the crusade. Even the worldly Marc Lescarbot, a companion of Poutrincourt, prefaced one of his works with the classic text ordaining the propagation of the faith: "the gospel of the kingdom of heaven [sic] shall be preached in the whole world for a testimony to all nations, and then shall the consummation come." [6]

The biblical stricture applied to New France as elsewhere, and thither the Jesuits and Recollets eagerly rushed. Even after their first failures both orders—the Jesuits twice—scrambled to reestablish themselves in Canada. When they finally succeeded, their apostolic spirit did not die but endured down to 1763. Father Claude Dablon (1619–97) exemplified that spirit. He set up an Iroquois mission in 1655, only to flee it three years later. He

3. Arthur E. Jones, ed., *The Aulneau Collection* (Montreal, 1893), p. 123.
4. "Relation . . . 1635," VII, 259.
5. "Relation . . . 1661 & 1662," XLVII, 196.
6. "La Conversion des sauvages qui ont esté baptizés en la Nouvelle France cette année 1610," *Jesuit Relations*, I, 58. Matt. 24:14.

labored on Lake St. John with the indefatigable Druillettes in 1660, and in 1669 went west with Allouez and Marquette. Soon he forsook his companions to go alone to Lake Superior, in order, as he wrote, to care for the souls of the Ottawas who had taken refuge north of that lake.[7] Later Dablon became superior at Quebec, but he still worked to expand the missionary frontiers; to that end he assigned Marquette to accompany the explorer Joliet to the Mississippi, and edited the priest's accounts of his travels. Sixty-five years after Dablon's canoe had entered Lake Superior Father Luc Nau (1703–53) heard rumors about unknown tribes in the far-western plains. Despite the danger of being cut off by the English or the Sioux, Nau wanted to go out instantly: "if this story be true," he wrote, "there is another grand opening for the Gospel." [8] Nau's friend, Jean Aulneau (1705–36), joyfully anticipating a journey to the west, wrote that he "was about to penetrate into a region unknown, in view of making Jesus Christ known to savages who have never even heard Him spoken of." [9]

Pierre François Xavier de Charlevoix (1682–1761), a more mature and less enthusiastic contemporary of Aulneau, cherished similar hopes for the spread of the gospel, although he did little pioneering. Charlevoix first visited New France in 1705–09, before he was ordained. He returned in 1720 and traveled for two years, up the St. Lawrence and the Great Lakes, across Illinois, and down the Mississippi to New Orleans, whence he returned home. Later he wrote prolifically of America, and was popularly if not correctly regarded as the best French authority on the country. When a government official asked his advice on opening up the far west, Charlevoix remarked, "As we worked westward we could take measures for setting up in those vast territories establishments equally useful to religion and to the state. A priest could hardly spend three or four years in traversing those regions without having the opportunity of procuring the admission to heaven through baptism of several moribund infants." [10]

In Ireland, Bavaria, Formosa, or Canada, the goal of the missionaries dictated a procedure that was everywhere the same. As Charlevoix hinted, baptism always preceded salvation: the unbaptized lacked that sanctifying grace which allowed men to

---

7. "Relation . . . 1669 & 1670," LIV, 135.
8. Jones, ed., *The Aulneau Collection,* p. 26.
9. *Ibid.,* pp. 53–54.
10. Lawrence J. Burpee, ed., *Journals and Letters of Pierre Gaultier de Varennes de la Verendrye* (Toronto, 1927), p. 81.

accept God's saving grace. Now the means toward the final goal varied with the circumstances in which the unbaptized person lived. It was, for example, relatively simple to baptize an infant and then, as he matured, indoctrinate him with orthodox principles. With adults a more rational appeal was necessary: conversion demanded both faith and intellectual conviction; and adults were used to their old ways. In addition, once a person was baptized, it remained to fortify him in his new faith, under whatever circumstances he might have been living. Thus an Irish infant needed simply a sacramental rite, since he was born into an entirely Catholic community. But in continental lands like Bavaria, where many people had left the church, the priests had to prove the superiority of their faith over Protestantism. Yet Catholics and Protestants shared a common Christian heritage; a change of faith did not imply a social or economic revolution; hence the sophisticated methods of exposition and debate on dogma and morals seemed sufficient to overcome Protestanism. In distant lands like Formosa the missionaries found no such common bonds of tradition, although a highly developed culture existed. There, to make Catholicism comprehensible, the missionaries delved deeper and uncovered the basic ideas and institutions that related the European to other equally high cultures. But in Canada the missionaries found the people utterly foreign. The Indians were not simply heathens, like the people of Asia and Islam: their supernatural ideas partook of totemism and animism. True barbarians, they had no written language, and they spoke in tongues that were extremely elusive in structure and impeded communication of even the simplest religious concepts. In addition, the Indians lived under tribal governments, with little agriculture and few permanent communities. They seemed to share nothing with Europeans except the fact of their humanity. Under such extreme conditions, the Canadian missionaries resorted to the most basic reasoning and the simplest sentiments of humanity.

Yet even in America the Jesuits followed the same principles that they used in the most Catholic country of Europe. They knew thoroughly the dogmas and doctrines of the church. They studied their catechumens as closely as possible and adapted themselves and their morality to local customs in order to establish the broadest rapport with the Indians. Then they simplified their religious teachings to a point at which the Indians could grasp them. Lastly, as Ignatius Loyola had directed, the priests schooled themselves in eloquence—not Latin, but Micmac or Algonquin or Huron— as the most effective—here perhaps the only—means of spreading the Word. Nevertheless, no matter how keen their observation, how sympathetic their understanding, how close their adaptation, the Jesuits still experienced much difficulty with the Indians. However saintly and zealous, the priests remained European; their success depended upon their ability to transcend their natal inheritance while retaining their inspiration, and then to bridge the broad abyss between European and Indian culture. To overcome the obstacles that choked the path to conversion, the missionaries found themselves driven to the most diverse expedients.

Because they were pioneers Biard and Massé faced all the difficulties that exotic novelty could provide. The secular priest Fleché alone had preceded them; and he, ignorant of the native tongue, had not instructed his neophytes properly before baptism. As a result, his conversions were as temporary and superficial as they had been sudden. Biard found that their new faith had not improved the morals of these "Christians" and was shocked to see many of the men still keeping eight wives.[11] Fleché had not laid a solid foundation for Indian Catholicism; the Jesuits resigned themselves to making a fresh start. They began by learning the language and customs of the Etchemins and Micmacs.

After Biard and Massé, it became standard practice for every missionary to study first the language of the tribe to which he was assigned. Command of the language immediately opened the door to conversion, as Le Jeune pointed out: "First we take steps to go and attack the enemy on its ground with its own arms, that is to say, by the knowledge of the Montagnais, Algonquin, and Huron languages."[12] Sometimes a recruit could pick up the rudiments of the local tongue from a trapper or priest in Quebec; otherwise, he set out in total ignorance and relied on signs or chance interpreters until proximity instructed him. In 1625 Father Brébeuf wintered with the Montagnais and composed a grammar of their speech for the benefit of his successors. When he went out to the Hurons the next year, he followed the same procedure; while he found Huron much more difficult, he succeeded so well that later Le Jeune could write down a list of tips on what to say to the Hurons to win their friendship.[13] After the grammar came

11. "Lettre au R. P. Christophe Baltazar," *Jesuit Relations,* I, 161, 165.
12. "Relation . . . 1638," XIV, 124.
13. "Relation . . . 1637," XII, 117–123.

the catechism, which not only taught the savages doctrine but also showed the teachers how to simplify their speech and ideas so as to be understood. One of the earliest catechisms, the *Doctrine chrestienne* (published in Rouen, 1630), set out the French and Montagnais in parallel columns.

Once the problem of language was solved, there arose the greater problem of proving arguments that the Indians could aurally understand. A life according to Catholic precepts, based on the mass, a chapel, and a permanent community, seemed the most practical demonstration. Both before and after baptism the missionaries labored constantly to persuade the Indians to forsake their nomadic existence for an agricultural domesticity. Consequently they urged the tribes to make peace in order to till their fields in security; and they fostered colonization by Frenchmen who, they hoped, would portray the sweet virtues of the settled life. The first policy became confounded with the tradition of military intervention that Champlain had originated in 1609. The second coincided frequently with the aims of the Hundred Associates, the Society of Notre Dame, and other colonizing agencies. Hence, in the interest of conversion, the men of the church came to sanction conquest and colonization, although at times they objected strenuously to the military and mercantilist concomitants of such programs.

During his administration at Quebec the shrewd Le Jeune strove to combine the patronage of Richelieu and the experience of Champlain for the greatest possible benefit of the missions. In 1634 the superior sketched three great measures for speeding up the rate of conversion. First the French had to check the progress of the Iroquois—enemies of Christianity who were even then slaughtering the Hurons and destroying French prestige—and strike fear into their hearts. Then his priests could induce the nomadic natives to settle down, after the example which capable French farmers would set them. Lastly, Le Jeune advocated schools for Indian boys and girls, under the direction of "some brave woman and her companions" whom the Jesuits would supervise.[14] The next year he again emphasized salvation of souls as the ultimate goal of the French. A thriving trade, populous towns, royal prestige, and armed strength may have had other uses; but their primary use was to impress the Indians and thus expedite their conversion.[15]

14. "Relation . . . 1634," VI, 145, 153.
15. "Relation . . . 1635," VIII, 15.

However urgent military conquest appeared in 1634 to a man at Champlain's elbow, it had not seemed so important to Biard and Massé in 1611. The Acadian Indians were peaceable, and force seemed both repellent and superfluous. Biard relied on colonization alone to help spread the gospel. He reminded his provincial in Paris that "if they are savages, it is to domesticate and civilize them that people come here." In 1611 colonization did not seem urgent to Biard. He felt that the success of the Acadian mission depended upon divine aid and royal favor, and secondarily upon the pious generosity of the nobles and the climate of Acadia. But at that time Biard was content to petition the queen mother for a permanent subsidy.[16] Later, when in one stroke Argall wiped out his work, the need for colonists became more evident. In 1616 the ex-missionary resumed his clamor for royal patronage of a Canadian mission. Addressing the young king, he wrote that the noblest work man could undertake would be to make a garden out of the wilderness of Canada by introducing order and discipline to subjugate the satanic monsters who ruled there. The best means would be to establish a Christian colony among the Indians "to convert and civilize them." "New France should be cultivated to call the savages to a knowledge of Christ and the church." But, Biard asked, why should the king put himself to so much trouble? and replied, what better reason than to save souls? He also set forth a baser consideration: the French had already poured much wealth and effort into New France, and if they abandoned the country now they would become the laughingstock of Europe; their prestige could not afford such a blow.[17] (Even this zealous theologian did not scorn worldly arguments to accomplish his spiritual goal.) Two years later Biard again pleaded for conversion and colonization, with similar hints of political and economic gains but with no mention of conquest. In the same period Father Jamet, the head of the Recollet mission at Quebec, sketched out a more concrete plan. The French should not, he wrote, put their orphans and unwanted children in convents at home; they should send them to New France, where they would fill a real need. Every nobleman should send over fifteen men, and the king as many as his proportionately greater wealth would permit.[18]

The charter of the Company of New France seemed at last to

16. "Lettre au R. P. Christophe Baltazar," *Jesuit Relations,* I, 141, 179–183.
17. "Relation de la Nouvelle France," III, 35, 137–139; IV, 113–117.
18. Denis Jamet, "Relation au Cardinal François de Joyeuse," *La Nouvelle France,* XIII (Québec, 1914), 442.

promise fulfillment of Jamet's and Biard's demands. But from the beginning the company failed to live up to its commitments, particularly with regard to colonization. In addition, the monopolies the company secured practically nullified whatever prospects New France held out to enterprising settlers. Yet even if the country had offered a free field to all comers on their own terms, its bleak aspect and cold weather would scarcely have enticed many French farmers or traders from their own rich fields and towns. The Huguenots, who might have immigrated after 1629, were barred by the charter of the company. As a result, desirable colonists arrived in a thin trickle. When the failure of the associates first became apparent, Le Jeune, reiterating that colonists constituted the surest auxiliaries of the Canadian church, begged Richelieu to remind them of their duty.[19] But at the moment European affairs absorbed the cardinal. When Le Jeune received no answer he turned to a wider public, in search of a sympathetic hearing.

In the Relation of 1635 the superior argued the case for colonization at length. He decried the frivolity of individual adventurers who dissipated the energy and talent of France over all the nations of the earth. Would it not be better to have all emigrants concentrate in New France? Many in France were poor or needed work or land; let them come over! A populous American colony would immensely fortify the power of the king; those who left France for neighboring European lands did not help him and might even injure him.[20] Le Jeune's eloquence did not call forth a swarm of settlers, although the rich and pious responded warmly with grants of money and land. In 1638 Le Jeune reported on the first fruits of such largess: the funds had made possible the reservation at Sillery, where the blessings of a secure domestic existence moved the Christian Algonquins to transports of joy.[21] Settlements, he concluded, furnished the best means of conversion and further colonization. There conditions favored a stable family life, which on the one hand supplied the seminary with new recruits to spread the gospel and on the other hand cultivated the land to make communities richer and even more permanent. Then Le Jeune informed his generous readers that Christian marriages among the Indians cost about twenty-two livres apiece.[22] But such a sum

19. "Lettre à Monseigneur le Cardinal," *Jesuit Relations,* VII, 239, 245.
20. "Relation . . . 1635," VIII, 9–13.
21. "Relation . . . 1638," XIV, 215–217.
22. "Relation . . . 1639," XVI, 251.

must have covered merely the initial costs, for later Father Vimont reckoned that it took three hundred livres to finance a home for an Indian family and thereby insure its firm adherence to Christianity.[23]

The largest single donation to the missions came in 1641, from the two associates who purchased the Isle of Montreal. When the laymen enlisted the aid of Jean Jacques Olier, the cause of colonization and conversion won a stout champion. At this time Olier was an important figure in Paris. His association with Vincent de Paul assured him of rich and powerful patrons, and he won further respect by his thorough reform of the corrupt parish of St. Sulpice. In 1643 Olier organized the Society of Notre Dame to raise funds for the new settlement. To publicize his scheme he anonymously issued "Les Véritables motifs de messieurs et dames de la Société de Notre Dame de Montréal." In this tract he stated the religious motives and the necessity for colonization more systematically than any of the missionaries themselves; for beyond the zeal that he shared with the priests in the field distance gave his arguments a perspective they could not achieve.

Olier regarded the obligations of Frenchmen to Canada as essentially religious in nature. Accordingly, he relied primarily upon theological arguments and used economic and political considerations simply to strengthen his main thesis. From his reading of St. Matthew 24:14, he concluded that divine revelation had bound man to aid in the propagation of the Word.[24] Without doubt God could accomplish the work alone. But just as He does not save us without our cooperation, so has He resolved to save us through each other, so that we may need one another. Olier drew a parallel between individual salvation through cooperation with God and the salvation of the infidel by the faithful through the same cooperation. In the latter task the missions took the first steps. Therefore they deserved support from the city of Paris as well as from the church; since Paris "at present seems to be falling heir to the riches of ancient Rome and following the holy traditions that Rome has bequeathed it." [25]

Olier stated his point most typically in his "third motive." Here he first posited that good spiritual works were preferable to good

23. "Relation . . . 1640," XVIII, 117.
24. Cf. n. 6 above.
25. "Les Véritables motifs de messieurs et dames de la Société de Notre Dame de Montréal," *Mémoires de la Société Historique de Montréal,* IX (1880), 9.

temporal works. The act of conversion was a spiritual work. Alms-giving was a temporal work; but it could partake of the merits of spiritual works if its purpose was conversion, for under such circumstances it became true charity. He then distinguished charity from the giving of alms solely out of humanitarian compassion: the latter was simply temporal, because it neglected any super-natural end. Charity, then, became an obligation upon the faithful, while humanitarianism remained proper only for good infidels who could look merely to natural ends, knowing no other. Now, con-tinued Olier,

to know what a spiritual work is, we must judge by what distinguishes it from temporal works. For it is not by their principle which is grace joined to our will, nor by the last end which is God, nor by the manner of producing them freely out of the motive of charity. For both being meritorious have all these conditions. But they are distinguished by the effects and proximate ends toward which they tend. Thus, those which concern only the body are purely temporal; those which con-cern the welfare of the soul are purely spiritual. This is not remark-able, since causes and actions arise from the excellence of their effects and ends and since the nobility of the latter determines the dignity of the former.[26]

Then Olier repeated the obligations of the Christian.

Thus it is clear that it is harmonious with the orders of the Master of charity to contribute according to one's condition where there is more need and misery, and particularly where this misery is caused by orig-inal sin from which Christians are freed at infancy by the grace of baptism. Consequently they are more culpable of present sins than the savages and infidels, who are ruined and ravaged in body and soul by the depredation of this cursed original sin, for the remedy of which our Lord came into the world. And so these sins are more excusable in infidels than in evil Christians, who by their faults render themselves unworthy of the compassion which they received at baptism.[27]

And the sinner could infer that contributions to the missions ac-complished not merely a positive work of charity but also partial expiation for his own sins.

After discussing the general question of charity, Olier turned to consider who was most worthy to receive it, and decided in favor

26. *Ibid.*, p. 22–23.
27. *Ibid.*, p. 34.

of the Indians. For "Whoever examines closely the necessitous circumstances of the savages, their country, the temperature of the climate, their birth, and the vitality of their life, and their barbarous idolatry, will easily conclude that their misery is inevitable, irreparable, and without resource, unless it be assisted." [28]

The author also anticipated some of the objections that his arguments might raise. The chief of those was that, since the Indians possessed natural reason, they could save themselves if they but obeyed the law of nature. Olier replied that obedience to natural law might save men from damnation, but it could not effect their salvation, even if they lived unblemished by sin. It had never been taught that any infidel attained salvation before or after the promulgation of the written law. In their present condition the poor savages could scarcely be expected to avoid mortal sin. But even if they did possess a perfection that the first men lacked, all the more reason for the faithful to cause to be achieved in them by grace what God had started working by the gifts of nature.

In conclusion Olier could not resist touching on worldly matters. With a bow to what he doubtless considered good temporal works, he predicted that conversion would increase the native population. Thus France, to her great honor and benefit, would acquire many more subjects to fight her battles and consume her goods.[29]

The concern for effects that permeated Olier's principal arguments closely reflected congruist doctrine. In his criteria for the evaluation of works Olier adapted Molina's distinctions between efficacious and sufficient grace and deduced from the Molinist theology an analogous theory of charity.

In regard to colonization Olier also believed with the Jesuits in France's historic *mission civilisatrice*. Usually that mundane mission has involved a land policy: either of *défrichement*, to plant civilization in a barren land; or of conquest, to improve a civilization that already existed. Because Catholicism has pervaded the development of France, it has always accompanied the execution of any land policy; and especially in the seventeenth century, when France felt the full impact of the Counter Reformation. But while the concept of a *mission civilisatrice* has remained distinct from religion and has served economists and strategists as well as missionaries, yet it emerged from writings about Canada clothed in a bright religious light. With conversion always before them

28. *Ibid.*, p. 41.
29. *Ibid.*, p. 58–59, 63.

as a goal, the missionaries thought that an improvement of man's natural morality usually accompanied, if it did not inevitably follow, the improvement of his supernatural morality. Cartier, Champlain, Lescarbot, and even Louis XIV subscribed to this parallelism also; indeed it colored the whole of French policy in Canada. Each group among the French perceived the use to which the *mission civilisatrice* could be put, but each had in mind its own desired end.

None of the missionaries, certainly, questioned his goal. But as the years rolled on, the goal seemed to come no nearer in spite of all their faith, zeal, and knowledge. As Biard had in time come to stress the importance of colonization, so did his successors give ever more thought to the means by which to reach their goal. They relied increasingly upon the attritive effects of French civilization. If barbarism and the wilderness depressed early enthusiasms, the wiser missionaries did not despair but took refuge in firmest patience and fortitude. Thierry Beschefer, for instance, after three years in the field, insisted that Canada was not so savage as people imagined; time alone would make New France like old France.[30] At the end of the century Father Antoine Silvy (1635?–1711), who had served the missions more than thirty years, accepted the process of slow seepage as the surest means of conversion. In a mood of resignation he wrote: ". . . infinite pains and time would be necessary to free these people [from evil] and to be able to persuade them to accept our customs and habits. It will only be brought about by continued application on them and little by little we can succeed; it is, I assure you, a work of several centuries." [31] But not all missionaries shared Silvy's disillusionment. Many sought to hasten the progress of French civilization without the aid of settlers, soldiers, and trappers; if not by preaching at the altar, then by teaching in the classroom.

It would have been very odd if the Jesuits had failed to practice in Canada the pedagogy that they had already perfected in Europe. Yet they were not the first who thought it necessary to educate the Indians. In 1621 Champlain had called a meeting of colonists in Quebec to consider what policies should be undertaken for the preservation of New France. Aside from agreeing upon the dissemination of royal justice and Catholicism, the assembly petitioned the home government to assist them in erecting a seminary specifically

30. "Trois lettres," *Jesuit Relations,* L, 171–173.
31. *Relation par lettres de l'Amérique Septentrionale* (Paris, 1904), p. 62.

to instruct the savages.[32] But at the moment the condition of the missions forbade any such ambitious enterprise. As soon as he could after 1632, Father Le Jeune set about building a college and seminary in Quebec. In the college, which antedated "the famous Puritan establishment" of Harvard, he immediately put the *Ratio studiorum* into effect, although it was never possible to offer the full curriculum. Most of the Jesuits had served in some capacity in the colleges at home; their assignment to New France did not imply any deficiency as teachers. Later the Jesuits also proposed a college for the Hurons, but the destruction of that nation thwarted the plan.

Alongside the college they conducted classes in their residences. In the wilderness, when the missionaries had finished their masses and private devotions, sick visits, and other duties, they turned schoolmasters. Always their chief problem was to master the tribal tongue; that accomplished, they had to create images vivid enough to convey to their auditors the ideas they wished them to grasp. When they made rapid progress, the missionaries went far beyond the basic principles of religion and undertook to teach their charges French and even rudimentary facts about French geography, government, and customs.

For female education, a task they had not been authorized to assume, the Jesuits cast about among the orders of French nuns. In 1633 Le Jeune wrote that baptism could have no lasting effect unless both sexes were guided along Christian paths, and he begged some sisters to come to New France to take charge of the Indian girls. The next year, in outlining his broad scheme for conversion, he again mentioned the necessity of such instruction. Resuming the same theme in 1635 he wrote that many nuns wished to cross the ocean to Canada. Some noble patroness should gratfy their pious ardor to serve God by endowing a convent in Quebec. Such a handsome act would be a work of charity and make a start on the great task of teaching Indian women Christian morality. A second reference to the pious anxiety of the sisters brought tangible results: Mme. Marie Madeleine de la Peltrie and three Ursuline nuns landed in Quebec in 1636 and there founded a convent.[33] That lady, diligent in her duties, was soon urging her relatives and friends to send more money to the missions. Like Le Jeune and Vimont she fell a victim to the fever of calculating the cost of conversion; at one time

32. Chrétien le Clercq, *First Establishment of the Faith in New France,* trans. John G. Shea (2 vols., New York, 1881), I, 164–172, 195, 198.
33. "Relation . . . 1635," V, 145, 257, 261; "Relation . . . 1636," VIII, 234–237.

she sighed: ". . . how many souls the price of a single dinner and a single ballet lasting only two or three hours would save here!" [34] In 1636, too, the Duchesse d'Aiguillon, niece of Cardinal Richelieu, donated funds for the Hôtel-Dieu in Quebec. The feminine enthusiasm did not die after the first surge but grew with the years. In 1657, for example, Marguerite Bourgeois sued for permission to establish the Congregation of Notre Dame at Montreal; her deep interest in "the advancement of the Catholic faith, by good instruction of persons of her sex, as much savage as native French" led the king to approve of her project.[35]

Yet, however essential instruction was for the future colony, the moral and theological reasons for colonization did not attract many Frenchmen. Therefore the missionaries appealed to the natural interests of man and depicted the easy life and huge profits that New France offered just for the taking.

The country was another France, Biard wrote in 1616, similar in climate and terrain. The soil lay richly fertile and would yield abundant harvests if only it were cultivated. But rich farm land could be duplicated at home; this country also offered vast opportunities for trade. In the rocky coves along the shore Biard had seen the fur trade flourishing. Each year more than five hundred vessels returned to Europe crammed with cod and piled high with beaver, elk, marten, seal, and otter.[36] When the French sailed up the St. Lawrence they discovered other riches. Le Jeune, for example, devoted twenty-four pages of one Relation to describing the geography, soil, minerals, crops, and beasts of New France.[37] The immense forests would provide the navy with timber for masts; copper, iron, and other metals could be worked out of the ground and shipped home. Grain grew there, too, as easily as in France.

Fish and furs, being most accessible, offered by far the richest profits. But the Normans, Bretons, and Basques had pre-empted the fishing waters early, and the charter of the Company of New France had in effect confirmed their prescriptive rights. Consequently late arrivals turned to the fur trade. The demand for pelts, particularly beaver, rose sharply in Europe after 1600. The animals retreated ever westward before the Indians who decimated them in a hot struggle to meet the demands of the insatiable

34. "Relation . . . 1639," XV, 232.
35. *Edits concernant le Canada,* I, 69–70.
36. "Relatio rerum gestarum," II, 199–201; "Relation de la Nouvelle France," IV, 111–113.
37. "Relation . . . 1635," VIII, 13; "Relation . . . 1636," IX, 151–183.

French. Thus, while Cartier and even Biard saw the fur trade
thriving along the coast, by 1650 the best trapping lands lay
perhaps a thousand miles inland. The trappers and explorers in the
forests blazed the paths of an advancing French civilization with
their clearings and occasional forts; and their inroads seemed
to presage a more settled and populous colony. Hence the missionaries, along with interested laymen, stimulated interest in the
fur trade by favorable reports on its profits.

In 1627 Father Charles Lallemant wrote that each year Canada
exported from twelve to fifteen thousand beaver skins valued at
ten livres apiece, and twenty-two thousand in the single year 1625.
After 1632 trade boomed, owing chiefly to the efforts of the
Hurons and their Algonquin allies, who brought to Quebec beaver
worth between 200,000 and 300,000 livres each year. At the same
time transactions at Tadoussac amounted annually to about
250,000 livres. After the Huron dispersion both prices and quantity fell off sharply, but trade soon revived. In 1660 the Ottawas
brought furs to Quebec worth 200,000 livres.[38]

As royal control expanded and Laval and the Sulpicians intruded, the Jesuits lost many of their nonreligious functions;
naturally they lost their previous intimate knowledge of the economic affairs of the colony. In addition, as the beavers were harried
westward by trappers, illicit gains and smuggling increased; the
official figures no longer reflected the true profits of the trade.
English competition in New York and Hudson Bay, moreover,
made the volume of French trade less predictable. As a result, the
Jesuits' reports for the later period lost their comprehensive nature.

The last general account by a Jesuit came from Father Claude
Coquart (1706–65). In 1750 Coquart, then at Tadoussac, was
commissioned to make a survey of the business at the royal trading posts. At Tadoussac he found the average annual turnover
to be three or four packets of beaver, over a hundred marten pelts,
thirty lynxes, a few foxes, and five to six hundred sealskins. At
Chicoutimi beavers brought about 13,000 livres, martens 10,000,
and bear, lynx, and otter another 15,000. At Seven Isles the pelts
were fewer than up the Saguenay but of higher quality: eight

38. "Lettre du Père Charles l'Allemant Supérieur de la mission de Canadas de la
Compagnie de Jésus, envoyée au Père Hierosme l'Allemant son frère," *Jesuit Relations*, IV, 207; "Relation . . . 1653," XL, 211; "Journal des PP. Jésuites Québek
jan-dec 1648," *Jesuit Relations*, XXXII, 103; "Journal . . . 1649," *Jesuit Relations*, XXXIV, 59–61; "Journal . . . 1652," *Jesuit Relations*, XXXVII, 117;
"Journal . . . 1659 & 1660," *Jesuit Relations*, XLV, 163.

hundred martens and many caribou and sealskins besides.[39] Coquart made no attempt to report on the western trade, which by
this time was flowing largely through New Orleans. But evidently
the fur trade, even in the older regions, was still yielding profit.

Yet it was not furs that had first attracted the French to America. Cartier, emulating the Spanish, had come looking for gold.
Although he and his successors failed in their quest, still the
precious metal lured the French westward as magnetically as did
the Northwest Passage. In 1674, for example, when Jacques Marquette began his explorations, he presented two motives for his
plans. He wished first to find the passage, but also "to verify what
has been said before concerning the two kingdoms Theguaio and
Quivira, bordering on Canada, where gold mines are supposed to
abound." [40] But Quivira remained a mirage. Canada did not yield
up her treasures to the French. The seekers after riches consoled
themselves with the discovery of baser metals that possessed great
if not absolute economic value.

When he described Acadia, Biard mentioned that if the country
were inhabited profit could be drawn from its mines; "for there
is a silver one at the Baye Ste. Marie, according to the Sieur Champlain: and two of beautiful and pure copper, one at the entrance
to Port Royal, and the other at the Bay of Mines; one of iron at
the river St. John, and others elsewhere. Sandstone, slate, mica,
coal, and all sorts of stones are not lacking here." [41] As the missionaries pushed west they cooperated with the intendants and
explorers to find the riches that lay in the soil. In 1660 Jérôme
Lallemant passed on to the French reading public the following
description of Lake Superior:

This lake which is more than eighty leagues long and forty wide in
certain places, is studded with isles scattered pleasingly along the
shores; its shore is bordered all around with Algonquin nations, where
fear of the Iroquois has made them seek refuge. It is also enriched in
all its shores with mines of lead in a nearly pure state; with copper
so excellent that pieces as large as a fist are found all refined; with
large rocks which have whole veins of turquoise.[42]

39. "Mémoire sur les postes du domaine du roi, 1750," *Jesuit Relations*, LXIX,
95, 111, 121.
40. "Le Premier voyage qu'a fait le P. Marquette vers le nouveau Mexique,"
Jesuit Relations, LIX, 86.
41. "Relation de la Nouvelle France," III, 68.
42. "Relation . . . 1659 & 1660," XLV, 218.

Ten years later Claude Dablon had become more familiar with Lake Superior and gave this description of the copper desposits there:

> . . . the slabs and lumps of this metal that we have seen weigh each a hundred or two hundred pounds, and much more; that large rock of copper of seven or eight hundred pounds, that all who pass see near the head of the lake, and besides a number of pieces found at the water's edge in various places seem to leave us no doubt that some place there are mother mines which have not yet been discovered.[43]

When Marquette passed through the Illinois country he located what "had all the appearances of an iron mine," and relayed many rumors about the riches of the Mississippi Valley.[44] As the French opened up Louisiana the reports about mineral wealth increased. In 1700 Father Jacques Gravier, who accompanied D'Iberville, mentioned a "very rich lead mine" in the present region of Missouri; and twelve years later Father Marest wrote from the mission of the Immaculate Conception concerning the land to the south: "It is alleged that there are silver mines there: what is certain is that there are in this country mines of lead and tin, and that, if trained miners came to dig in this earth, they would perhaps find mines of copper and other metal." [45] Again in 1750 an Illinois missionary expatiated at length on the mines of Louisiana, which "in no way differ from the mines of Mexico and Peru," and mentioned specifically lead, silver, borax, gold, and copper.[46] The accounts of the Jesuits gave a seemingly disinterested corroboration to the advertisements of the laymen and undoubtedly stimulated the interest of both traders and investors in New France. It will be recalled that one of the chief attractions of John Law's Mississippi scheme of 1719 was the mineral wealth of the territory.

Nevertheless, events proved that New France could not attract colonists, even were it El Dorado, unless its rulers also provided some guarantee of military protection. From the first the hostility of both natives and English menaced the country. While Biard and Massé had found the Indians of Acadia and Norumbega friendly, an English freebooter from Virginia had speedily ruined

43. "Relation . . . 1670 & 1671," LV, 98.
44. "Le Premier voyage qu'a fait le P. Marquette," *Jesuit Relations,* LIX, 107.
45. "Relation ou journal du voyage en 1700 depuis le pays des Illinois jusqu'à l'embouchure du fleuve Mississippi," LXV, 104; Gabriel Marest, "Lettre au Père Germon," *Jesuit Relations,* LXVI, 226.
46. Louis Vivier, "Lettre du Père Vivier, de la Compagnie de Jésus, à un père de la même compagnie," *Jesuit Relations,* LXIX, 222.

their work. Inland, after the battle of 1609, Champlain's first concern had been to return to Quebec and fortify the palisade, and thereafter he kept a vigilant guard against Iroquois reprisals. In the early period the Iroquois did not seriously threaten the French. As Jamet wrote in 1615, if they were terrible, they were few in number; a little blood and money spent immediately would secure the land for the king and lead to both its conquest and colonization.[47] While the Iroquois harassed Frenchmen who strayed too far from the St. Lawrence, down to 1629 the English menace remained much more dangerous.

After 1632 the missionaries, like Champlain before them, soon clashed with the Iroquois on behalf of the Algonquin alliance. They promptly cried out to France for stronger military support. The tiny garrisons of such posts as Tadoussac and Quebec could not effectively ward off the power of the five tribes. In 1634 Le Jeune made the first plain plea for conquest when he declared that the future of the missions depended upon terrorizing those enemies of Christianity.[48] While Champlain shared Le Jeune's solicitude for the faith, he possessed more tact as well as more intimate knowledge of Indian warfare: he wished to avoid the endless expense and bloodshed that conquest would involve. Accordingly, in 1635, for the last time in his life, the governor went among the Indians, to persuade them to submit peacefully. He urged them to become Christian in order to become civilized; for, once Christian, they would become allies of the French, receive military protection, live in peace, and grow rich.[49] If in his argument the governor seemed to make conversion the means to civilization, he thought he was appealing to the heathens more forcefully by dangling the more obvious rewards before them. The argument exemplified the interdependence of Champlain's aims: both conversion and empire seemed equally paramount.

Le Jeune's appeal for arms went unheeded; at home the government was deeply entangled in the Thirty Years' War. The Jesuits, in constant collision with the Iroquois, clamored ever more loudly. In 1640 Le Jeune returned to France to beg for military aid. But he was ignored and soon came back to Quebec, where he worked in the missions until 1649. In that fatal year the utter ruin of Jesuit hopes among the Hurons and the cruel death of his beloved Brébeuf drove him to France again. He never returned to Quebec;

47. "Relation au Cardinal François de Joyeuse," *La Nouvelle France*, XIII, 442.
48. "Relation . . . 1634," VI, 145, 153.
49. "Relation . . . 1635," VII, 288.

but neither did he cease to agitate for the adequate arming of New France when later he became procurator of the missions. In the years 1648–51 the government was too distracted by Frondeurs to concern itself over savages three thousand miles away. During the next decade, without arms or escort, the priests invaded the villages of the Iroquois, perhaps as much to allay their hatred of the French as to save their souls. But they failed; by 1658 the five tribes again took the warpath. At that time the superior, Jérôme Lallemant (1593–1673), who had spent his first seven years in Canada among the Hurons, warned that the Iroquois had to be crushed immediately and completely. Otherwise, he predicted, the French would lose forever the opportunity of trading or preaching among the Indians west of Montreal. Therefore the government should despatch two royal regiments to New France at once.[50] No regiments came, and the Iroquois continued to raid along the upper St. Lawrence.

Two years later Father Paul Ragueneau (1608–80) sounded a further warning. Ragueneau had worked faithfully beside Brébeuf among the Hurons; it was he who had shepherded the Huron survivors to safety on the island of Orléans in 1650; later he spent a year among the Onondagas. Now he wrote to his patron and former pupil, the Prince de Condé, that at least one regiment was absolutely indispensable to vanquish the foe to the south. Any further conversions in New France depended upon arms— an opinion that most missionaries then shared. The governor, seconding Ragueneau, also wrote Condé and stressed the more worldly advantages of such a conquest. Quebec "would be the finest, strongest, and greatest port in the world": it had the natural terrain and arable land sufficient to sustain a city of a hundred thousand, and a fine harbor.[51] His Majesty made no response.

In 1665 Father François le Mercier (1604–90) took up, along with the duties of superior, the plea for protection. He compared the Iroquois to the ancient tribes of Germany and Gaul, and chided the French (who boasted of their descent from Rome) for lacking the same courage to reduce these new barbarians that the ancient Romans had shown in their wars.[52] Soon afterward, whether Le Mercier's thrust found its mark or not, a regiment arrived and

50. "Relation . . . 1659 & 1660," XLV, 181–201.
51. "Deux lettres addressées à M. le Prince de Condé," *Jesuit Relations*, XLVI, 147–151.
52. "Relation . . . 1664 & 1665," XLIX, 215.

undertook a series of punitive expeditions. As a result Father Dablon, who became superior in 1671, reported that the Jesuits could then carry the gospel more than four hundred leagues in every direction without opposition.[53] Dablon's comment needed qualification: four hundred leagues south would have taken the French to Florida; in 1671 the Jesuits could not have moved about independently even in French territory. But Dablon was probably thinking only of Indian opposition.

Indeed, the home government intruded more and more. The troops did not come to New France simply to do the will of the missionaries: under the command of the governor, they served also to control all Frenchmen, whether lay or religious. The Jesuits welcomed the regiment, but they expected it simply to keep the peace, guarantee the present frontiers, and extend them when and where missionary policy demanded. While the government contemplated that arms would abet the cause of religion, they contemplated no subordination to that cause and quickly disillusioned the priests. In fact, after about 1690, external pressure made the missions more and more dependent upon the military. As it became increasingly necessary to police troubled areas, the governor often used the fathers as his agents to pacify the Indians.

Originally the missionaries had regarded conquest simply as a necessary means to insure a peaceful colonization. But the interest of the crown in territorial gains antedated the arrival of Biard and Massé by seventy years; similarly, the dispatch of a regiment started a drive for imperial conquest, which the exploits of La Salle intensified. In the eyes of the government conquest by religion had not succeeded; conquest by arms, then, became an aim in itself, as important as colonization or conversion—more important when it promised a more rapid success. The attitude of the Sieur de Cadillac reflected the official sentiment. In 1703 Cadillac called conversion unimportant in itself but useful if it could strengthen political ties between the French and the Indians. When he founded Detroit, he asked for some priests there to teach the savages the French language. That, he felt, and not Christianity, would surely civilize them. Later the missionaries could teach their religion, but: "subjects of the king, and afterwards . . . Christians." [54] Louis XIV himself also yielded to the secular arguments for conquest; but to him the religious and

---

53. "Relation . . . 1670 & 1671," LIV, 251.
54. Antoine de Lamothe Cadillac, "Papers," *Michigan Pioneer and Historical Society Historical Collection* (Lansing, 1904), XXX, 99, 166-167.

political aspects of his own absolutism became indistinguishable. In 1700 the king stated that the Huguenots had fled to New England in order to wrest New France from him; as the implacable enemy of the Huguenot fury he would save the country. Otherwise the work of a century would be lost, and the benedictions of heaven denied to the house of Bourbon.[55] Thus the military manifestations of absolutism threatened to overwhelm the benevolent missionary activity dedicated to ends that harmonized with that same absolutism. But the missionaries themselves had summoned the soldiers; thereafter they remained powerless to control their secular allies.

Subordinate to the primary corporate aim of conversion, the missionaries made use of whatever means seemed fit to advance the faith. They hoped to create a new France in America by their preaching, teaching, and religious ministration; and by enlisting the resources of auxiliary groups having economic, social, political, or military interests in the land. To procure such support as they deemed necessary, the missionaries deluged France with letters and petitions. While personal emissaries were rare, such priests as Massé on his two returns from America or the Recollet Piat who appealed to Ventadour for aid in 1624 or Le Jeune in 1640 did spread news about the missions by word of mouth. But generally the missionaries relied on written reports, which they published. Of these documents the most informative and abundant were the Jesuit Relations.

The idea of Relations apparently originated with Francis Xavier, who, soon after he established his order in India, ordered from all the missionaries under his jurisdiction periodic reports of their activities. These reports, sometimes edited or consolidated, he forwarded to Rome. Their purpose, he stated, was to bear witness to the faith, to describe the spread of the gospel and the experiences and obstacles the missionaries encountered, and to edify readers generally, for the greater glory of God.[56] The authorities in Rome approved of Xavier's practice and soon made it standard for all foreign missions.

After 1632 the Jesuit superior at Quebec forwarded an annual Relation to his chief, the provincial in Paris. Sometimes the superior wrote a completely original narrative from notes and interviews he had made during the past year. But more often the report

55. Collection de manuscrits, II, 341.
56. Léon Pagès, ed., Lettres de Saint François-Xavier (2 vols., Paris, 1855), II, 51, 115–117, 340–341.

consisted of accounts that he received from various Canadian posts and either edited or simply passed on to Paris without change. After any deletions that he thought proper, the provincial passed the documents on to the publishers. The Relations were intended primarily for public consumption; and as suited their complex organization, the Jesuits had other regular means of communicating information concerning personnel, administration, and finances.

The Relations have been truly labeled "works of propaganda and not scientific reports." [57] Nevertheless, it is essential to define "propaganda" as dissemination of information and to eschew the suspicion that the Jesuits had an ulterior motive concealed in their writings. They always made their purpose explicit; indeed, they publicly devoted themselves to the propagation of the faith. So stern a critic as Parkman defined the nature of their propaganda when he wrote that "the closest examination has left me no doubt that these missionaries wrote in perfect good faith, and that the Relations hold a high place as authentic and trustworthy documents." [58] The fathers themselves frankly avowed the true purpose of their writings. In 1616 Biard prefaced his Relation thus: "Now (dear reader) it is the ardent desire and zeal of seeing this New France conquered for our Lord that has made me take pen in hand to describe for you briefly and in all truth what I have discovered in these countries." [59]

From 1632 to 1674 the Jesuits published a Relation each year, and its contents made the purpose of each report clear. In 1653 Francesco Bressani, the lone Italian in this French mission field, compiled a Relation in his native tongue because he wished to make the work of the missions known in as many languages as possible.[60] In the same year Paul Ragueneau published *Progressus fidei Catholicae*, which included an excerpt from the Canadian Relation of 1648–49 with similar accounts from Asia. He was appealing, he wrote, especially to "the orthodox reader desirous of the propagation of the faith." [61] Many years later Le Mercier

57. Gilbert Chinard, *L'Amérique et le rêve exotique dans la littérature française au XVIIe et XVIIIe siècle* (Paris, 1913), p. 64.

58. *Jesuits in North America in the Seventeenth Century*, p. vi.

59. "Relation de la Nouvelle France," III, 36.

60. "Breve relazione di'alcune missioni de PP della Compagnia de Gesu nella Nuova Francia" [Macerata, 1653], XXXVIII, 217.

61. *Progressus fidei Catholicae in Novo Orbe* (Coloniae Agrippinae, 1653), Introd.

echoed Ragueneau: "I hope that there will be found here material to satisfy the curiosity of those who take pleasure in learning what occurs in foreign nations, and at the same time material to edify the piety and animate the zeal of apostolic men." [62] It is noteworthy that in 1670 Le Mercier should have hinted at a division between the curious on the one hand and the apostolic on the other. After 1674 interest in missionary activity flagged in France, and the Relations ceased to be published in an annual series. Once again it seemed expedient for missionary writers to state their purpose. In 1724 Joseph Lafitau presented his critical résumé of American manners as a continuation of the spirit of the earlier Relations.[63]

When the reports were published regularly, the fathers imagined that "a great part of France awaits [them] with some excitement," [64] and did not hesitate to appeal for specific assistance when necessity dictated. Thus Le Jeune begged for money, an endowed convent in Quebec, and military protection. In 1645 Vimont took to task those readers who were skeptical about conversions: ". . . doubts that may exist in France . . . are one of the greatest impediments that can be offered . . . God may withdraw His favors from these infidel lands, because in the midst of storms confidence in Him has been withdrawn." [65] The Relations, then, not only transparently reflected the official aspirations of the missionaries but also served as vital instruments in encompassing more intermediate aims. Weapons of eloquence and persuasion, of the essence of the missionary task, they were indeed propaganda.

But they were also truthful documents. They presented the American Indians in their daily drabness and their wildest orgies to the French reading public. They fed that curiosity about natural man in a state of nature—as opposed to supernatural man or to man in a state of highly artificial society—which so occupied the Europeans in the eighteenth century. The great majority of Jesuits did not anticipate the use to which their material was put; it was the result rather than the purpose of their work. They worked simply and steadfastly for the conversion of the heathens, in accordance with the wishes expressed and the means permitted by God, their general, and their king.

62. "Relation . . . 1669 & 1670," LIII, 24.
63. *Moeurs des sauvages américquains* (2 vols., Paris, 1724), I, 5.
64. "Relation . . . 1640," XVIII, 60.
65. "Relation . . . 1644 & 1645," XXVIII, 62.

V

THE PERSONAL INTERESTS
OF THE MISSIONARIES

IN New France the missionary sought to fulfill not only the
corporate aims that his superiors ordained but also certain
personal goals. While submission to a rule bound the Recollets,
Jesuits, and Sulpicians more strictly than other men in Canada,
it destroyed neither their individual personalities nor their entire
freedom of action. Thus in conduct and attitude they frequently
resembled the traders and explorers, who also faced the barbarism
and harshness of the frontier. On the other hand, if, for instance,
Biard and Champlain felt alike about the necessity of conversion,
they had come to such agreement along entirely different paths.
The explorer would have insisted that he had formed his opinion independently, as a result of his experience and his personal
religious feelings. The priest had voluntarily submitted to the
higher authority of the Jesuit order, whose dictates he thereafter accepted; and conversion in New France happened to be a
Jesuit policy. Early in life a missionary abdicated the utter freedom that a layman enjoyed until death. In exchange the missionary sought a regulated liberty; aided by the limitations of his
vows, he also sought personal realization. The conditions of life
and nature in Canada shocked the priests by the radical contrast
with what they had known in Europe. While they strove to spread
the faith by the accepted means of knowledge, adaptation, and
eloquence, individuals often found themselves forced into independent action of startling boldness or originality. As a result, a
broad variety of personal interests developed among the missionaries.

While the founders of the Jesuit and Recollet orders intended
to train their novices under a discipline, they did not desire absolute uniformity. The Recollets dedicated themselves principally
to contemplation yet recognized that not all friars could attain
the same mystical level. The Jesuits dedicated themselves to more
worldly goals; accordingly the *Spiritual Exercises* and the *Ratio*

studiorum allowed for a greater variety of individual taste, mental capacity, and spirituality. Indeed, as the Society of Jesus became more intimately related to the work of the Counter Reformation, a diversity in its membership became ever more desirable. It was their very versatility and adaptability that made the Jesuits so useful to the church and justified the broad mandate that Paul III had given the order in 1540. The nature of Jesuit education was orthodox and classical. It was also liberal, in that it did not train men for specific duties but provided them with a general attitude of Catholic humanism. Thus, as "the shock troops of the papacy," the Jesuits stood ready for any given task. Their number (approximately sixteen thousand in 1640, and over twenty-two thousand in 1773) generally made it possible to assign men to tasks that suited their individual abilities and tastes. The provincial in France also considered the fitness of the men he ordered to Canada and used volunteers whenever he could. In Quebec the superior tried to dole out the missionary tasks on a similar basis.

Despite a common discipline and a common call to the religious life, the Jesuits who went to New France were not all alike. While, no doubt, "the priest who saw monsters and almost demons in the savages and the old professor of rhetoric at La Flèche who could not forget the Latin poets and historians in the depths of the American forests" dwelt to some degree in each missionary,[1] he also possessed personal characteristics that duty and training could not completely stifle. The prompt solution of new problems in an alien land demanded of the Jesuits an ingenuity, perception, and decision that formal education could only sharpen but not originate.

The Canadian missionary served in many capacities: he taught and administered in the college and residences; he preached and confessed in French villages and forts; he did anything and everything among the Indians; and, in addition, he occasionally explored, traded, or acted as a government agent. Not all missionaries were equally well suited for all kinds of work. But most filled their roles with competence, and many brilliantly. While Le Jeune, for example, proved a superior of imagination, prudence, and initiative, Charles Lallemant hated the responsibility and the conditions of life in Quebec. Paul Ragueneau, the beloved pastor of the Hurons on their final trek in 1650, made a tactless and interfering superior, whom the governor finally exiled to Three

1. Chinard, *L'Amérique et le rêve exotique*, p. 138.

Rivers. Brébeuf, who could not endure the strain of teaching at Rouen, created his destiny among the Huron villagers. Charlevoix, undistinguished as a missionary, rendered his colleagues high service as their publicist in France. In contrast to such men of affairs scores of men worked among the savages in silence, like Ennémond Massé, who wrote in 1611: "I admit to you that I said then freely to God: here I am: if you choose what is feeble and despicable in this world, to overthrow and destroy what is strong, you will find all that in Ennémond. Here I am: send me, and make my tongue and my word intelligible, so that I may not be a barbarian to those who will hear me." [2]

Massé had already adjusted himself to his task. Each missionary faced a similar adjustment. But each was an individual in a different assignment, contending with its peculiar circumstances; each made his own personal adjustment. The interests of the missionaries colored their descriptions of the Indians. Therefore the expressions of the attitude they adopted toward their duties are significant.

The personal interests may be classified as spiritual or secular. Spiritually, the missionary attained one of four ascending states of mind. Simple devotion to duty characterized perhaps the majority, who prosaically reported like clerks on their progress in the vineyard. Above the simply dutiful stood the resigned, whom Massé typified: reflective, yet perhaps without any great capacity for aspiration. Next were men gifted with a higher religious consciousness, who derived a rich consolation from suffering. At the peak of aspiration stood those—especially the martyrs—who not simply learned, but distilled glorification, from their hardships. The secular interests represented personal extensions of the intellectual and moral—in contradistinction to the purely supernatural—motives of the missionaries. Many cherished a natural curiosity and eagerly scanned the American woods for exotic novelties. Others, equally inquisitive about human nature, studied the Indians.

If the corporate motives remained external to the spiritual progress of the individual, they nonetheless circumscribed its course. The salvation of souls played a doubly virtuous role: it not only would bring about the consummation of the world but also sped the missionary to his own salvation. Such work was Christian

2. "Lettre au R. P. Claude Aquaviva, Général de la Compagnie de Jésus," *Jesuit Relations*, I, 184.

par excellence: to act without selfishness but in charity, simultaneously for the highest good of society and of oneself. The devoted servant could offer up to his merciful Master the pains and triumphs that accompanied the performance of his earthly mission.

A sense of duty ruled every missionary, except for those rare few who gave up the spiritual life. The priest who did nothing more than he was ordered usually failed to inject his personality into his reports; his devotion must be gauged by the record of his actions. Jérôme Lallemant regarded his duty in such simple and literal terms. Jérôme was born in 1593, the younger brother of Charles who became procurator of the mission and vice-provincial in Paris. Jérôme's life followed a more ordinary pattern. Before coming to New France in 1638 he had taught philosophy and natural science in Jesuit colleges for almost twenty years. In America he first worked among the Hurons and in 1645 succeeded Vimont as superior. He visited France in 1651 to beg for military protection, and on his return to Quebec buried himself in the Montagnais missions. In 1656 he went to France again, acted as rector of La Flèche for a year, and accompanied Laval back to New France in 1659, as the prelate's vicar-general. After a second term as superior, he resigned in 1665 to help Laval organize the new diocese. He died in 1673. Lallemant wrote his share of fifteen Relations, several journals, letters, and memoirs. His writings reveal candor, great energy, and a wry humor. But his religious sentiments remained obscure; he did not express them on paper, and they must be deduced from his varied activities.

Antoine Silvy held no such exalted posts as Jérôme Lallemant, but he displayed the same devotion to duty. After the usual course in studies and terms of teaching philosophy and theology in France, Silvy came to New France in 1673 and remained until his death in 1711. He was first stationed at St. Ignace for four years and then came east to Tadoussac, where he worked until 1686. Next he joined an expedition to Hudson Bay as chaplain and stayed there among the Indians until 1693. Later he retired to Quebec, where he taught mathematics in the college and preached and baptized in the nearby missions. Beside a fragment of the Relation of 1676–77, Silvy left a *Relation par lettres* which apparently supplied Charlevoix with much information. The latter included many prudent observations about the conduct and the aims of the missions, but it revealed little about the author. Once again, in the face of personal reticence, long years of service alone proved a missionary's devotion.

The abbé Maillard, a secular who lived with the Micmacs from 1735 to 1768, stated the mood of simple devotion most clearly. In one letter he wrote: "Whatever happens, I am determined to stay with the savages . . . having the confidence in J.C. that in forcing myself to fulfill all the duties of my ministry, the stubborn indocility of my hearers will not be any obstacle to my salvation." [3] Whether Maillard felt more deeply the grace, love, or fear of God that inspired other priests is unknown; but at least zeal for souls sustained him.

As the quotations from Massé and Maillard indicate, the missionaries found New France a harsh land, which often provoked them to express their frustration. Yet few Jesuits persisted in a mood of resignation. Divine grace and love counteracted despair. The glory of their sacrifices, ranging from trivial physical discomforts to murder, sustained many who would have found the mere dutiful conversion of pagans an inadequate compensation for the loneliness, poverty, filth, and exposure of their lives. Thus tales of cruelty and hardship can no more be ascribed to self-pity than can the records of native virtue and conversions to fatuous self-congratulation. Furthermore the missionaries, anxious to tell what went on in New France, regarded their accounts of hardship as edification for their readers.

"Surely we sow in great poverty and tears," Father Biard admitted in 1611; but, he added, "may the Lord deign to grant us to reap some day in joy." [4] Cast forlorn upon the rocks of Acadia and the dubious friendships of Poutrincourt and Membertou, Biard and Massé did not despair. When they were driven back to France, they continued to urge others to carry on their work, the one by his books, the other by his talks with the fervent young priests and scholastics at La Flèche. Later men found similar hope in their trials. In 1635 Le Jeune forwarded to his provincial the *Divers Sentiments and Advices of the Fathers Who Are in New France.*[5] These testimonials catalogued in full the magnitude and variety of hardships that could be anticipated. But they also demonstrated how the writers had risen above resignation and

3. Antoine Simon Maillard, "Lettres," *Collection de documents inédits sur le Canada et l'Amérique* (3 vols., Québec, 1888–90), I, 63.

4. "Lettre au T.-R.P. Claude Aquaviva," *Jesuit Relations,* I, 190.

5. "Relation . . . 1635," VIII, 168–193.

derived solace and moral instruction from such situations. One of the first described the journey to Quebec:

Truly, to make 900 leagues upon the floods of the sea, and with hundreds of encounters with Turks, icebergs, reefs, perfectly terrible storms—that can stun a man's nature and make the human heart throb; there one experiences what David means, *Anima mea in manibus meis semper.* I hold my heart always in my hands, and I am ready at every moment to sacrifice it to God; alas, only too happy to be able to make many times a precious holocaust of myself. . . I confess that I have learned better upon the sea than upon the land, what the infusion of God into a well-formed soul is.

Another saw himself in the track of the Apostle of the Gentiles:

I was for twenty-four hours, seeing ourselves pursued by the Turks on leaving the English Channel, expecting nothing else than to fall into their hands and to be covered with chains and to live in slavery. Among these natural alarms, lo a strong thought comes to seize my heart, and says to me: ah, what fortune it would be to be able to imitate Saint Paul, and to see myself enchained for the love of Jesus, who was bound for me and treated like a slave and like the king of thieves.

Zeal led one priest, once in the new country, to write:

. . . they say that the first to found churches usually are saints: this thought so much softens my heart that, although I see myself very useless here in this blessed New France, I must admit that I cannot prevent one thought which presses on my heart. *Cupio impendi, et superimpendi pro vobis:* Poor New France, I desire to sacrifice myself for your good, and though it should cost me a thousand lives, if thus I can help to save a single soul, I shall be too happy, and my life very well spent.

Instances of the spirit of self-sacrifice also appeared without reference to the church. The finest of these was the following:

Three powerful thoughts console a good heart, which is in the infinite forests of New France or among the Hurons. The first is, I am in the place where God has sent me, where He has led me as by the hand, where He is with me, and where I seek Him alone. The second is, what David says: according to the measure of the pains which I endure for God, His divine consolations rejoice my soul. The third, that one never finds either cross, or nails, or thorns, without finding J. C. in the midst, if one looks closely.

One pious father summed up all the virtue of his poor lonely existence when he wrote that "to lose all in order to find God is a sweet loss and a holy usury." However heavy their burdens or poor their prospects of success, these men knew that a "well-formed soul" could not but find glory in the missions. And, they showed, it was not always cloistered meditation alone that led to an intuitive apprehension of God.

One year Jean de Brébeuf described his life among the Hurons. He elaborated on the rough traveling conditions, the crude shelters and food, and the suspicion and rude manners a missionary could expect. The work was hard, he cautioned, but it also was full of glory.[6] Later, when Paul Ragueneau recounted the Iroquois massacre of the Hurons, he bemoaned the collapse of the Jesuit schemes for that western nation. But the sober man was not embittered. "Where," he reflected, "would our merit and faith be, if we did not wander among these obscurities?"[7] More than the official aims of their order, their personal resources sustained such priests in the face of disaster—even when they more than half knew that hostile forces would wreck what they had not yet built.

To other missionaries New France meant hardships that were more physically immediate. François de Crépieul, whose faithfulness to the Montagnais had led him to the killing winters, marshlands, and vicious insects of the far north, chafed under the conditions of his life. In 1697 he admitted:

The life of a Montagnaix missionary is a long and slow martyrdom—
    Is an almost continual exercise of patience and mortification—
    Is a life truly penitential and humiliating, especially in the cabins and on the journeys with the savages. . . .
    The missionary almost all day sits or is on his knees exposed to an almost continual smoke during the winter. . . .
    His usual drink is water from a stream or some pond, sometimes melted snow or broth, pure or mixed with snow in a dish usually quite greasy. . . .
    He always sleeps with his clothes on . . . to protect himself from vermin. . . .
    He is . . . sometimes made ill by the stink . . . of those who have scrofula. . . .

6. "Relation . . . 1636," X, 97–115.
7. "Relation . . . 1648 & 1649," XXXIV, 200.

I have even been often obliged to drink from ponds in which I saw toads, etc.

Crépieul closed his litany of misery in fitting fashion: "Suffering and hardship are the appanages of these holy and arduous missions—*Faxit Deus ut iis diu immoretur et immoriatur servus inutilis missionum Franciscus S.J.*" [8]

Crépieul mentioned martyrdom; but only in a manner of speaking, because martydom was not "long and slow." It meant death; it came in an instant, with violence, as a direct consequence of a voluntary testimonial to the faith. Indeed, many missionaries attained true martyrdom when they refused to yield to mortal menaces in their quest for complete personal fulfillment. Aside from those like Isaac Jogues, whom the church has explicitly designated as such, surely Sébastien Rasles at Nanransouock and Jean Aulneau in the far west also rank as martyrs. Their actions and writings demonstrated their intentions and bespoke the intense aspiration that they wrung from their experiences.

Isaac Jogues, born in 1607, studied under the Jesuits until he set sail for New France in 1636. He worked with Brébeuf among the Hurons for six years; then his ordeal began. The Mohawks captured him in a battle with the Hurons and subjected him to the inevitable torture of burning and mutilation. One savage approached to cut off his nose, hesitated, and approached the priest again. But again he refrained, and Jogues suspected the cause: ". . . you know, my God, what I said to you then in the depth of my heart. Indeed I know not what invisible force repulsed him a second time." [9] Then his captors drove him, bleeding and feverish, to their village, where they racked and burned him again —"Oh my God! what nights"—and finally adopted him. One night Jogues had a vision that filled him "with a consolation wholly divine and completely inexplicable," but which convinced him that his death "was delayed" and seemed to indicate a divine wish that he baptize the Iroquois. [10] For over a year he shunned every chance to escape, hoping to win some convert. But the savages remained adamant, and in the autumn of 1643 he fled, with the help of the Dutch, and sailed from the island of "Manate" for

8. "La Vie d'un missionaire montagnaix," *Jesuit Relations,* LXV, 42–48.

9. Jean de Brébeuf, "Epistola ad R. P. Mutium Vitelleschi, Praepositum Generalem Societatis Jesu," in *Jesuit Relations,* XXIII, 246–253; "Relation . . . 1647," XXXI, 34.

10. "Relation . . . 1647," XXXI, 66–68.

France. At home his colleagues and the great ones of the world
—even Anne of Austria—gazed at his scars and crushed hands.
But Jogues did not relish their sympathy, and after building up
his strength he speedily returned to New France, intent on his
mission.

In the spring of 1646 the French signed a truce with the Iroquois, and Jogues's superior ordered him back to the Mohawks.
Jogues himself wished to resume the work, but his reply to the
superior's letter betrayed his presentiment and revealed the am-
bivalent state of mind every martyr must share:

. . . would you believe that upon opening the letters of your R[ever-
ence] my heart was as though seized with fear at the beginning, apprehending lest what I desire and what my spirit should most prize
might happen. My poor nature which remembered the past trembled,
but our Lord through his goodness has calmed it and will calm it still
more. Yes, my father, I wish all that our Lord wishes at the peril of a
thousand lives. . . . [I] undertake this journey . . . against all
the inclinations of nature.[11]

Jogues went to the Mohawks and founded the Mission of the
Martyrs in memory of his dead colleagues and perhaps also out
of premonition, for he knew he had walked into the jaws of death.
In October, as he was entering his cabin, a savage stepped from
behind the door and split open the priest's head with his hatchet.
Jogues had conquered his nature. Jérôme Lallemant wrote that
he died "the death of a martyr before the angels." [12]

If Jogues knew his murder was certain, Sébastien Rasles (1652–
1724) had only less palpable intimations of martyrdom. Rasles's
early life followed the usual Jesuit pattern of study interspersed
with terms of teaching until 1689, when he was sent out to the
Canadian mission. He spent his first two years with the Abenakis
and after two years with the Illinois returned to the Abenakis
at Nanransouock in 1693 for the rest of his life. In contrast to
Jogues Rasles worked among tribes that were friendly and already
partially Christian. While the Dutch had instigated Iroquois
resistance to the French, they had not singled out Jogues for
special hatred; but the English, anxious to rule the Abenakis, did
aim particularly at Rasles. The mission of Nanransouock stood
near the Kennebec, well within the English claims; thus, even

11. *Ibid.*, pp. 106–108.
12. *Ibid.*, p. 120.

though Rasles did not insist that his flock swear allegiance to the
king of France, his Catholicism constituted a patent threat to
English political rule. After 1713 especially, the English strove
hard to push the French back through Maine to the St. Lawrence,
and marked out Rasles as the leader of the Franco-Indian resistance.

At first the English sent Protestant missionaries north from
Boston, but they made little headway against Abenaki Catholicism. Then the English tried to frighten Rasles into running away.
In January, 1722, they sent out a war party to capture him, but
with a few faithful Indians he fled to the woods. There the English

came within eight paces of the tree that hid me, and where *naturally*
they must have seen me; for the trees were stripped of their leaves;
nevertheless, as if they had been repulsed by an invisible hand, they
suddenly retraced their steps and again took the path to the village.

Thus, by a special protection of God, I escaped their pursuit.[13]

The missionary had noted, like Jogues, an invisible means of deliverance; his will to do God's work was fortified. In October,
when the English again threatened Nanransouock, his neophytes
urged him to withdraw to Quebec. But he refused:

What will become of the flock, if it is deprived of its shepherd? Death
alone can separate me from them. . . . I say to them, do not be
anxious about what concerns me: I do not fear the menaces of those
who hate me when I have not deserved their hatred, and I do not value
my life more precious than myself, so that I may finish my course,
and the ministry of the word that has been entrusted to me by the
Lord Jesus.[14]

The more Rasles determined to remain, the more the English determined to be rid of him. In 1723 Rasles believed the enemy had
set a high price on his head. He stood firm:

I shall be only too happy if I become their victim, and if God judge
me worthy of being loaded with irons and of pouring out my blood
for the salvation of my dear savages. . . . It is true that for a long
time they have vowed my destruction; but neither their ill will toward
me nor the death with which they threaten me will ever be able to

13. "Lettre à M. son neveu," *Jesuit Relations*, LXVII, 114; italics mine.
14. *Ibid.*, p. 118.

separate me from my old flock; I commend them to your devout prayers.[15]

In August, 1724, a large party of English and their Indian allies surprised Nanransouock when most of the villagers were away. Hearing the uproar that their appearance had caused, Rasles came out of his cabin and was struck dead by a volley of musketshot, among his dying followers. "The victim of his charity and of his zeal," he won "a glorious death, which was always the object of his desires." [16]

Ten years after Rasles fell at Nanransouock, Jean Pierre de la Touche Aulneau arrived in New France. Fresh out of school, this young priest came to dread the task to which he had dedicated his life. "I have already seen a few of almost all the tribes," he wrote his mother two months after landing, "and there is no more repulsive sight, but they have been ransomed by the blood of God. How happy shall I be if He deigns to make use of so unworthy an instrument as myself to bring them to love and adore Him in spirit and truth." [17] In 1735 Aulneau was sent out to the Lake of the Woods at the utter extremity of French America. Contemplating the prospect with gloom, he relied upon the succor of Christ. "Happy the one who is deemed worthy to die for Him." A month later he wrote that out there he should "resemble the first missionaries of this poor country who watered it with their sweat and blood." [18] The following year hostile Sioux ambushed the party of friendly Indians and French whom he accompanied, and Aulneau was killed with a hatchet. The pious pessimism of his last letters seemed to presage such an end. In death Aulneau escaped the dilemma into which his zeal and sensitivity were perhaps leading him. Less robust of temperament than Jogues or Rasles, still he resembled the former in an awareness of spiritual conflict, and the latter in determination.

To judge by the conduct of the martyrs any missionary might have made the same sacrifices under similar circumstances. But fortunately the circumstances made no such uniform demands; and to have sought out the martyr's crown would have entailed sinful pride. Therefore the missionary, while prepared to sacrifice all, remained content to overcome whatever obstacles—petty or colos-

15. "Lettre à Monsieur son frère," *Jesuit Relations,* LXVII, 204, 228.

16. Pierre de la Chasse, "Lettre au Père ———," *Jesuit Relations,* LXVII, 230–235.

17. Jones, ed., *The Aulneau Collection,* p. 13.

18. *Ibid.,* pp. 46–47, 54.

sal—lay in his way. Thus he attained the spiritual goal of which he was capable.

Parallel to the supernatural interests there also ran in many missionaries secular interests of an intellectual or moral nature. The principles of adaptation and sympathy so vital to successful conversions made curiosity about the Indians and their country inevitable. In addition, Europe was bursting with a curiosity about exotic new regions that even cloistered monks could not ignore in the seventeenth and eighteenth centuries. Before Biard landed in Acadia explorers, fishermen, and religious refugees had already stimulated French interest in America; and the progressive schools of the time (including the Jesuit colleges) gave courses in the natural sciences. Secular curiosity, then, came easily to the French missionaries.

Ordinarily the secular concerns of the priests did not conflict with their spiritual interests: they remained subordinate. It was not the new land that fascinated the missionaries; it was the people who lived there. But since it was necessary to understand the Indians before attempting to convert them, it became also necessary to know the physical, political, social, and moral conditions of Indian life; and then, of course, to publish them, in order to explain the progress of the faith. If the accounts of natural phenomena in the Relations pale beside those of more worldly men, it should be borne in mind that the missionaries did not sail forth to find new marvels or El Dorado or even the Northwest Passage; they wanted souls. On the other hand, the missionaries could not avoid some knowledge of the Canadian climate and terrain. Indeed, nothing is more conducive to knowledge of a region than covering it step by step and paddle stroke by paddle stroke, counting the rapids, pacing the portages, marking the springs, skirting impassable cliffs and swamps, welcoming sheltered valleys and pine-needled forest floors. Thus did the missionaries track back and forth across New France.

Exploration attracted many of them. Biard and the early Recollets had followed paths cut out by trappers and explorers, as missionaries continued to do, so long as their posts stood along the routes of the fur trade. But after 1632, when the priests ventured further up the Saguenay, into the New York forests, and out across the Great Lakes, they systematically charted their progress. As they moved out ever farther they found fewer competent Indian guides; often they assumed the entire burden of exploration themselves. Especially after 1670 did the priests experience the exciting novelty of entering unknown country. When Claude Dablon, for example, followed the Ottawas north of Lake Superior, he explained his action on two grounds. He was first of all concerned for "the conversion of these people"; also he wished

to discover at last that North Sea, of which so much has already been said and which has not yet been found overland.

The motives of this discovery are first to know if this sea is the bay to which Hudson penetrated in the year 1612, or some other, by comparing the longitudes and latitudes of this place with those of that sea. . . . Secondly to learn if it is possible to communicate with that sea from Quebec by following all the northern shores, as had been tried some years ago. . . . Thirdly, to verify the rather strong conjectures that have been held for a long time, that a passage was possible from there to the Sea of Japan.[19]

The same Relation bearing word of Dablon's scheme to Quebec (whence it probably reached Colbert) also included an early hint of Jacques Marquette's interest in exploration. Marquette (1637–75) had arrived in Canada in 1666 and was assigned to work with Allouez in the western missions. In 1669 Marquette received a visit from some Illinois, who, to reach him, had had to

cross a great river which is almost a league wide: it flows from the north to the south and so far that the Illinois, who do not know what a canoe is, have not yet heard any mention of its mouth . . . . a nation that they call Chaouanou [Shawnee?] came to see them last summer . . . . [who] are laden with beads, which shows that they have communication with Europeans. . . . It is hard [to believe] that this great river discharges its waters in Virginia; and we think rather that it has its mouth in California. If the savages who promise to make me a canoe do not break their word, we shall go along that river as far as we can . . . We shall visit the nations who live there, to open a passage to those of our fathers who have waited for this good fortune for such a long time. This discovery will give us a full knowledge of either the South Sea or the Western Sea.[20]

But Marquette had to postpone his plans. In 1671 the Sioux drove him out of his post in Wisconsin, and he moved north to St. Ignace, where he labored for two years. Then he set out with the adventurer Louis Joliet; they explored the Mississippi down to its juncture

19. "Relation . . . 1669 & 1670," LIV, 134–136.
20. Ibid., pp. 188–190.

with the Arkansas. Marquette's motive remained primarily religious: "to seek toward the south sea nations new and unknown to us, in order to make them know our great God of whom they have been up to now ignorant." [21] When the two explorers made their reports to Quebec, they aroused the ambitions of Frontenac and La Salle, who thereupon launched their own project for the conquest of inland America. In 1675, on his way back to St. Ignace from a second voyage, which led to no new discoveries, Marquette died.

Three years later a Recollet, Louis Hennepin (1640?–1706?), appeared in the west. Hennepin had come to New France in 1675 and spent two years among the Iroquois at Kenté before he was assigned to La Salle as chaplain of his expedition. He joined La Salle eagerly because, as he once wrote, "All my life I have loved to travel and my natural curiosity has driven me to many parts of Europe. But not being satisfied with this, I have searched farther and wished to see more distant lands and the most unknown nations." [22] Sailing up the Great Lakes from Niagara, the party reached the Illinois in 1679; there Hennepin founded the mission of Crèvecoeur. In the next two years he explored the Mississippi above its juncture with the Illinois, and then, after an alleged capture by the Sioux, he returned to Quebec.

Closely related to exploration, if less vital for the missions, was interest in the exotic plants and animals that the missionaries spotted on their travels. The richness of the soil, its products, and minerals provided, it is true, inducements with which to attract colonists to New France. But frequently the missionaries departed from utilitarian considerations, and once they had discovered a bizarre novelty they obviously delighted to unveil it to their wonder-struck readers.

Anxious to discredit the magic of the native sorcerers, the missionaries examined the herbs with which the Indians charmed away mental and physical sickness. A Jesuit account of a journey into Iroquois country listed the advantages of that region over the rest of New France: ". . . grapes, plums, and other fruits common to the fine provinces of Europe," chestnut and walnut trees, nuts from which "an excellent oil is extracted," stoneless cherries, and "apples as large as goose eggs." "But the commonest and most marvelous plant of these countries is what we call the universal plant, because

21. "Relation . . . 1672 & 1673," LVII, 262.
22. Louis Hennepin, *Nouvelles découvertes d'un très grand pays* (Utrecht, 1697), p. 5.

its leaves, when mashed, cure all sorts of wounds in a short time; these leaves, broad as a hand, have the shape of a lily as depicted in heraldry, and its roots smell like laurel." [23] On the Mississippi Marquette came across the wild oat, cactus, mulberry, a fruit that tasted like an orange and looked like an olive, and the persimmon, which he described as follows:

. . . and another fruit as big as a hen's egg, we broke it in two and two divisions appeared, in each of which eight to ten fruits are encased, almond-shaped and good when ripe. Yet the tree that bears them has a very bad odor, and its leaves resemble those of the walnut tree. There is also in the prairies a fruit like hazelnuts but more delicate.[24]

The animals of America attracted even more attention. Naturally the missionaries, like the laymen, treated of the beaver fully, since it was virtually the coin of the realm and a knowledge of its habits became essential to the colony's prosperity. But they reserved their chief interest for more freakish beasts like the giant catfish and the bison that Marquette observed on his Mississippi journey. Of the catfish he wrote: ". . . a monster that had the head of a tiger, a sharp nose like a wildcat's, with whiskers and ears sticking straight up, the head was grey and the neck all black . . ." and of the bison:

. . . they have a very large head, a forehead that is flat and a foot and a half wide between the horns, which are exactly like those of our oxen, but black and much larger; they have under their neck a sort of dewlap that hangs down, and on their back a rather high hump. The whole head, neck, and part of the shoulders are covered by a great mane like that of a horse, it is a crest a foot long which makes them hideous and, falling over their eyes, prevents them from seeing in front of them . . . . they are very fierce . . . . they do not usually move very fast, except when angered. They are scattered over the prairies as in herds; I have seen one of four hundred.[25]

When Rasles visited the Illinois, he remarked that no tribe lived so abundantly as they, and listed the fowl and animals that they hunted. He also described the bison, which he called oxen, and

23. "Relation . . . 1656 & 1657," XLIII, 256–258.
24. "Le Premier voyage qu'a fait le P. Marquette," *Jesuit Relations,* LIX, 93, 138.
25. *Ibid.,* pp. 108–112.

stated that he had seen as many as five thousand in a herd.[26]

The curiosity about nature extended to the American heavens as well. Here too scientific interest was tempered by the desire of the missionaries to discredit the religious myths of the Indians, particularly those dealing with creation. In 1639 Jérôme Lallemant used observations of an eclipse to determine the latitude and longitude of his position in Huron country, "according to the rules of geography." [27] In 1674 Father Pierre Milet took rather unfair advantage of the superstitious Oneidas in predicting a lunar eclipse. "Everything," he complacently observed, "happened as I had announced, and they were constrained to admit that we knew things better than they." [28] But the French had not always been so omniscient, as Biard revealed when he first observed the aurora borealis:

We were still a league and a half from the island when twilight ended and it became night. The stars were already appearing, when suddenly toward the north a part of the sky became as blood red as scarlet, and spreading little by little in streaks and flashes, came to rest directly over the settlement of the men of St. Mâlo. The red glow was so bright that the whole river was tinged and made luminous by it. This apparition lasted half a quarter-hour, and as soon as it disappeared, another started up with the same form, direction, and substance.

There was not one of us who did not think this meteor a portent.[29]

In 1671 Claude Dablon on Lake Superior recounted with rapture the appearance and course of the winter sun and its parhelia, even to including in his Relation a drawing of the "highly pleasing spectacle." [30] When Aulneau moved west, although bent on conversion, he nevertheless bore in mind his obligation to report the natural phenomena of the unknown territory he was entering. He begged his friends not simply to pray for him but also "to send me the reckonings of the eclipses of the sun and moon visible in France and America. I shall endeavor to turn them to account to the best of my ability, in determining the longitude of the new regions to which Providence is sending me." [31] Even in so subjective a nature

26. "Lettre à Monsieur son frère," *Jesuit Relations*, LXVII, 167–169.
27. "Relation . . . 1639," XVI, 224.
28. "Relation . . . 1673 & 1674," LVIII, 182.
29. "Lettre au R. P. Provincial," *Jesuit Relations*, II, 26–28.
30. "Relation . . . 1670 & 1671," LV, 173–179.
31. Jones, ed., *The Aulneau Collection*, p. 55.

as Aulneau's, then, the spark of natural curiosity was not entirely dead.

Most manifestations of secular interest came in the later days of the missions. In the earlier period the missionaries concentrated more intently upon their spiritual goals, both corporate and individual. Only when their zeal failed to win over the Indians in swarms as they had anticipated did the missionaries turn to a more serious consideration of means; these in turn led them to stress the natural environment. At the same time men everywhere were valuing knowledge more for its natural than for its supernatural meaning. Even when they did not deny religious values, many priests took them for granted, and many laymen forgot them. As early as 1670 it had occurred to Father Le Mercier to justify his Relation as both satisfying the curious and edifying the apostolic.[32] By 1724 Joseph Lafitau, while professing to carry on the spirit of the relators, set forth this justification of his book: "The religious zeal which obliges a missionary to pass overseas is also to serve as his motive and to direct his pen, when in leisure he labors to elucidate the discoveries which he has made there and the information he has acquired. That is the aim of a worker of the gospel." [33] Le Jeune or Biard might have agreed with Lafitau, but they would not have couched the missionary's aim in such unspiritual terms.

Lafitau in fact was not a mere relator. He was a Jesuit historian who had served a tour of duty in New France; and the title of his book betrayed his primary interest in the Indians: their manners. Lafitau simply emphasized an intellectual interest of the missionaries that had already played a large role but had never loomed larger than the spiritual aims. Indeed, as an essential foundation for their primary task of conversion, missionaries since the days of Biard had paid special attention to the characteristics of the Indians themselves.

32. Cf. Chapter IV, n. 62.
33. *Moeurs des sauvages amériquains*, I, 5.

VI

THE PHYSICAL ASPECTS OF INDIAN LIFE

BIARD and Massé must have formed some idea about the Indians before they landed at Port Royal. Probably they had read of them; certainly they had heard talk about them on the docks of Dieppe or on shipboard. But with the sight of the Americans in the flesh, paddling out to meet them or waving a frantic welcome from the shore, they no longer needed to rely on secondhand accounts. From the very first they put their impressions down on paper; as long as the French ruled Canada, later missionaries imitated them.

Such accounts could not be absolutely objective, in view of the corporate and personal interests of the writers. Also, as Montaigne had remarked about travelers, "your sophisticated men are more curious observers, and take in more things, but they glose them; to lend weight to their interpretations, and induce your belief, they cannot help altering their story a little. They never describe things as they really are, but bend them and mask them according to the point of view from which they see things." [1] Even though the Jesuits tried honestly to write the truth, it was as they saw it; and Montaigne's warning is sound. If the modern reader approaches the writings of the Jesuits as their contemporaries did, he experiences little difficulty in plucking out the objective truth from their accounts. But the modern critic labors under a handicap: the Jesuits were more than simply Jesuitic; they reflected other ideas common to their times and country. Seventeenth-century Frenchmen, sharing the same ideas, could the more easily identify the peculiarly Jesuitic element in the Relations and thus, casting that element aside, regard only the facts about the Indians.

The inaccuracy and incompleteness of the Relations arose from the circumstances of missionary expansion. At first, in a rush to capture the essence of the Indian character, the Jesuits set down whatever they saw; without thought or discrimination they min-

---

1. Michel Eyquem de Montaigne, *Essays*, trans. E. J. Trechmann (New York, 1946), pp. 175–176.

gled bland generalizations about the whole race with precise comments about members of tribes whom they knew intimately. Biard, for example, attributed traits of the Acadian tribes to Indians in general. Later, as the missionaries ventured deeper into the forests and met other tribes, their observations became more exact. They rarely generalized, except to contrast the distinguishing marks of one tribe with those of another that they already knew.[2] If the progress of the missions had followed the plan of Le Jeune and the paths laid out by nature, the Relations might have presented a systematic survey of the Indians, tribe by tribe. But many external factors, chiefly the temper and polity of the natives themselves, diverted the priests in their travels; as a result they knew few tribes well and some not at all. Where evidence was slight, as with the Sioux, the tendency to generalize persisted; then the Relations presented merely a blurred image. On the other hand, the Relations were packed with detail about tribes among whom the missionaries had long sojourned; here it was not vagueness but a profusion of facts, sometimes contradictory, that impeded accuracy.

As the missions spread, comments about individual traits took up more space in the reports. The relators sent home whatever facts they thought would inform or edify. In later years the novelty of recounting personal traits wore off. The missionaries devoted more space to native feasts, dances, and councils, which the early narrators had not considered very relevant to baptism and salvation. At a time when religious fervor was waning and secular curiosity was growing, pious authors needed the sharp spice of marvels and diversion to hold an audience. But even then missionaries professed interest in such external phenomena because they shed light upon the personality of the Indian.

As long as they remained ignorant of the local tongues the missionaries depended upon their senses for impressions of the Indians. They could note physical appearances, but no more. Once the barrier of language was overcome, intimate contact allowed them to study the daily life and prejudices and ideas of the Indians and then to consider the best means of bringing them to baptism.

The misery and crudeness of the native culture struck Biard immediately. He had assumed, he confessed, that experience gained in the passage of time would have led these people to some stage of perfection in philosophy, the arts, and sciences; but he found

2. Cf. "Lettre du Père Charles l'Allemant," *Jesuit Relations*, IV, 211–213.

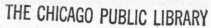
them barren of all accomplishment. And he saw no indications of religion: they lacked doctrines, ceremonies, ritual, temples, and sacred edifices. He offered two explanations for such an abject condition; both became standard in the Relations. The simple, natural need to satisfy the pangs of hunger had forced the Indians to put aside intellectual development, literature, and medicine. Secondly, since they lived outside the grace of Christ and the way to eternal salvation, they could not share in the natural happiness that God contemplated for all His creatures.[3] With a complacency perhaps natural in a former professor of rhetoric, Biard was inclined to condemn the Indians for their barbarism. In later years Father Le Jeune also recognized this backwardness—which no one in fact denied—and deplored it. But he was far more tolerant; he never entertained the idea that such a condition would endure. The Germans, Spanish, or English, he wrote, were no more civilized before they became Christians. In his detailed account of the clothes and ornaments of the Montagnais Le Jeune indulged in further reflections—as pertinent to Europeans as to Americans —on the subject of progress:

It was the opinion of Aristotle that the world had taken as it were three steps in order to arrive at the perfection which it possessed in his time. At the first men contented themselves with life, seeking purely and simply the things just necessary and useful for its conservation. At the second they united the agreeable with the necessary, and civility with necessity. They found food first, then the seasoning; they covered themselves in the beginning against the rigor of the weather, and afterward they gave grace and charm to their dress; they made houses in the first ages simply to use, and afterward they made them to be seen. At the third step men of intellect, seeing that the world was enjoying the things which were necessary and pleasant for life, gave themselves to the contemplation of the things of nature and to the investigation of the sciences, so that the great republic of men has perfected itself little by little, necessity marching ahead, civility and well-being coming after, and the sciences bringing up in the rear.

Now I wish to say that our savages [both] the Montagnais and the nomads, are still only at the first stage of the three which I have just mentioned; they think only in order to keep alive; they eat so as not to die, they cover themselves to banish the cold, not for appearance;

3. "Relation de la Nouvelle France," III, 111, 115; "Missio Canadensis," *Jesuit Relations*, II, 75.

grace, civility, the knowledge of the arts, the natural sciences, and much less the supernatural truths, have as yet no dwelling in this hemisphere, at least in these countries. These people do not believe that there is any other science in the world than to live and eat, that is their whole philosophy. . . . In short they have nothing but life, yet they are not always sure of that, since famine very often kills them.[4]

On the other hand, the Jesuits found that the effects of barbarism were not all harmful. True, the Indians were ignorant; but as compensation they enjoyed "the innocence of the first centuries."[5] If the Americans did not know all the pleasures that their European contemporaries so avidly pursued, they were nevertheless content.[6] Jérôme Lallemant even blessed the poverty, suffering, cold, and hunger to which ignorance subjected the Indians: he felt that such hardships discouraged the sensual vices and allowed of little opportunity to sin.[7] If the relative freedom from sin did not approximate the state of nature, at least, according to Vimont, "everything there has the freedom of the earliest times."[8] One of Vimont's colleagues elaborated upon the pristine atmosphere of Canada. "It seems that innocence, banished from the majority of the empires and kingdoms of the universe, retired into the great forests where these people live; their nature has something of the goodness of the terrestrial paradise before sin entered it; their customs have none of the luxury, ambition, avarice, or pleasures which corrupt our cities."[9] "Vice," another missionary observed, "reigns in towns much more than in the woods . . . association with animals is not so harmful as that with men, and our savages live in . . . great innocence."[10] As time passed the relators placed more emphasis upon the lesson to be drawn from such a condition of ignorant innocence, until what had originally been a consolation for the benighted heathen became a reproach to the civilized men of France. Father Charlevoix, who scolded his readers for abandoning the purity of the old faith, occasionally conveyed the impression that it was the Indians themselves, not the missionaries, who established the moral standards. Americans,

4. "Relation . . . 1632," V, 33; "Relation . . . 1634," VII, 6–8.
5. "Relation . . . 1651 & 1652," XXVII, 152.
6. "Relation de la Nouvelle France," III, 135.
7. "Relation . . . 1647," XXXI, 223–225.
8. "Relation . . . 1644 & 1645," XXVII, 208.
9. "Relation . . . 1647 & 1648," XXXII, 282.
10. "Relation . . . 1661 & 1662," XLVII, 168.

he wrote, scorned French riches and conveniences because they wished to show that they were the true philosophers. But, he added honestly, they at least envied the French the abundance and delicacy of their food.[11]

Indian innocence encouraged the missionaries immensely, since it boded well for their task. "The silence of the forests seems more fit to receive its influence [i.e., the gospel's] than the great bustle of Louvres and palaces." [12] Certainly such opinions sprang rather from aspiration than from a stern regard for objectivity; but the missionaries grasped at every hopeful sign to buoy up their efforts.

The conviction that the Indians possessed a great potentiality for goodness, if not present innocence, sustained Father Le Jeune in his heroic struggle to entrench the missions solidly on Canadian soil. In 1634 he wrote that "our savages are not so barbarous that they cannot be made children of God; I hope that where sin has reigned grace will triumph over it." [13] Indeed, Le Jeune did not believe in their actual innocence; he knew them too well. But he did suspect that at one time the Hurons had had clearer and more natural knowledge of God, although later vice and low habits clouded even that knowledge. Thus he once wrote the equation, "in barbarism, that is, in inconstancy"; and he reached the saddening conclusion that, no matter how diligently the Indians struggled to grasp the enlightenment of civilized Christianity, relics of their past condition clung to them and dragged them backward.[14] Had Le Jeune revisited Canada a century later, he would have found the retrogressive tendency still present. According to Charlevoix, even if the Indians were raised by the French from infancy, they nevertheless betrayed an inherited preference for the old ways.[15] Le Jeune and his contemporaries, more naïvely optimistic, would not have tolerated such an admission; they had always expected that inconstancy could be sloughed off, since they saw it as a mere consequence of paganism. But certainly by 1720 the missionary experience seemed to justify Charlevoix's conclusion.

As long as they hoped to convert large numbers of Indians the Jesuits attributed the barbarism that they saw on every hand

11. Pierre F. X. Charlevoix, *Journal d'un voyage fait par l'ordre du roi dans l'Amérique Septentrionale* (Paris, 1744), VI, 32. Hereafter cited as *Journal*.
12. "Relation . . . 1651 & 1652," XXXVII, 192.
13. "Relation . . . 1634," VI, 140.
14. "Relation . . . 1637," XII, 108; "Relation . . . 1636," X, 125.
15. *Journal*, VI, 33.

to pagan innocence. Accordingly, they felt it was urgent to intro-
duce God and a law and manner of life that the savages had not
led for perhaps four thousand years.[16] If the tribes waged in-
cessant war on each other, they were not to blame. As Father Jean
Dequen once argued, the savages were ignorant of God's law,
and Christians had to recognize this deprivation and be patient
with them. Besides, he added, those who professed to know God
and boasted of it should know that He is a God of peace, and
Christians who went to war were much more guilty than the benighted heathens.[17] The author of the Relation of 1657–58 (probably Dequen again) went further and stated that the Indians did not
lack intelligence but merely education and the knowledge of the
true God. They were indeed less attractive than the nations of
the earth who clothed themselves in silks, had fine manners, and
ruled empires and republics; but Jesus had preached rather more
to the savages, for among them dwelt faith, virtue, and holiness.[18]
The basic fault of the savages was a failure to recognize and hence
adore with fitting gratitude the true source of their gifts. Since,
moreover, the Word had so far been denied them, this failure could
not be a fault of their own willing; it was a deficiency that the missionaries had to fill. Upon such a position concerning natural innocence the Jesuits were henceforth content to rest.

Le Jeune had stated that conversion and cultural progress were
closely related, and most later missionaries agreed with him. But,
in passages similar to his reference to Aristotle already quoted,
he also opened another line of argument for the consideration of
his readers and the elaboration of his successors. By comparing
the stages of Indian development with parallel stages among Europeans, he applied the attitude of relativism to one more area of
the earth's surface. With respect to America Montaigne had of
course already led the way. But Montaigne's superficial knowledge
of the Indians, coupled with his skepticism, did not carry the
weight of the Relations, which were steeped in orthodoxy and drew
upon intimate contact with the Indians.

Not only did savage ignorance lead to a higher morality than
the luxury of Europe, also the two societies differed qualitatively.
Such a difference never occurred to Biard, who questioned the
superiority of French culture no more than he did the superiority

16. "Relation . . . 1642," XXIII, 205.
17. "Relation . . . 1655 & 1656," XLII, 223.
18. "Relation . . . 1657 & 1658," XLIV, 209, 250.

of Christianity. The later Jesuits were not so confidently Gallic. It was, in fact, one of those savages Biard scorned so loftily who stated most succinctly the reason for the cultural disparity. When a priest happened to scold him for a barbarous action, he retorted, ". . . if God had taught you no better [than He did us] . . . perhaps you would not be any better people than we are." [19] Perhaps not; and until the savages could understand the teachings of God, the missionaries hoped to awaken in Europeans a sympathy for the strange morals and manners of the Indians.

Granted they were foreign, nevertheless they were fundamentally like other men. Le Jeune first hinted at a relativistic attitude in 1633 when, without acknowledging his debt, he introduced the following reflection into his report: "Oh, how feeble is the judgment of men. Some find beauty where others see only ugliness. The most beautiful teeth in France are the whitest, in the Maldive Islands whiteness of the teeth is a deformity, they redden them to be beautiful. And in Cochin China, if I recall aright, they paint them black. Who is right?" [20] Jérôme Lallemant later observed that Indians of the same district were as closely united to each other as peasants in France; and, similarly, they constantly indulged in petty quarrels. He concluded that "men are men everywhere, at the ends of the earth as well as in the middle"; therefore, as he stated elsewhere, "this new world has the same nature as the old; it has its virtues and vices just like Europe." [21] The relator of 1657–58 felt that the French and the Indians differed mainly in taste and customs, and agreed with Le Jeune and Lallemant that they were similar in temperament. Everything, he wrote, after considering the Indian use of musk, the favorite songs of the two lands, their ways of seasoning meat, using cosmetics, dressing their hair, and clothing their bodies, was relative. But at the same time the relator took the opportunity to preach to his readers: "The world is full of variety and inconsistency, and one will never find permanence. If someone went up on a very high tower whence he could see at his ease all the nations of the earth, he would have trouble in telling those who are wrong or right, foolish or wise, in such strange varieties and such confusion." [22]

It might have seemed that relativism would sap the very reli-

19. "Relation . . . 1639," XVI, 158.
20. "Relation . . . 1633," V, 106; cf. Montaigne, *Essays,* p. 409.
21. "Relation . . . 1647," XXXI, 190; "Relation . . . 1647 & 1648," XXXII, 252.
22. Relation . . . 1657 & 1658, XLIV, 277–296.

gious aim that drove the missionaries on. Indeed, some Hurons once insisted to Le Jeune that what was good for France was not necessarily good for Canada, and that each country was entitled to its peculiar customs.[23] So much might be conceded, in an attempt to win the friendship of the Indians. But when another Huron pushed the same line of reasoning one step further and asked whether, since the French had one God and the Indians the god they had learned from their fathers, each people could not be allowed to retain their own beliefs, the missionaries balked. They admitted—Father Le Mercier in this instance—that there could be as many ways of conducting the affairs of this world as there were peoples in it. But God was one, and all nations should unite to worship and serve Him in the same way.[24] The priests never forgot the clear distinctions between nature and supernature; they believed that in each sphere the essential qualities of thought and deed differed. Therefore they saw nothing inconsistent in allowing great latitude in one sphere while insisting upon absolute cohesion to one standard in the other.

Relativism permitted the Jesuits to plead with their countrymen to tolerate the natural conduct of the barbarians. One Indian, through the pen of Le Jeune, addressed the French thus: "Perhaps you had as much trouble as we in abandoning your old ways when they began to preach the faith to you." Thereupon the missionary admonished "some of our Frenchmen" to "correct the idea they have of our savages, imagining them as ferocious beasts, with nothing human about them but the manifest structure of their bodies." [25] Ten years later Paul Ragueneau advised the French to be extremely wary in condemning Indian customs simply because they differed from customs in other parts of the world. It was easy, he wrote, to call stupidity irreligion, but it was not necessary to brand as criminal things that were done with an innocent intent.[26] Because the Indians were unenlightened by faith, necessity and appetite bound their wills; they were not free to know, and hence do, good or bad.

Although men were men everywhere and vice contended with virtue in primitive America as in civilized Europe, yet differences

23. "Relation . . . 1635," VIII, 119.
24. "Relation . . . 1637," XIII, 171–173.
25. "Relation . . . 1638," XIV, 132, XV, 76.
26. "Relation . . . 1647 & 1648," XXXIII, 145.

remained; it did not follow that the same vices and virtues occurred in each place, or to the same degree. The Crees might dance and jest like the Gascons, and the Assiniboins act phlegmatic and sedate like the Flemish, but few exact parallels appeared.[27] The Jesuits spent more energy pointing up the moral lessons that could be derived from relativism. The Indians could help the French repair many of their deficiencies in exchange for enlightenment in the true religion. Ragueneau wrote that in regard to morality the French owed as large a debt to these barbarians as to the Greeks.[28] Jérôme Lallemant waxed even more didactic when he learned how sternly some tribes punished women for adultery: "If barbarians, who are instructed only by the law of nature, have such noble sentiments of honor, what reproaches will they, who obey the precept to cut out their eyes rather than let anything prejudice their salvation, some day make to the libertine Christians?"[29] In later years Jouvency concluded that while the Indians differed from Europeans in at least six hundred ways, their customs were as good as or better than the European.[30] And the earnest Charlevoix never ceased to shame his countrymen for their lack of virtue beside the ignorant savages. The latter, he wrote, were happy merely because they believed they were; they possessed the most precious of all the gifts of nature and did not know about those false goods that the French esteemed so highly and for which they sold their true virtue. Claiming to be the most enlightened of men, the French groped in irremediable ignorance of the most vital knowledge. This ignorance, at least, did not grip the Indians so firmly.[31]

As they roamed over New France the Jesuits confirmed the popular conception that the Indians were truly barbarians. But even though they recognized the fact, they did not crush or scorn the savages. The discovery of barbarism may have made a Biard or a Charles Lallemant feel superior. But men like Le Jeune, Ragueneau, and Charlevoix searched barbarism for its advantages. They turned ignorance to use in preaching the gospel and construed virtues out of an innocence that could be held up as a model

27. Gabriel Marest, "Lettre au Père de Lamberville," *Jesuit Relations,* LXVI, 109.

28. "Relation . . . 1651 & 1652," XXXVII, 151–153.

29. "Relation . . . 1659 & 1660," XLV, 236.

30. "Canadicae missionis relatio," I, 285.

31. *Journal,* VI, 32, 61.

to Europeans. In addition, by adopting a relativistic attitude, they strengthened the opinion that all men were fundamentally the same despite superficial variations in their manners.

Even at first no Jesuit remained content simply to generalize about barbarism, ignorance, innocence, and the relative value of civilizations. Before engaging the Indians in conversation, he tried to glean some indications of their character from their appearance.

If their appearance gave any hint as to their mental or spiritual qualities the missionaries anticipated little trouble in converting the Indians. Straight off Biard declared the Micmacs and Etchemins to be as handsome and well proportioned "as we would be if we remained in the condition we were in at twenty-five." [32] Le Jeune found the Montagnais also well proportioned and with good figures, which were not so stocky as he had been led to believe. Two years later, after wintering with them, he confirmed his first impression, at some length:

If we begin with the gifts of the body, I shall say that they possess them in abundance: they are tall, upright, strong, well proportioned, agile, nothing feminine appears in them. Those little dandies who are seen elsewhere are just caricatures of men in comparison with our savages. Once I almost believed that the pictures of the Roman emperors represented rather the idea of the painters than men who had ever existed, so great and powerful are their heads; but I see on the shoulders of these people the heads of Julius Caesar, Pompey, Augustus, Otto, and others that I have seen in France, drawn on paper, or in relief on medallions. [33]

Vimont came across a noble Algonquin named Barnabé Otsinonannhont whom he found remarkable in every respect: "In a word he is one of those people who bear on their foreheads something, I know not what, worthy of empire, and to see him with a bow or a sword in his hand one would say that he is an animated portrait of those ancient Caesars of whom we see in Europe only copies all blurred with smoke." [34] Apparently New France preserved not only the simple life but also the heroic mold, after both had vanished from Europe. But even more: the Indians also retained the old standards of beauty, favoring black eyes set in a large face,

32. "Relation de la Nouvelle France," III, 74.
33. "Relation . . . 1632," V, 25; "Relation . . . 1634," VI, 228.
34. "Relation . . . 1643 & 1644," XXVI, 308.

after the style of the ancients.[35] By general consent the Indians everywhere appeared to be handsome, strong, and graceful, whether they were Micmacs, Montagnais, and Hurons, or Illinois, Abenakis, Crees, or Assiniboins.[36]

The Indians appeared not only more pleasing to the eye than Europeans but also healthier. Biard, for example, could not

find a potbellied, hunchbacked, or deformed man among them; they do not know what it is to be leprous, gouty, afflicted with gravel, or insane; those among us who have some defect, like one eye, squint eyes, a flattened nose, etc., are noticed right away by them and generally laughed at, especially behind our backs and when they are by themselves.[37]

When Father Bressani came to the Iroquois, they did not know "even the names of many of the diseases common in Europe, like stone, gout, rupture, etc. They do not appear either hunchbacked or dwarfed or very corpulent or with goiters . . ." And they possessed four qualities that Bressani particularly admired: their senses, endurance, knack of direction, and memory.

. . . first their senses which are most perfect; although they pass almost six months without seeing outdoors anything but snow and in their cabins anything but smoke, they have with all this very acute vision; an excellent and musical ear; a rare sense of smell, different from ours only [in] that they consider musk stinking and are unconcerned with the odors of things that are not edible, and with this sense they often discover fire long before seeing it, especially at night. They have a most delicate touch and skin, [their sensibility] being perhaps increased by the ointments common among them, as anciently among the Gentiles and Hebrews.[38]

In depicting the hardships of their primitive existence, Biard had already remarked that the Indians—"born, so to speak, of boreas and ice"—endured extreme hunger and cold in order to get the barest necessities of life.[39] Bressani conveyed a clearer idea of savage stamina in his description of the Iroquois:

35. "Relation . . . 1657 & 1658," XLIV, 285.
36. Charlevoix, *Journal,* VI, 3; Marquette and Sr. Joliet, *Voyages et découvertes de quelques pays et nations de l'Amérique Septentrionale* (Paris, 1845), p. 21; Rasles, "Lettre à Monsieur son frère," *Jesuit Relations,* LXVII, 137; Marest, "Lettre au Père de Lamberville," *Jesuit Relations,* LXVI, 107.
37. "Relation de la Nouvelle France," III, 74.
38. "Breve relazione," XXXVIII, 256–258.

Secondly, they have an admirable fortitude in hardships; they suffer from hunger for ten or fifteen days, sometimes out of superstition, more often out of necessity; [they suffer] fire without crying out, to which the youths accustom themselves at the age of ten or twelve years, two of them binding their arms together and then putting a coal between the two arms to see who will shake it off first and be despised for it; [they suffer] cold, heat, pain, illness without complaining, and although among pains the sacred scripture considers that of childbirth the greatest, the women to set an example of courage bear their children without giving any sign of pain, for if they cried out they would be deemed cowardly and be despised, and they would not find husbands again.[40]

Years later Charlevoix condensed Bressani's characterization and loosely applied it to all American Indians. He added that they surpassed the French with respect to both external and internal senses. He attributed the savages' strength and suppleness to their practice of taking their mothers' breasts even into their sixth or seventh year. Charlevoix also pointedly drew the attention of the effete French to the utter disregard in which the Indians held their bodies. They were constantly abusing them: going everywhere naked, through thickets, water, mud, and snow; making forced marches in wartime; and intemperately fasting, gorging themselves, and swilling much brandy. Only the most robust frames could survive such immoderate treatment; yet unless they met a violent end, these people generally lived a long time.[41]

The Indians enhanced their herculean appearance by their manner of dress. In many tribes the men went naked, "except for a piece of hide with which they covered themselves from just below the navel to the thighs." The women were generally "decently covered" from the shoulders to the knees. When Le Jeune first saw them dressed in furs, they reminded him of St. John the Baptist or of "that Greek philosopher, who wore nothing that he had not made." [42] The missionaries devoted many pages of the Relations to the garments of the Indians, which they found universally bizarre. But even when they raged against immodesty of dress they could not refrain from praising its rude simplicity.

39. "Missio Canadensis," *Jesuit Relations*, II, 76.
40. "Breve relazione," XXXVIII, 256–258.
41. *Journal*, VI, 3–5, 36.
42. "Relation . . . 1632," V, 24.

VII

SOCIAL CONDUCT OF THE INDIANS

ACCORDING to the Jesuits the richest fruits to be gathered in the vestigial paradise of America were the souls of its inhabitants. The priests welcomed whatever primitive innocence survived amid the boreal barbarisms, but they did not rely entirely on such favorable accidents for a full harvest. In order to derive the greatest benefit from the simplicity of Indian life they studied the daily round of activity. Then they tried to establish a common ground between Indian standards and their own dogma and morality. On that basis the missionaries hoped to construct a religion at the same time native and Catholic, and thus bring the Indians to salvation—a salvation that they deserved by their very nature and that God desired for them.

Because the Indians were pagan their conduct could not be called in any strict sense moral, as Le Jeune once pointed out.[1] But in the wilderness theological distinctions between morality and an ethical code were easily forgotten. Generally the missionaries looked at the Indians more broadly and classified their actions and attitudes according to the analogous categories of Christian morality. Such a moral outlook was perhaps inevitable for the missionaries, given their preconceptions, no matter how relativistic they tried to be. Furthermore, they could not avoid giving spiritual significance to any phenomenon that they thought relevant to both man's nature and his supernature. But the priests, regarding the Indian either strictly as unredeemed or laxly as unregenerate, understood him more sympathetically as they learned more about his environment, faculties, and conduct.

Depending upon the personalities, motives, and experiences of the relators as well as upon actual differences among the various tribes, the Relations contained numerous divergent opinions about each aspect of Indian life. But all the missionaries saw in the Indians the mixed good and bad that made them fallible human beings. As a result, the savages emerged from these pages as real

1. "Relation . . . 1634," VI, 240.

people, whom the variations of the individual writers made more credible.

The native trait that opinion almost unanimously acclaimed was liberality. As a rule the Indians gave most generously to those with whom they were most closely united, and naturally the French received the least consideration. Yet few missionaries complained of Indian niggardliness; most of those who did complain had already formed a strong prejudice against the barbarians. In addition, even the friendliest missionary did not usually anticipate genuine hospitality, since, as he realized, he was intruding upon the closed society of the tribe, and his very presence boded change. Their generosity to the black-robed strangers, then, did the Indians all the more credit. Hence the missionaries described native liberality in two separate contexts: on the one hand as information and advice with regard to their own reception by various tribes; on the other hand as evidence of the true native character, with regard to the conduct of the Indians among themselves.

If sometimes the Indians revealed their liberality obscurely, it was fortunate that the Jesuits marked it. The reasonable hope of being offered potluck at the next village gave the missionaries a confident, footloose independence. Otherwise they would have moved about New France much more slowly, encumbered with provisions and perhaps accompanied by armor-clad musketeers rather than half-naked trappers. Here Biard, who depended heavily upon the good will of the local tribes, may be considered a first authority. In 1612 he described the savages' generosity among themselves and added, "the same . . . has been seen for the benefit of the French upon any occasion when they were distressed." [2] The next year he put his bland assumption to the test. The English had captured him and his followers at the mission of St. Sauveur; and

While we were actually hovering between the dubious alternatives of death and imprisonment, when the report of our calamity had spread among the barbarians whom we knew, they came to see us in great numbers, greatly pitying our misfortune and most obligingly offering the meagerness of their goods for the entire following year if we would remain among them.[3]

Biard cited this as a rare instance of savage goodness.

2. "Missio Canadensis," *Jesuit Relations,* II, 78.
3. "Relatio rerum gestarum," II, 260.

Charles Lallemant, the next superior after Biard, detested the Indians. In a letter to his brother Jérôme written in 1627 he called their heartless lack of generosity their chief treachery. As proof he cited how the Recollet fathers, in preparing to journey up the Ottawa River to the Hurons, had to take a year's supply of food, "or the means of buying it; for to expect that the savages would give you any is folly, unless they have taken you under their protection, and you should wish to live in their villages and cabins; for then they will feed you for nothing." [4] Lallemant was manifestly unfair; yet other priests, much less harsh, made similar comments. About the Montagnais Le Jeune wrote:

They are very liberal among themselves, indeed they claim to love nothing, to be attached to none of the goods of the earth, in order not to grieve themselves if they lose them. . . . One of the great insults among them is to say "that man loves everything, he is a miser." . . . they do not open their hand halfway when they give; I say among themselves, for they are as ungracious as possible toward strangers.[5]

Since a stranger was anyone not under the Indians' protection, many Frenchmen did not experience their generosity. It was vital for the missionaries that strangers should be received and offered protection as new friends. Then as a matter of course the savages willingly led them into their villages, inside their cabins, and around their stewpots. Many a wandering, half-frozen mission-ary was welcomed to some isolated hut after he had abandoned the hope of ever seeing a human face again. Even if the proffered hospitality meant wriggling under ill-cured skins to lie beside some filthy children in a reeking, smoke-filled den, the guest was grateful, however nice he may once have been back at La Flèche or Clermont. Le Jeune himself often testified to the Jesuits' gratitude for such rude but warm hospitality. Others were even luckier, like Brébeuf, the second time he arrived among the Hurons. Until the villagers completed his cabin he moved in with "one of the richest of the Hurons"—lest the length of his stay should work a hardship on a man of less means—and lived in comparative luxury. As he explained:

You can lodge where you wish, since this nation above all others is very hospitable to all sorts of people, even strangers; and you stay

4. "Lettre du Père Charles l'Allemant," *Jesuit Relations,* IV, 194–196.
5. "Relation . . . 1634," VI, 236–238.

there as long as you please, always well treated in the fashion of the country, and on leaving they are repaid for their hospitality with a *ho, ho, ho, outoecti,* or many thanks, at least among themselves. Now from the French they expect some recompense, always at your discretion. It is quite true that all are not equally hospitable, some more and some less. . . .

So I lived with this man, where I stayed with two of our fathers and one of our people, for the period of more than a month and a half, until we moved into our new cabin. Regardless, these poor savages performed for us all possible kindnesses, some influenced by their good nature, others by the consideration of some little presents which I had made them, and the hope of some others.[6]

In 1644 Father Druillettes went to Sillery to meet some natives with whom he was to spend the winter. The Indians knew that on the long trek home through the snow food would be scarce and that the priest, unskilled in foraging or trapping, would prove just one more mouth to feed. Nevertheless "they welcomed him not in the fashion of the court but in a manner of sincerity and frankness."[7] Among the Illinois Father Allouez usually met a cordial reception wherever he went. "I find," he wrote, "all those among whom I have worked affable and humane, and they say that when they meet some stranger, they give a cry of joy, caress him, and render him all the testimonies of friendship they can."[8] Farther south, on the Mississippi, Father Marquette found the Arkansas very liberal in giving the explorers supplies, and generally solicitous of their welfare.[9]

Unless the Indians were waging war, they showed greater generosity to natives outside their own tribes than to the French. In the Relation that mentioned how ungracious the Montagnais were to French "strangers," Le Jeune also told this tale: famine had gripped the winter-bound country, and some unknown Indians stumbled starving into a village where the inhabitants had just returned from a successful moose hunt.

Now please admire the love which these barbarians bear toward one another; no one asked these new guests why they came onto our boundaries, if they did not know well enough that we were in as great

6. "Relation . . . 1635," VIII, 92–96.
7. "Relation . . . 1644 & 1645," XXVII, 204.
8. "Relation . . . 1666 & 1667," LI, 50.
9. *Voyages et découvertes,* p. 39.

need as they, that they were coming to take the crumbs from our mouths; but on the contrary they were received, not with words but with deeds, without external courtesy, for the savages have none, but not without charity: they threw them some large pieces of the freshly killed moose, without saying another word to them but *mitisoukou,* eat . . . while they ate a feast was prepared, at which they were treated generously, I assure you.[10]

But regardless of how they received strangers, among themselves the Indians were uniformly openhanded, as instances already cited disclose. "The nature of our savages," Biard wrote, "is in itself liberal and not at all malicious." They shared everything with each other and thus created a mutual obligation of gratitude; "no one would dare to scorn the request of another or to eat without giving him a part of what he possesses." As Biard hiked from one Micmac village to another he noted that

Among themselves they are marvelously liberal; no one may enjoy any good fortune by himself without giving away the largest part of it to his neighbors, and whoever holds a *tabagie,* as they say, that is, whoever asks others to a feast, does not himself sit down with the rest but serves, and sets aside no part of the food for himself but distributes it all, so that the host is forced to suffer hunger that day, unless one of the guests takes pity on him and gives him back some from what remained over from his share.[11]

Once Le Jeune told about a young Montagnais who was known to have stolen a cache of food from his village. In spite of the theft, his family coming again to the point of starvation, the villagers took the man into their cabins, along with his wife, whose legs were paralyzed, his infant son, and another relative. "They were made most welcome and treated like members of the family." [12] The rich Huron who played host to Brébeuf in 1635 once donated "two bins of grain—at least one hundred or one hundred and twenty bushels—" to ward off a famine that threatened his village after fire had wiped out their other stores.[13] Such instances are numerous, and it may be concluded, as Jouvency did, that the

10. "Relation . . . 1634," VII, 176.
11. "Relation de la Nouvelle France," III, 72, 94; "Missio Canadensis," *Jesuit Relations,* II, 78.
12. "Relation . . . 1634," VI, 236.
13. "Relation . . . 1635," VIII, 94.

Indians were very free with what little property they owned and asked for little in return.[14]

Inside the tribe, as ties of blood reinforced those of friendship, liberality became affection. "You notice among them," Brébeuf wrote of the Hurons, "in the first place a great love and union, which they are careful to cultivate by means of their marriages, their presents, their feasts, and their frequent visits." [15] As the Montagnais relieved even thieves of starvation, so the Hurons tended the last days of the sick:

The father who came back here this year remarks with reason that our Hurons are more praiseworthy for their humanity than the Algonquins; for instead of abandoning each other in their sickness, as the latter usually do, the Hurons on the contrary put themselves out to care for a person who is sick unto death. He says he has seen them make litters and carry their languishing carcasses over the rapids, so that if one of them happened to die they would enshroud him with as much care as if they had been in their home country; instead the Algonquins often leave their dead without burial.[16]

When he lived with the Montagnais Le Jeune had ample opportunity to observe the course of family relationships.

On the 12th of November winter advanced, beginning to besiege us with its ice. Having been for a long time that day in a large cabin of the savages, where there were many men, women, and children of all conditions, I remarked their admirable patience; if there were as many families together in our France, there would be nothing but disputes, quarrels, and insults; the mothers do not get impatient with their children, they do not know what it is to swear, their only oath consists in this word *taponé;* in truth there is no jealousy among them; they aid and support each other magnanimously because they hope a return of the favor; this hope failing, they do not respect whoever it may be.[17]

It was natural for the Jesuits to explain the usual harmony of a tribe by reference to family life. The organization of the family, with its ramifications in the clan, constituted the tribal structure and hence provided the standard of individual conduct. The Jesuits exalted the Indian family as a model to Europe, where Catholic reformers were striving to maintain the same unit as a

14. "Canadicae missionis relatio," I, 275.
15. "Relation . . . 1635," VIII, 126.
16. "Relation . . . 1638," XV, 134.
17. "Relation . . . 1633," V, 104.

nucleus of orthodoxy. From this point of view, then, when Le Jeune described the Montagnais as treating the thief and his people "like members of the family," he gave them the highest possible praise. No group showed more proper or more intense sympathies. After telling that story Le Jeune went on to state what such treatment meant:

You will see them care for their relatives, the children of their friends, widows, orphans, old men, without ever reproaching them for anything, abundantly giving them sometimes whole moose; it is truly a sign of a good heart and of a generous soul.

As there are several orphans among this tribe—for since they have abandoned themselves to drinking wine and brandy, they die in great numbers—these poor children are distributed in the cabins of their uncles, their aunts, or other relatives; do not suppose that they are snubbed, that it is made a reproach to them that they eat the food of the house; nothing of the sort, they are treated like the children of the father of the house, or at least little different, and are dressed as well as possible.[18]

As Father Jouvency epitomized in admiration: by alleviating the poverty and the grief of their unfortunate fellows the Indians avoided family quarrels and civil wars; their domestic life resembled an idyl.[19]

Of all the aspects of family life, parental love appealed most to the Jesuits. "The savages love their children supremely," Le Jeune reported, "they are like monkeys, they smother them by embracing them too tightly." Vimont also testified to the "strange passions" with which they loved their children, adding that "their loss is the only one for which they manifest any sorrow." [20] Others also observed that such lavish affection spoiled the children and contributed heavily to the self-indulgent license of their adult years. Charlevoix, who never saw one child punished, felt that Indian parents did not know that judgment came only with discipline. "The mothers and fathers neglect nothing to inspire in their children certain precepts of honor, which they cherish all their lives"; but when each new generation put such precepts into practice, it transformed courage into brutality.[21] Yet the Jesuits derived consolation from the fact that a good sentiment, at least,

18. "Relation . . . 1634," VI, 238.
19. "Canadicae missionis relatio," I, 275.
20. "Relation . . . 1639," XVI, 68; "Relation . . . 1642 & 1643," XXV, 182.
21. *Journal,* V, 401; VI, 10, 37; cf. Jouvency, "Canadicae missionis relatio," I, 277.

had caused such a deplorable corruption; optimistically they relied upon baptism and grace to guide parental love to more benevolent ends and remedy the defect caused by pagan ignorance.

If Indian liberality delighted the Jesuits, the manner in which it was extended pleased them fully as much. The Americans, they found, regulated their social relations with free and affable candor, which a dignified calm made even more admirable. Although at times policy demanded that the Indians show a friendship for the French that they did not sincerely feel, in many regions no rivalries, European or American, existed to color their conduct. While, for instance, Biard deemed the Micmacs and Etchemins to be very friendly by both nature and policy, on the other hand he reported that the Excommuniquois were implacable enemies; for, he hinted darkly, "certain Basques tried to commit an evil outrage" against them.[22] Nevertheless, several tribes had not seen white men before the priests appeared; and, not knowing how to act in front of them, they acted naturally. Thus Marquette, pioneering in the west, found the Illinois "nice and tractable by nature" and very humane. "At the limit of the discoveries that the French have made," he encountered three tribes: "Miamis, Maskoutens, and Kikabous, the first are the most civil, the most liberal, and the most shapely . . . they are very docile, and they listen peaceably to what is said to them. . . . The Maskoutens and the Kikabous are coarser and seem to be peasants in comparison with the others." [23]

A similar affability prevailed among most of the tribes that the missionaries visited. On Cape Breton Island, twenty years after Biard, Father Perrault was very favorably impressed by the Micmacs:

You do not see in their gestures and bearing any foolishness or nonsense, but rather a certain gravity and natural modesty, which makes them amiable. . . .

Now what consoles us in the midst of this ignorance and barbarism and what makes us hope to see the faith widely planted there is in part the docility which they show us in wishing to be instructed and in part the honesty and decency which we remark in them.

22. "Relation de la Nouvelle France," III, 68–70.
23. *Voyages et découvertes*, p. 20; "Le Premier voyage qu'a fait le P. Marquette," *Jesuit Relations*, LIX, 100–102.

. . . the honesty and decency which we see shining in them like two bright rays of light in the midst of darkness.[24]

Le Jeune passed the same judgment on the Hurons, whom the Jesuits came to esteem as the ideal Indians. Here, he wrote, on most occasions they respectfully maintained "the reserve natural to young savages before their elders." Later Le Mercier added to the sum of Huron virtues a "modesty and devotion" that "would put many Frenchmen to shame." Brébeuf gave a fuller account:

Omit some evil persons who are found almost everywhere [and] they have a gentleness and an affability almost unbelievable for savages; they are not easily irritated: and even if they believe they have received some injury from someone, they often disguise the resentment that they feel; at least one finds here very few who give vent in public to anger and vengeance. They maintain themselves in such perfect harmony as this by frequent visits, the mutual help which they give each other in their sicknesses, by feasts, and by [marriage] alliances.[25]

On this count even the Iroquois won praise. Bressani, despite his cruel treatment at their hands, wrote that in general they "are affable to one another and do much visiting and like to pass for liberal and disinterested." He noted further "a certain seemliness in their behavior, which prevents a thousand levities that are rather common among European youths." [26]

The gentleness of their comportment seemed so general to Vimont that he was surprised when he came across one Indian scolding another for his clumsiness in learning the Pater Noster.

Who would understand the savages will be astonished at the liberty which he took in reproving his comrade: for I shall say in passing that it is a striking thing, the respect which the savages bear one another on this point, although they are deprived of humility and have an entire liberty to do and say all they wish in their cabins; nevertheless in the matter of reproving one another, they go about it with a rare circumspection and prudence.[27]

Father Allouez came across another odd blend of manners among the Pottawattomies, when curiosity drove an Indian to an impertinence that his courtesy soon mended:

24. "Relation . . . 1635," VIII, 160–162.
25. "Relation . . . 1638," XIV, 252; "Relation . . . 1653 & 1654," XLI, 140; "Relation . . . 1636," X, 210–212.
26. "Breve relazione," XXXVIII, 256, 266.
27. "Relation . . . 1642 & 1643," XXIV, 82.

Once when I had gone to see one of their elders, he cast his eyes on my shoes, which were made in the French fashion; curiosity moved him to ask me for them, to inspect them at his ease; when he gave them back to me, he refused to let me put them on myself, but I was constrained to permit him this service, even wishing to fasten my thongs; with the same marks of respect as servants show to their masters, when they render them this service: being at my feet he said to me, this is how we treat those whom we honor.[28]

Such handsome conduct induced comparisons with European manners. Jérôme Lallemant, describing how contact with French ways had changed the Tadoussac Indians, was similarly inspired. After some were baptized, he found

they begin to imagine that to be good Christians they ought to live entirely in the French fashion, and with this thought in mind they act polite. . . . The savages and the French hold the two extremes in the matter of compliments: the former are insipid and boorish in the little respect they pay to each other, and the French annoy by the excess of their ceremonies, and [are] very often insincere in the too great demonstration of friendship. Rustic candor is preferable to a feigned courtesy, excess was never good in anything: if these good neophytes assume it, they will soon be weary of it.[29]

In this light rustic candor was indeed attractive; but there was another side of Indian complacence that did not find the same favor in Jesuit eyes. Few of the missionaries were prudes; but many concluded that sexual immorality among the barbarians rivaled the worst depravity of Europe. If more of the relators did not bemoan such promiscuity, it was probably because they considered it a natural consequence of heathen barbarism, which they hoped to change. In the meantime they tolerated strange customs as broadly as possible; or else they consoled themselves that even the worst license did not destroy parental love and tribal harmony.

Biard first took up the subject of Indian sexual relations in 1616, in a chapter on their marriages. He began with a brief account of courtship among the Abenaki tribes; then he considered their morality in general. Before marriage "the immorality of the girls is not so important, nor do they fail for this reason to

28. "Relation . . . 1666 & 1667," LI, 26–28.
29. "Relation . . . 1645 & 1646," XXIX, 126–128.

find themselves husbands; yet it is always shameful." He went on to explain why the Indians permitted premarital relations:

According to the custom of the country, they can have several wives; nevertheless the majority of those whom I have seen have but one: many of the sagamores claim they cannot do without this plurality, not indeed out of lust (for this nation is not very incontinent) but for two other reasons: one in order to retain their authority and power by having several children, for in that lies the strength of houses, in a multitude of allies and cousins; the second reason is their maintenance and service, which is great and laborious since they have great families and followings, and therefore require a number of . . . housewomen, for they have no other servants, slaves, or laborers but their wives.

Then Biard listed the tasks of the women, which amounted to the entire daily management and support of the household. The men did not treat their women well but beat them, "often for very slight cause." Yet despite harshness the marriages apparently were permanent. "Few divorces occur among them and (as I believe) little adultery. If the wife forgot herself in that, I do not think that it would cost less than death for both of the adulterers." [30] As their disregard of premarital chastity indicated, then, these people had a different morality: they punished adultery not so much because it was bad as because it infringed a man's property rights. As Biard concluded, the Indians did not know "the blessing of Christian marriage"; wives simply represented property. Nevertheless, even savages saw something "shameful" in those acts that the European priests called immoral.

Several western tribes regarded adultery in the same light as the Micmacs and Etchemins. Polygamy prevailed among the Miamis and the Illinois; the penalties for adultery were similarly harsh: the wives had their noses or ears cut off, although their seducers escaped punishment. The Natchez also permitted polygamy. But here matriarchy prevailed. A woman of noble blood could punish an unfaithful husband by having him clubbed on the head.[31]

In his description Biard next took up Indian dress, bearing, and manners: ". . . the women and girls are very modest and bashful,

30. "Relation de la Nouvelle France," III, 98–102.
31. Marquette, *Voyages et découvertes*, p. 20; "Le Premier voyage qu'a fait le P. Marquette," *Jesuit Relations*, LIX, 127; Charlevoix, *Journal*, VI, 182.

the men also are not immodest and are very scandalized when some French fool dares to amuse himself with their women." [32] But Biard's statement could not apply to Americans in general. In fact modesty of appearance and conduct seemed to depend as much upon the prejudices and attitudes of the individual priests as upon the customs that existed in the tribes. Father Le Jeune, who always hoped for conversion and hence inclined toward indulgence, nevertheless tried to present a true picture. The Montagnais, for instance, blended virtue and vice in a mode of conduct that he could describe only as natural.

I had been told that the savages were quite chaste; I shall not speak of all, not having visited them all, but those whom I have talked with are very loose, both men and women. God, what blindness! How great is the happiness of Christian people! How great the chastisement of the barbarians! Instead of saying, as we do rather often, JESUS, what is that! My God, who did that? these villains and rogues pronounce the names of the shameful parts of man and woman. Their lips are incessantly soiled with these obscenities, even the little children. . . . The older women go about almost naked, the girls and young women are decently clad, but among themselves their language is stinking like the sewers. But I must admit that if the freedom to be gorged with this filth existed among some Christians, as it does among these people, one would see very different displays of excess from those that are seen here; for notwithstanding the divine and human laws, depravity strides more openly there than here. For here my eyes are not offended. The sorcerer alone has committed any brutish action in my presence, the others offended my ears alone, but seeing that I heard them, they were ashamed.[33]

Perrault, who perhaps loved his charges too blindly or his vocation too well, praised the Micmacs extravagantly:

As to decency, they hold it in such esteem, at least as far as external appearances go, in their actions and words, that they will probably arise on the last day and condemn many Christians, who will have cultivated it less in the law of grace than these people do in that of nature.

We have never heard them say evil words, nor seen them do anything too freely, although we have lived intimately with them, inside and outside their cabins.[34]

32. "Relation de la Nouvelle France," III, 102.
33. "Relation . . . 1634," VI, 252–254.
34. "Relation . . . 1635," VIII, 164.

The manner in which the priests treated Huron morality showed how their personal tastes and experiences colored their accounts. Charles Lallemant, who never saw the Hurons at home, first described their morals. He conceded that the clothes of the men "decently hid the parts which modesty demands should be covered"; but that was all. In spite of the fact that they were more settled and prosperous than the Indians around Quebec, "yet they are more savage in their customs, committing without any disgrace or concealment all kinds of shameless acts." Lallemant did not specify what the "shameless acts" were. He simply remarked that "religious eyes cannot support so much lewdness as they carry on openly there: that is why the RR. PP. Recollets have been compelled to build their cabins apart." [35]

To read Brébeuf, a more acute judge of Huron character, the truth must have been somewhat less outrageous. In 1635 he admitted that "as to conduct, the Hurons are lascivious, although in two main points less so than many Christians, who will some day blush before them. You will not see among them any immodest kissing or caressing; and in marriage a man will live for two or three years, apart from his wife, while she is nursing." But evidently Brébeuf did not yet know his charges well enough, for later he revealed that virginity after the age of seven was "a very rare quality among them." In addition, weighing the prospects of conversion, he felt that "conjugal continence and the indissolubility of [Christian] marriage seemed to them [i.e., the Indians] the greatest obstacle to the progress of the gospel." [36]

Yet even the Hurons had their limit. Le Mercier discovered one woman whose "excessively lewd" conduct made her notorious in her village, even though the other women were not exactly temperate. Exceptions on the side of virtue also existed. Le Jeune came across one paragon who "has never lived in the license to which these girls and women abandon themselves." But he too found such chastity "astonishing" and concluded, with resignation, that they tended naturally to all sorts of sensuality.[37] Ragueneau was not so surprised to see continence prevail among the Hurons after their flight to Quebec in 1650. But then most of them had settled down and become Catholic. Knowing one neophyte who so loved virtue as to remain a virgin through three marriages, Ragueneau

35. "Lettre du Père Charles l'Allemant," *Jesuit Relations,* IV, 194–196, 202.

36. "Relation . . . 1635," VIII, 126; "Relation . . . 1636," X, 62, 166.

37. "Relation . . . 1637," XIII, 136; "Relation . . . 1638," XV, 106, 121; "Relation . . . 1639," XVI, 61.

attributed such conduct mainly to piety. But also, he maintained, tribal custom fortified her, since

these people conduct themselves ordinarily, for the first two, three, or four months of their marriage, as if they were brothers and sisters, giving as a reason for their mode of conduct that they love each other with the affection of near relatives, who have a horror of carnal actions. This love of kinship is greater and stronger among pagans than conjugal love, into which it finally degenerates. So that in these first months, if they become distasteful to each other, they separate without scandal, remaining as they were before.[38]

Needless to say, Ragueneau saw what he wished to see: baptism notwithstanding, Charles Lallemant would not have interpreted such an arrangement as a marriage but as a "shameless act."

Elsewhere the reports on sexual morality varied in proportion to the cordial reception that the tribes extended to the priests and their preaching. Thus Dequen wrote, during his sojourn with the Iroquois, that seduction "is so common . . . that it is done almost publicly and without shame." [39] And Allouez reported that the Ottawas were "utterly abandoned to idolatry, superstitions, fables, polygamy, unstable marriages, and every sort of libertinism, which makes them renounce all natural shame."

The mainspring of their religion is libertinism; and all these various sacrifices usually end in debauches, indecent dances, and infamous acts of concubinage; the men direct all their devotion toward having several wives and changing them when it pleases them; the women to leaving their husbands; and the girls to living in depravity.[40]

On the other hand, the tribes of the north received Father Buteux very kindly in 1650; he was "delighted to see what God had done without us," in preparing the way for conversion. As samples of His ingratiating work, the good father adduced "two young women, very well formed, but modest, as modest as any European Christian." Charles Albanel, who knew the northern people far better than most of his colleagues, also praised their morals. Around Hudson Bay polygamy was rare; with some tribes which were docile, intelligent, and peaceful, it "passes for an infamous thing." "As for the rest, they are very discreet and live very in-

38. "Relation . . . 1651 & 1652," XXXVII, 154.
39. "Relation . . . 1655 & 1656," XLII, 140.
40. "Relation . . . 1666 & 1667," LI, 20, L, 290.

nocently." Indeed he found that polygamy, when it did exist, stemmed from barbarian charity: "I have even noticed that the second wife of those who have two was almost always some close relative; and having asked the reason that they could have such a custom, I was told that when a woman has lost her husband, it is up to the nearest relative to take care of her and to support her and not to keep her in the quality of a slave but of a wife." [41] Similarly, Marquette, finding the Illinois affable, praised their women for the modesty of their dress as well as their discretion and poise; and the men's going practically naked most of the year did not disturb him at all.[42] In contrast the moralistic Charlevoix inveighed against the Natchez: they were more given to prostitution than any other tribe on the continent; indeed, their looseness had contaminated their northern neighbors. This condition he blamed on the immodest clothing of the women and on the refusal of the Natchez—alone of all the tribes—to vilify wives whose adultery became publicly known.[43]

If complacency often seduced the Indians into license, the missionaries found, on the other hand, that serious affairs made them act with candor and dignity. Only the fiercest eloquence could turn their usual calmness to anger or enthusiasm. But such composure prevailed chiefly within the limits of ordinary experience —normally coterminous with the tribal boundaries. In unusual circumstances stoicism and friendliness gave way to the most brutal violence.

Biard attributed the savage phlegm as much to the hard conditions of life as to natural humanity. The dignity of the Indian councils, which became proverbial, did not greatly impress the Jesuits, for even in Europe state business was carried on with some degree of gravity. Much more remarkable seemed the composure of the Indians in the most routine matters. Le Jeune wrote about the Montagnais:

They profess never to get angry, not for the beauty of the virtue, for which they have not even a name, but for their contentment and pleasure; I mean, to free themselves from the bitterness which anger causes. The sorcerer said to me one day, speaking of one of our Frenchmen, "he has no sense, he gets angry, as for me nothing is capable of up-

41. "Relation . . . 1650 & 1651," XXXVII, 52; "Relation . . . 1669 & 1670," LIII, 88; "Relation . . . 1671 & 1672," LVI, 216.

42. *Voyages et découvertes*, p. 22.

43. *Journal*, VI, 4, 181–182.

setting me; famine may oppress us, my nearest relatives may pass on to the other life, the Hiroquois our enemies may massacre our people, I never get angry . . ."

Who professes not to get angry should also make a profession of patience; the savages surpass us so much in this respect that we ought to be ashamed: I saw them in their hardships, in their labors, suffering with cheerfulness. . . . I have never seen anything so patient as a sick savage; let them cry, storm, leap, dance, he almost never complains. . . . they will endure all kinds of scorn and discomfort and all sorts of trials and injuries very patiently.[44]

In short, as he wrote later, the Indians prized "a certain gentleness or apathy" above all things and deprecated nothing more than a show of anger.[45] Once Vimont saw a man flare up at some trifle, but he abandoned his rage as quickly and threw his hatchet into the fire: "If there are barbarous actions among these people, there are thoughts worthy of the Greeks and Romans." [46] They retained this calmness under most circumstances—in disgrace or captivity, when losing at gaming or mourning their dead.[47] Men endured grievous insults without rising up in wrath, however righteous; victims of torture never groaned.[48] According to Charlevoix they learned self-control early in life and thus acquired a "natural and modest gravity." [49]

Apparently the Indians regarded stoicism as a universal human trait: when they learned that white men lacked it they were stunned. One woman, watching a Frenchman lose his temper, exclaimed: ". . . is it possible that a Christian suffers with impatience, when he is promised paradise, where it is so beautiful, as a reward for his patience? 'We others,' she said, 'have not the hope nor the promise of those benefits, and yet we are not angry in the horrible pains which we are made to suffer when we are taken in war by our enemies.' " [50]

The Jesuits often attributed to Indian temperament acts that resulted merely from ignorance or custom. They told how the Indians preferred their own hardships to milder French ways, and saw here again a noble simplicity. For instance, "Although they have a tenderer and more delicate skin than the French . . .

44. "Relation . . . 1634," VI, 230–232.
45. "Relation . . . 1639," XVI, 164.
46. "Relation . . . 1644 & 1645," XXVII, 242.
47. "Relation . . . 1639," XVI, 201; "Relation . . . 1649 & 1650," XXXV, 118.
48. "Relation . . . 1639," XVI, 208; "Relation . . . 1653 & 1654," XLI, 152.
49. *Journal,* VI, 8–11, 38.
50. Relation . . . 1640, XIX, 30.

these good people have not the softness nor the delicacy of our Europeans. They find sleep sweeter upon a bed of earth and on a pillow of wood than many persons do upon down." [51]

Notwithstanding a certain rude nobility, the barbarians had many habits that the missionaries found utterly disgusting. Most priests would have agreed with Charles Lallemant that they were "dirty in their eating habits and in their cabins and have many vermin that they eat when they catch them"; though none, apparently, reacted quite so violently.[52] Le Jeune, the savages' most ardent apologist, admitted that they ate lice; "not," he hastened to explain, "that they have any taste for them, but because they wish to bite those who bite them." [53] The lice were simply enemies to be destroyed in the perpetual struggle for existence. Like Le Jeune, most Jesuits kept American barbarism constantly in mind; hence they were prepared against the bizarre, the shocking, or the repulsive.

To the gluttony of the Indians the Jesuits objected more strenuously, on grounds of morality, health, and economy. The vice scandalized Charles Lallemant: "As to the customs of the savages, it is enough to say that they are completely savage. From morning to evening they have no other concern but to fill their stomachs. They do not come to see us except to ask for food, and if you do not give it to them, they make their displeasure clear." [54]

Le Jeune concurred. But again indulgent, he connected the habit with tribal hospitality:

Eating among the savages is like drinking among the drunkards of Europe: these dry and ever-thirsty souls would expire willingly in a vat of malmsey and the savages in a stewpot full of meat; those over there talk of nothing but drinking and these here of nothing but eating. It is a sort of insult to a savage to refuse the pieces which he offers. . . . an old woman told me that if I wished to be loved by their nation, I had to eat a great deal. . . . the greatest satisfaction that they can have in their paradise is the stomach.

In short, gluttony caused all their sickness and famine. But soon Le Jeune and his colleagues found that drinking brandy rivaled gluttony in baleful effects. Primarily for moral reasons the priests

51. "Relation . . . 1657 & 1658," XLIV, 280.
52. "Lettre du Père Charles l'Allemant," *Jesuit Relations*, IV, 198.
53. "Relation . . . 1634," VI, 244.
54. "Lettre du Père Charles l'Allemant," *Jesuit Relations*, IV, 196–198.

railed against the sale of liquor to the natives by French traders; brandy brutalized the Americans, and thus the French were debauching the very people whom they should convert and civilize. Beyond that, the missionaries feared lest the Indians lose their vigorous health or be defrauded of their goods. In addition, they worried about the safety of the French settlers; for life meant nothing to Indians on a spree. Le Jeune was one of the first to complain of the imported vice.

The savages have always been gluttons, but since the coming of the Europeans they have become such drunkards that although they see clearly that these new beverages of wine and brandy which are brought to them depopulate their country, and of this they themselves complain, they cannot abstain from drinking, thinking it glorious to become drunk and to make others drunk. . . . give two savages two or three bottles of brandy, they will sit down and without eating will drink one after the other, until they have emptied them. . . .

When the Indians insisted that liquor was a demon which possessed them and made them the passive agents of his will, the full evil of brandy became apparent: then they had an irrefutable excuse for whatever violence and destruction they committed.[55]

Even the Hurons were slaves to meat and drink. "For the most part," remarked Le Mercier in disgust, "they think only of their stomachs and the means of prolonging this miserable life." [56] Naturally, a thoughtful colleague might have remarked—adding that while gluttony (like so many other habits) was deplorable, it was not incurable; nor, since they were heathen, did it contribute to their damnation.

When Biard called the Indians "a race of utterly brutal disposition and customs," he referred not merely to gluttony but also to their boldness and cunning. He was loath to grant them courage, chiefly because they "never placed themselves in battle order" but fought from cover or ambush; and he concluded they were "by nature fearful and cowards." But, he added, "to have the name of great heart. . . . is the supreme virtue among them." [57] On the other hand, later missionaries, better acquainted with native

55. "Relation . . . 1634," VI, 248–252; "Relation . . . 1632," V, 49–51.
56. "Relation . . . 1637," XIII, 126, 165.
57. "Relatio rerum gestarum," II, 276; "Relation de la Nouvelle France," III, 90–92.

military tactics and bearing in general, did not doubt savage courage. Charlevoix, a century after Biard, lauded their valor; he remarked especially on how their discreet use of bushes, trees, and ditches in attack helped to compensate for the limited effectiveness of their weapons.[58]

The Indians did indeed pride themselves on their courage; the Jesuits extolled it when it was passive, fortified, and stoical. The following incident illustrated the bravery of one of them:

Although the savages are subject to fear, like other men, and are less resolute and courageous in their attacks than our Europeans, yet the fact remains that they glory in not wavering or recoiling when someone wishes to strike them, either in earnest or in feint. A Frenchman holding a halberd and pretending to thrust it at a savage in fact wounded him, because he stood still, without dodging the blow.[59]

Their courage was instructed and self-conscious: they prized "the name of great heart" more than the heart itself. Le Jeune wrote, in summing up their "good things": "They have only their own pleasure and contentment in view, add the fear of blame and the glory of appearing to be good hunters; there is all that moves them in their conduct." [60] But they could also be stirred by self-esteem, as Le Mercier showed in an incident that occurred at Three Rivers. The Iroquois constantly attacked the settlement, and finally the Indians there, "seeing themselves hemmed in and so often harassed, took courage, preferring to die fighting"; they turned on the invaders and routed them.[61] To Charlevoix even this action in self-defense showed merely the sinful pride of the warrior, and he castigated the Indians for remaining "the slaves of human respect and public regard." Such haughtiness, he moralized, brought with it a great fall—as the Hurons, whom the Iroquois had brought so low, proved.[62]

The Iroquois themselves, of course, best exemplified the warrior qualities of courage, pride, cunning, and brutality. In battle they were "Proteuses, who change their appearance every moment; and it should not be thought that they lack either leadership or courage." When they had planned an attack, the braves rose early

58. *Journal,* VI, 10–11.
59. "Relation . . . 1645 & 1646," XXIX, 226.
60. "Relation . . . 1634," VI, 240.
61. "Relation . . . 1652 & 1653," XL, 98.
62. *Journal,* VI, 12.

from their earthen beds, dressed in their finest, and filed out of the villages into the forest, "with no other chief to command them but their own courage." [63]

Although the Jesuits seldom denied the courage of the Indians in battle, they were generally so situated as to be unable or unwilling to report upon it very objectively. The bravest tribes were the most warlike and therefore those who resisted most successfully the advance of the French, whether missionaries or soldiers. Their courage, then, often appeared to the priests as treachery, made more heinous by the stealth which Biard and many others decried. But by far the weightiest explanation for the infrequent praise of valorous actions in the Relations lay in the motives and consequences of those actions. The courage of the warpath was not a corollary to composure and dignity; it was excited by blood lust and a desire for vengeance. Once a tribal council had determined upon war, oath takings, feasts, and dances whipped enthusiasm to a high pitch. After the warriors had departed the villagers waited tense and uneasy for their return; when the issue was known, the tension found release in triumphal orgies for the victors and in death, captivity, or torture for the victims. Consequently, the missionaries who dwelt with the victors saw only the wild preparations and the sadistic consequences of savage bravery. On the other hand, the priests who lived among the victims witnessed a treacherous surprise, the bloody massacre of their charges and perhaps their colleagues, and cruel tortures inflicted upon the captured survivors. The missionaries, whichever side they were with, knew cruelty at first hand, and the memory of it gripped their minds so vividly that when they came to write their reports they forgot whatever details about valor or skill they might have heard at second hand. The nobility of the virtue was obliterated by its effects.

The Jesuits deprecated such excesses constantly; no Relation lacked its tale of massacre, scalping, flaying, burning at the stake, or mutilation. The Indians murdered at least a dozen priests and cruelly mutilated as many more: Bressani managed to reach the Dutch on the Hudson River with just one finger left on each hand. Jérôme Lallemant must have been filled with compassionate rage when he penned the account of the martyrdom of Isaac Jogues; Bressani must have wept, remembering his own experiences as he

63. "Relation . . . 1649 & 1650," XXXV, 212; "Relation . . . 1669 & 1670," LIII, 138.

dictated the story of the massacre of Brébeuf and Daniel.[64] But it was not on their own account that they condemned this violence, for at the stake martyrs found glory. As one of them wrote: "We can say that we are like perpetual victims among them, since there is not a day when we are not in danger of being massacred; but it is that also which makes the pinnacle of our joy and the source of our purest consolations." [65] The Jesuits hated cruelty for the simple human reason that it inflicted pain upon other men. In addition, most of the victims were heathens, who were thus snatched from the saving embrace of the church. Finally, and worst of all, the high orgies of torture and killing intensified the vicious brutality of the perpetrators. From every aspect the cruelty into which courage degenerated became a weapon against the faith and rendered the task of conversion longer and more difficult. Therefore the Jesuits continued to include such horrible tales in their Relations: what better arguments for the necessity of conversion and—ever more urgently—of French conquest?

The Iroquois were the scourge of the French and of the tribes who had the misfortune to be their neighbors; but they were not the only Indians guilty of cruelty. Once Brébeuf told how the Hurons slow-burned their enemies—Iroquois, of course—for five or six days, roasted their hearts, and gave the cooked flesh to the youths of the village to eat; "they think this makes them courageous," he observed dryly.[66]

But whatever the practices of other tribes, the Iroquois were the most assiduous and committed the worst atrocities—men "who breathe only blood and slaughter, who glory in killing and burning men." [67] Jérôme Lallemant once depicted their attack upon a Huron village: "they throw themselves upon the old men and the children and the women . . . they wrench, they cut, they gash, they burn, they turn everything to fire and blood; they beat, they strike, they tear out the nails of those whom they wish to lead in triumph into their country." [68] Like their Huron cousins, they reached the peak of ferocity in cannibalism. In 1642 they surprised an Algonquin village, and, having slaughtered the braves and

64. Cf. "Relation . . . 1647," XXXI, 26–50; "Breve relazione," XXXIX, 240–242, 252–254.
65. "Relation . . . 1669 & 1670," LIV, 74–76.
66. "Relation . . . 1636," X, 226–228.
67. "Relation . . . 1669 & 1670," LIV, 74.
68. "Relation . . . 1647," XXX, 236–240.

secured the women and children with strong cords, "they prepared their supper in the house of the vanquished":

They dismember those whom they have just massacred, cut them in pieces, and throw the feet, legs, arms, and heads into the stew, which they set boiling with so much joy, that the poor captives who remain alive are heartbroken. . . . Supper being cooked, the wolves devour their prey; one throws himself upon a thigh, another upon a breast. Some suck the marrow from the bones; others open a skull to take out the brain. In a word, they eat men with as much appetite as and more joy than hunters eat a boar or a stag.[69]

With such horrors in mind Charlevoix felt justified in writing that all Indians were brutal, treacherous, vindictive, and motivated by a desire for revenge in all their actions.[70] But war and its frightfulness seemed abnormal to most missionaries even in the time of Charlevoix. While tribal anarchy intensified under pressure from the Europeans and forced the missionaries to give up their efforts in many regions, strife was still negligible inside the tribes where the missionaries sojourned. What conflicts did arise were settled in the customary ways and tempered by austerity and liberality. Moreover, few Jesuits sensed the increasing turbulence as acutely as Charlevoix, whose travels afforded him broader vistas.

Yet in the most peaceful villages there existed individual traits to disturb the daily routine. In 1634 Le Jeune devoted a long chapter to the imperfections of the Indians; comparing the Montagnais and the Hurons, he found them both proud and reckless of the evil effects of their loose tongues. They were also "slanderous beyond belief"; they gossiped maliciously and wittily; but in this they were like children. Their deceit, on the other hand, was more adult:

Lying is as natural to savages as talking, not among themselves but to strangers: so that it can be said that fear and hope, in a word, interest is the measure of their fidelity, I would trust them only so far as they would fear to be punished if they failed in their duty or hoped to be rewarded if they were faithful. They do not know what secrecy is [or] keeping their word [or] loving with constancy; especially those who are not of their nation, for they are harmonious among themselves, and their slanders and raillery do not disturb their peace and their friendly intercourse.

69. "Relation . . . 1642," XXII, 252–254.
70. *Journal*, V, 364–370; VI, 13.

I shall say in passing that the Montagnais savages are not thieves, they are always free to enter the dwellings of the French, because their hands can be trusted; but for the Hurons, if a person had as many eyes as they have fingers on their hands, still he would not prevent them from stealing, for they steal with their feet: they make a vocation of this, and expect to be beaten if they are discovered.[71]

Others who lived with the Hurons were not so scrupulous as to specify that they stole only from strangers. Brébeuf stated flatly that "Huron and thief are all one," while Vimont remarked that "it is a miracle when a Huron is not a thief." [72] The former admitted all the faults of his favorites but minimized the evil by emphasizing the good: "They are very lazy, lying, thieving, importunate beggars. Some call them vindictive, but in my opinion this vice is more noticeable elsewhere than here. One sees shining in them some rather beautiful moral virtues. One sees in the first place a great love and union . . ." [73] and for four pages he listed their virtues. Until he and his colleagues could be convinced of the worthlessness of any tribe, they gave them the benefit of every doubt; for, as he wrote: despite their many faults, they had natural good—"*leur bon naturel*." [74]

In his natural state, the Indian seemed to be capable at once of both high nobility and abysmal depravity. Out of his strange customs the missionaries collected a miscellany of virtues and vices. When vice appeared to predominate, they insisted that the appearance belied the reality, and for this conviction many of them paid with their lives. Even Charlevoix, superficial as he was, concluded that the Indians had truly a nobility and grandeur of soul that the French, with all their religion and philosophy, rarely attained— and that these qualities of the heart came from instinct and reflection.[75] Ragueneau or Vimont or Marquette would have agreed; if the Indians were brutalized, they were not brutes.

But they lived in the accursed darkness of heathendom. Accordingly, Le Jeune was once constrained to remark: ". . . all that I have said in this chapter is very true, and nevertheless I would not dare to assert that I have seen one act of true moral virtue done by a savage." [76] Again his fellow missionaries would have agreed. He

71. "Relation . . . 1634," VI, 246–248.
72. "Relation . . . 1636," X, 144; "Relation . . . 1642," XXII, 140.
73. "Relation . . . 1635," VIII, 126.
74. "Relation . . . 1635," VIII, 96.
75. *Journal*, VI, 8, 13.
76. "Relation . . . 1634," VI, 240.

was not by any means admitting defeat; he merely stated his conclusion, drawn from his observations. With these facts given, the new task was to be faced. No one stated the task more aptly than Father Brébeuf: "Our Lord Jesus Christ be forever praised. It is upon these dispositions and foundations that we hope with the grace of God to build the edifice of the Christian religion among these people, who besides already cherish us mightily and hold a great opinion of us. It is now ours to correspond to our calling." [77]

77. "Relation . . . 1635," VIII, 130.

VIII

NATURAL REASON AND NATURAL RELIGION

FOR success in their task the missionaries depended not simply upon their own zeal and ability but also upon the reception that they met among the Indians. Neither mute observation of savage conduct nor chance conversations furnished sufficient ground for the propagation of Catholic doctrines. Therefore the Jesuits examined the intelligence of the Indians and looked out especially for any religious predilections they might entertain. If men were men everywhere, it followed that their "souls are all of the same stuff." Like their European brothers, then, the Americans should possess rational means of apprehending dogma parallel to an intuitive growth of faith. The Jesuits also hoped to learn that the Indians derived spiritual as well as moral benefits from their primitive condition. Perhaps, in a reason that transcended the limits of natural activity or under the cloak of blind impulse, the Americans preserved intimations of God that civilization had destroyed in the old world.

Biard, in fact, did feel that he had found in Membertou, the Etchemin chief, a savage whom nature had instructed in the divine will; "for, even before he knew Christ, he could not be persuaded to take more wives than one: considering this more in harmony with nature and reason." [1] But this American Clovis was exceptional in many things. Seldom did missionaries come across conduct that so happily combined natural and supernatural morality. They were usually grateful to find instead the intellectual gifts of common sense, memory, and docility.

Even to Biard Membertou was an exception. The pioneer called most Acadian Indians "stupid," because they lacked respect for the French and were awkward in teaching the newcomers their language. Stupidity was natural to unlettered barbarians living outside the grace of Christ; they were completely earth-bound. As Biard explained,

1. Jouvency, "Canadicae missionis relatio," I, 214.

the very nature of the language, too, so deficient in words suitable for the expression of even the most common ideas, evaded the eager pursuit of our men and greatly disheartened them. Of those things, indeed, which fall under sight, touch, and the other senses, the names were obtained from the answers of the savages in one way or another, but for those things which elude the senses, there is the greatest scarcity of names among that race and also a profound ignorance of the things themselves.

But later, after Biard returned to France, recollection and a broader perspective tempered his opinion:

They have a fresh, clear intelligence in the evaluation and judgment of sensible and common things, and they deduce their reasons very nicely, seasoning them always with some pretty comparison. They have a very good memory of material things, like having seen you [before], the peculiarities of a place where they may have been, what might have been done in their presence twenty or thirty years before, etc. But to learn by heart, there is the snag: there is no way to get into their skulls an ordered sequence of words.[2]

Biard found, to his displeasure, that it took time and patience to learn their tongue and more of both to teach them the Pater Noster and the Ave Maria, early steps in their catechizing. Because he first broke the ground in Acadia and struggled against overwhelming obstacles, Biard judged the savages hastily and often harshly. His successors, more fortunate and consequently more lenient, credited the Indians with a high mentality.

In 1632 Le Jeune commented that the Montagnais "have pretty good sense; they do not all talk at once, but one after the other, listening patiently." Later, when reckoning up his baptisms, he estimated their intelligence more precisely. He had converted one "rather intelligent" man; but he did not anticipate rapid progress with the others, for evil had usurped their reason, and they resisted his advances subtly. "I could not tell you how cunning this nation is," he ruefully concluded.[3] Two years later, cataloguing "the good things that are found among the savages," he wrote thus about their reason:

. . . it is of good quality; I believe that souls are all of the same stuff, and that they do not differ in substance; that is why these barbarians

2. "Relatio rerum gestarum," II, 218–221; "Relation de la Nouvelle France," III, 72.
3. "Relation . . . 1632," V, 24–26, 72.

having well-formed bodies and well-arranged and well-regulated organs, their minds should work with ease: education and instruction only are lacking, their soul is a soil very good by its nature but burdened with all the evils that a land abandoned since the birth of the world can furnish.[4]

When he went among the Algonquins, he found them equally "intelligent"; Albanel concurred, several years later, that their minds were "good and facile." [5] The northern Indians did not monopolize such gifts; the Illinois, for example, Marest reported, "are naturally curious, they can turn a joke in a rather clever manner." [6]

Many missionaries, going beyond bare generalizations, compared the American barbarians very favorably "with certain villagers, since both are usually without education; yet our peasants are better off in this respect [i.e., of education]; nevertheless I have not seen anyone so far of those who have come to this country who does not confess and admit frankly that the savages have more wit than our ordinary peasants." [7] Like other barbarians, then, the Indians lacked knowledge, not sense. So Jérôme Lallemant argued in asking his readers to subscribe more generously to the support of the Huron missions. He counseled those whose interest was flagging, on account of the paucity of converts, to keep up their hopes.

For in truth it is easy to despair of the conversion of these people, even upon this conclusion alone, that since they are barbarian, hardly anyone can believe that they are men and that they can be made Christians. But it is wrong to decide thus, for I can say in truth that as to intelligence they have no less than Europeans and [even?] those who live in France.[8]

The following year, after Lallemant became superior at Quebec, Ragueneau took up the plea for the Hurons.

The savages are not so savage as is believed in France, and I can say with truth that the intelligence of several [of them] yields in nothing to ours. . . . It is true that their mode of expression is different from ours; but since the word of the heart is the same in all men, one cannot doubt that their language has also its beauties and graces, as much

4. "Relation . . . 1634," VI, 228.
5. "Relation . . . 1639," XVII, 198; "Relation . . . 1669 & 1670," LIII, 86–88.
6. "Lettre au Père Germon," *Jesuit Relations*, LXVI, 230.
7. "Relation . . . 1634," VI, 228–230.
8. "Relation . . . 1644 & 1645," XXVIII, 62.

as ours. Although they live in the woods, they are no less men for it.[9]

Already Le Jeune had marked the acumen of "their children, who are very bright and amiable." Thus when he first pondered how to catch "the strange and vagabond nations, like those at Quebec where we live," the stratagem of besieging the children occurred to him immediately.[10] They were the generation of the future; also tender years rendered them more susceptible to new ideas and less hardened in the old heathen beliefs. He decided to start classes for them. Father Brébeuf, out with the Hurons, supported Le Jeune's program wholeheartedly, for, as he wrote in 1636:

If there were nuns at Quebec—I believe that we could also send you some little seminarists—there is here a quantity of fine young girls, who if they were well trained, would yield in nothing to our young French girls. . . . I do not doubt in the least that the divine bounty will crown with great blessings those in particular whom it inspires to contribute to the foundation of these seminaries and to the education of these little seedlings of this infant Church.[11]

Once Le Jeune had herded a few children into his first schools, he proved the "admirable truth" of his assumption and found in fact "that education alone is wanting in these poor children, who have minds as good as our Europeans." [12] One worthy pupil was "so intelligent that she has learned the French language in less than two years and then to read and write [it], so that she outstrips the little French girls [who are in her class]." [13] A few years later Vimont assessed the results of the schools more fully: "The children who have been baptized upon reaching years of discretion have given evidence of a good mind, they apprehend promptly, retain easily, and have become very assiduous at the catechism; which has been not a little useful for the bigger ones who have learned their prayers from the younger." [14]

If the Indians were trained young enough, then, they could comprehend the ideas of immaterial as well as material things. And, once conceived, they could remember such ideas. Memory, indeed, constituted two of the traits that Bressani so admired in his Iroquois captors:

9. "Relation . . . 1645 & 1646," XXIX, 280–282.
10. "Relation . . . 1632," V, 32.
11. "Relation . . . 1636," X, 32.
12. "Relation . . . 1639," XVI, 178.
13. "Relation . . . 1652 & 1653," XL, 228.
14. "Relation . . . 1642 & 1643," XXIV, 92.

Thirdly their imagination is prodigious in remembering places and describing them to one another in guiding themselves in the woods, where they are hardly ever lost. I have tried many times in cloudy weather or at night to lead some barbarian astray, using the compass to try to make him lose the idea of the four directions of the world, and then to ask him where the east was, where the south, where the country of the enemy, where ours ; never have I found that they were confused ; they guided themselves as surely by their senses as I by my compass. . . .

Fourthly a very tenacious memory ; they have neither books nor writings, negotiations are carried on by embassies, in which I have been amazed to see how many things and how many circumstances they recall.[15]

Aside from a fund of common sense and a faculty for memory, as the preceding chapter has noted, the Indians had an affable manner. Thus they often appeared to believe the sermons of the missionaries. Brébeuf observed that the Hurons were "generally very docile" and not so dull as one would think ; they "can be led as you please," at least under the influence of "temporal considerations." [16] But the Jesuits praised such conduct only so long as they felt they were not preaching to stones ; what appeared to be docility among prospective Christians quickly turned to slyness among adamant pagans. Brébeuf could write indulgently about the Hurons, whose eventual baptism he took for granted. But Le Mercier complained bitterly about the Ottawas in a tone that recalled Le Jeune's comment on Montagnais cunning :

The dissimulation which is natural to these savages and a certain spirit of acquiescence in which the children are brought up in that country make them assent to all that is told them and prevent them from showing anything contrary to the sentiments of others, although they may know that what they are told is not true. To this dissimulation must be added stubbornness and obstinacy in following entirely their thoughts and desires ; which has obliged our fathers not to receive so easily in baptism the adults, who besides were raised in idolatry and license.[17]

Docile or cunning, the Indians were intelligent, as Le Mercier grudgingly admitted ; he railed not so much against their lack of

15. "Breve relazione," XXXVIII, 258–260; cf. Charlevoix, *Journal*, VI, 7–8.
16. "Relation . . . 1635," VIII, 146; "Relation . . . 1636," X, 40.
17. "Relation . . . 1668 & 1669," LII, 202–204.

wit as against their lack of virtue. Yet, by the missionaries' own premises, how could it have seemed otherwise?

The observer found the clearest index of the nature of the savage intellect not in actions, which could be variously construed, but in words. Although the rhetorician Biard scorned their narrow concepts and their consequently limited vocabulary, he valued their speeches highly. Later missionaries, more conversant with the native tongues, applauded the Indians for the mental qualities their eloquence revealed. The Iroquois, Bressani wrote,

> have a good understanding and express themselves well. They have an excellent narrative style and great eloquence, and they conduct those matters of which they understand the fundamental elements as well as the most sagacious Europeans. In France people have believed that their speeches and addresses, which we reported in our relations, were fictitious; but I am sure that most of these, when translated into another tongue, are much less forceful than in their own. They have often convinced us in negotiations of importance and made us change the resolutions which after many false starts we had taken for the good of the country.[18]

Father Brébeuf found the same gift among the Hurons: ". . . there is almost no one of them who is incapable of conversing and arguing well, and in good language, on things with which he is acquainted: what develops them still further in discourse is the councils which are held almost every day in the villages, upon any occasion: and . . . each has the right to express his opinion." The missionary gave proof of Huron eloquence: ". . . with a discourse which a captain named Aenons made me this spring, he was trying to persuade us to move our cabin over to his village." Then he quoted at length the speech of Aenons, in which "he employed all his rhetoric." Although Brébeuf did not move his cabin, he confessed the captain had stirred him: ". . . the harangue . . . would in my opinion have passed in the judgment of many for one of the speeches of Titus Livy if the subject had interested him; it seemed very persuasive to me." [19] In 1648, after the Iroquois had devastated their country and massacred three missionaries, the Hurons gave another notable display of their oratorical talents. They insisted that the surviving priests go with them to an island safely out of reach of the Iroquois. On that occasion they "spoke for

18. "Breve relazione," XXXVIII, 260–262.
19. "Relation . . . 1636," X, 212, 234–244.

more than three whole hours, with an eloquence as powerful to make us yield as the art of orators could furnish in the midst of France, where most people call these countries barbarous." [20]

Farther west Indian eloquence rose to equal heights. In 1691 the Illinois seized upon the arrival of Rasles among them as a pretext for parading the full repertory of their welcoming ceremonies.

When all the guests had arrived, they ranged themselves all around the cabin, sitting on the bare ground or on mats. Then the chief rose and commenced his harangue. I confess to you that I admired his flow of words, the aptness and the force of the arguments which he set forth, the eloquent turn which he gave them, the choice and delicacy of the expressions with which he adorned his discourse. I am persuaded that, if I had put down in writing what this savage said to us offhand and without preparation, you would readily agree that the most capable Europeans, after much meditation and study, could scarcely compose an oration more solid or well turned.[21]

Charlevoix, as usual, outdid his predecessors; everywhere he found their speech "full of luminous features which would have been applauded in the public assemblies of Rome or Athens. Their eloquence has that power, substance, and pathos that art does not confer, which the Greeks admired particularly in the barbarians." He regarded their accomplishment the more highly for its being a natural gift.[22] In a similar vein Father Bressani praised the Indians in their primitive state, while envisaging a brighter future for them, when he wrote: "I do not doubt that they are capable of the sciences, they have a harmonious and excellent ear for music, but theirs is different and somehow more martial than ours. It is not taught as an art, but the most proficient esteem it as one of the gifts of nature." [23]

Hitherto, since they had lacked both civilization and grace, the Indians had drawn all their lore from nature. But even the lessons of nature sometimes transcended the physical and became manifest to the Indians in other forms. On the subject of sorcery Brébeuf wrote in 1636 that "these people are not so stupid as not to see and to recognize something beyond the senses," and then

20. "Relation . . . 1648 & 1649," XXXIV, 208.
21. "Lettre à Monsieur son frère," *Jesuit Relations,* LXVII, 162.
22. *Journal,* VI, 6–7.
23. "Breve relazione," XXXVIII, 262.

lamented that vice had blinded the heathens to the vision of God.[24]
Father Dequen also observed that the Indians were aware of
some existence beyond the reach of the physical senses. Once,
describing an Iroquois council meeting, he explained what the
presents given on such occasions meant; after telling of the first
three, he went on: "These people believe that sadness and anger
and all the violent passions chase the rational souls from the
body, only the sensitive souls, which we have in common with the
beasts, remaining there at that time. That is why on these occasions
they usually make a present to restore the rational soul to the seat
of reason, and this was the fourth present." [25] Jouvency elaborated
upon this presentiment when he discussed Indian medical practices:

They believe there are two main sources of disease: one of these is in
the mind of the patient himself, which desires something and will vex
the body of the sick man until it possesses the desired object. For they
think that there are in every man certain inborn desires, often unknown to themselves, upon which the happiness of individuals depends. For the purpose of ascertaining desires and innate appetites
of this character, they summon soothsayers who, they think, have a
divinely imparted power to look into the innermost recesses of the
mind.[26]

Charlevoix agreed with these opinions. From the keen imagination and vivid perceptions that the Indians betrayed in their
speech, he concluded that they possessed internal senses no less
mature than their external faculties.[27]

Through the intellect of the Indians the Jesuits could perceive
their humanity and more fully understand their natural conduct.
But they also glimpsed other impulses at work in the Indian
mentality beyond the bare urge to gratify the instincts. Being
enlightened through faith, the Jesuits recognized the internal
senses. But by what means had the existence of these senses been
intimated to the heathens? Anxiously the priests searched to discover if there was something more than the silence of the forests
that made the word of God welcome among such primitive people.

24. "Relation . . . 1636," X, 192.
25. "Relation . . . 1655 & 1656," XLII, 50.
26. "Canadicae missionis relatio," I, 258.
27. *Journal*, VI, 6–8.

The missionaries found many elements of natural religion, along with evidence that the devil had been working on the ignorance of the barbarians. At most they hoped to find a simple, untutored sentiment of divinity. Even where they first failed to perceive any religious propensity, they continued to believe that it existed, embedded deep and obscure in the Indian ideas; and when they came to know the savages well enough, they could certainly uncover religious sentiments that would overcome ignorance and facilitate baptism. Naturally, in such a mood of stubborn hope the Jesuits sometimes saw religious predispositions where none really existed. Indeed, their conviction became necessary to sustain their apostolic zeal.

For those who had eyes to see it, the evidence was plain; the Jesuits often scolded their countrymen for harboring doubts on so vital a point. "I am not pleased," wrote Le Jeune, "with those who thought that one did not see in the mind of the savages any little ray of light, or of knowledge concerning the divinity"; he was speaking for his whole order.[28] When they themselves could not see this knowledge they grieved. About his Micmacs, for example, Father Perrault wrote:

What they lack is the knowledge of God and of the service which they are obliged to render Him, as also of the state of souls after death: it is marvelous that we have not yet been able to discover any trace of this, in what we know of their language. Perhaps we shall discover something more when we know more about it; for it is not credible that the light of nature should be completely extinguished in them in this respect, it not being so in other nations which are more barbarous . . .

And having admitted so much, the good man still read some hint of supernatural assistance in the courtesy and diligence with which the Micmacs heard his instruction. "I do not know whether it is through complacence, for they have a good deal of this naturally, or through instinct from above, that they listen to us so willingly." [29]

But Perrault's experience was exceptional; generally the missionaries drew more solid conclusions from native speech and conduct. Bressani, for instance, while supporting the argument of

28. "Relation . . . 1638," XIV, 190.
29. "Relation . . . 1635," VIII, 160–162.

Perrault based on probability and faith, was not forced to rely on it entirely when he described the religion of the Iroquois.

I had read in various authors, who write against the atheists, that atheism is a sin against nature, who herself inspires *sensum quemdam divinitatis:* I did not doubt it, but I have confirmed myself in this sentiment by what I have seen among our barbarians, who are so wholly uncultivated that nothing seems to remain but corrupt nature alone, and yet they are very far from the opinions of our libertines and from atheism. In the first place, they believe in the immortality of the soul . . . good and bad spirits . . . a divinity. . . . Thirdly, they pray. . . .[30]

If the Jesuits defined the Indian beliefs no more specifically than Bressani, few of them seemed as unsure as Perrault; most felt that the Indians possessed at least the idea of religion.

Charlevoix saw among them, even in their most indifferent moods, survivals of primitive religion. Their ideas about a prime being were very confused, and they had only the scantest remnants of worship left; but he was confident that these remnants would lead them along the path of salvation.[31] If any record of God's original generosity remained among these barbarians, the forces of evil abroad in the world since the fall of Adam had obliterated it. Their religion, then, was truly natural, deprived as it was of supernatural effect. The missionaries set themselves the task of salvaging the scraps from the past for the benefit of the future; to do so they leaned heavily upon the bounties conferred by the redemption.

However much primitive worship had degenerated among the Indians, nevertheless the Jesuits searched for its natural manifestations. Biard, indeed, cited Membertou as acting in harmony with nature and reason. Brébeuf knew at least one pagan "to whom our Lord had communicated, a year ago, several good impulses." Among the Hurons Le Mercier came across a veritable prodigy who possessed "natural advantages which surpassed not only the average among these barbarians but even those ordinarily encountered in France." This paragon was endowed with a well-formed body and a still better mind: his poise and strength of judgment placed him on a par with mature men, although he was but ten years old; he was docile, polite, devout, serious, and oblig-

30. "Breve relazione," XXXIX, 12.
31. *Journal*, V, 391; VI, 62.

ing. On one occasion, when a companion faltered in his prayers, " 'Courage, my cousin,' he said, 'pray earnestly to God, it is He who gives us all that we have, the corn, the fruits, the fish.' That is remarkable in a child. Now here is something to make us lower our eyes and admire in all humility the secret designs of God." But the prodigy died at eleven; and very few adults existed whose names were similarly "written in the Book of the Elect." [32]

Accordingly, the missionaries resorted to more general proofs of the existence of natural religion. In 1644 Jérôme Lallemant wrote from Huron country that he had

never seen in France illiterate people more susceptible to the mysteries of our faith. They penetrate them with so much intelligence and draw from them such solid sentiments about heavenly things that this alone convinces my mind that God wills to be acknowledged in the midst of this barbarism, that He has His elect here, and that were we to die a thousand times, the gospel must be preached here. [33]

The relator of 1657–58 stated "that the savages are as worthy of God as other more civilized nations. The gift of prayer, the love of suffering, charity for one's neighbor are found in some to an eminent degree: *ex ungue leonem*, from the sample the whole piece is known." [34] All Jesuits were not, then, like Perrault, forced to deduce the existence of religious sentiments. They had frequent opportunities to corroborate from observation the opinion of Bressani: the Indians believed in immortality of the soul, spirits, and a divinity, and they prayed.

Although the barbarians felt that a soul existed, they had great difficulty in defining its attributes and even greater difficulty in conveying their ideas to the priests. "They have a confused and vague idea of the immortality of the soul and of a future compensation for good and evil," Biard reported, "but beyond this point they do not seek nor care." [35] Yet Biard was probably as confused as the Indians. Their ignorance and totemism combined to preclude any such systematic body of religious thought as would appeal to a Jesuit theologian. Indeed, the Indians entertained

32. "Relation . . . 1636," X, 58–60; "Relation . . . 1637," XIII, 116–118; "Relation . . . 1639," XVI, 172.

33. "Relation . . . 1643 & 1644," XXVI, 212.

34. "Relation . . . 1657 & 1658," XLIV, 252.

35. "Relation de la Nouvelle France," III, 134; cf. Mathurin le Petit, "Lettre au Père d'Avaugour, Procureur des missions de l'Amérique Septentrionale," *Jesuit Relations*, LXVIII, 129.

many contradictory ideas about souls. They confounded human souls with other spirits that represented for them a crude hierarchy of ideal prototypes, as Le Jeune found when he wrote about the Montagnais. One member of that tribe said

that his people believe that a certain savage had received from Messou [a god] the gift of immortality in a little packet, with a mighty warning not to open it, while he kept it shut he would be immortal; but his curious and incredulous wife wished to see what was in this present; when opened, it all flew away, and ever since the savages have been subject to death.

They say besides that all the animals of each species have an elder brother, who is as it were the principle and origin of all the individuals, and this elder brother is marvelously great and powerful. . . . these elders of all the animals are the younger brothers of Messou.[36]

According to Brébeuf the Hurons also believed that the soul was immortal and corporeal.[37] Le Jeune recounted several other beliefs of the Hurons:

some say that the souls do nothing but dance after departing this life; there are some who admit the transmigration of souls, as Pythagoras did, and most imagine that the soul is insensible after it has left the body; all generally believe that it is immortal. They distinguish many souls in one body. One old man told us some time ago that some savages had up to two or three souls, that his had quitted him more than two years before to go off with his dead relatives, that he no longer had any other soul than the soul of his body which was to descend to the grave with him. From this it can be seen that they imagine the body has its own soul, which some call the soul of their nation.[38]

Jouvency adduced as further evidence of the Indian belief in immortality that they buried things with their dead, like the Egyptians.[39]

The confusion that this welter of ideas betrayed was, of course, ascribed by the missionaries to the ignorance of the Indians. They knew no reasons for the immortality of the soul, as Charlevoix pointed out, but believed in it only through tradition. He found further proof of the deficiency of their understanding in the belief that they would be rewarded in a future life for their good

36. "Relation . . . 1634," VI, 158.
37. "Relation . . . 1635," VIII, 121.
38. "Relation . . . 1639," XVI, 190–192.
39. "Canadicae missionis relatio," I, 261.

deeds on earth, but that their evil deeds would not be punished.[40] How could the Indians comprehend heaven and hell, when they had not yet received the grace that was essential to freedom of the will? But even more, the confusion that the Jesuits reported illuminated the flaws in their own observation. Since all the tribes looked alike and were neighbors, the priests assumed they held certain religious ideas in common. On the contrary, each tribe was to be understood by itself; the religion of the Hurons, for example, was simply barbarian, closer, perhaps, to the ideas of Asiatic heathens than to those of other American tribes. Therefore it was footless to construe a distinctly American worship.

If the Indians were only dimly aware of their own souls, they were much more acutely conscious of divinity. Even Biard, who in one place wrote that they had no religion, conceded elsewhere that they held "a tenuous notion of one supreme god"; but, he continued, they were so seduced by vice as to worship the devil. Elsewhere he noted with contempt that "they believe in a god, they say: but they can call him by no other name than that of the sun, Niscaminou." [41] Le Jeune, who esteemed the intuitions of the Indians more highly than Biard, wrote with discernment of the Montagnais:

I shall say that it is a great mistake to believe that the savages have no knowledge of any divinity: I was astonished at this [mistake] in France, seeing that nature had given this sentiment to all the other nations of the earth. I confess that the savages have no public or common prayers, nor any rite which they offer regularly to him whom they take for God, and that their knowledge is only shadows; but it cannot be denied that they recognize some nature superior to the nature of man; as they have neither laws nor police, also they have no ordinance concerning the service of this superior nature, each one does as he understands it; I do not know their secrets, but from this little that I am going to tell, it will be clear that they acknowledge some divinity.

Then Le Jeune told the legends of Atahocan, who made all things and who dwelt in the sky; and of Messou, who "restored the world when it was lost in the waters." [42]

40. *Journal,* VI, 75–77.
41. "Relation de la Nouvelle France," III, 132; "Missio Canadensis," in *Jesuit Relations,* II, 76.
42. "Relation . . . 1633," V, 152–154.

When Father Brébeuf first knew the Hurons, he utilized the same arguments as Perrault had, to deduce a belief in God from his own Christian premises: "That there is a divinity who made heaven and earth is so clear and so evident that our Hurons cannot entirely ignore it. And although they have the eyes of their mind very clouded by the darkness of a long ignorance, their vices and sins, nevertheless they do see something." But he could not descry what they saw. The following year, more familiar with their ideas, he ceased to argue the question. Instead he filled a chapter of his Relation with proofs "that the Hurons recognize some divinity."

They have recourse to the sky in almost all their necessities and respect the great bodies in it above all creatures and perceive in it something divine: it is indeed after man the most vivid image that we have of divinity. . . . I say this to show how easy it will be with time and the divine assistance to lead these people to the knowledge of their Creator, because they honor already so particularly a creation which is such a perfect image of him.

Then, as Le Jeune had done for the Montagnais, Brébeuf proceeded to relate the Huron legends: of the creation of the world by Eateantsic, who also nourished the souls of her creatures; of her son Jouskeha, who protected living beings; of the first men; and many other stories.[43] Such myths strikingly resembled those of Greece and Asia, and in Jesuit eyes testified to the universality of divine providence. Later Ragueneau wrote about the Hurons in a tone similar to Brébeuf's. Although they had received no idea about the God of the Christians, yet they retained

a secret sentiment of the divinity and of a first principle author of all things, whom they invoked without knowing it. . . . So true is what Tertullian said of the most infidel nations, that nature in the midst of perils makes them speak with a Christian voice, *Exclamant vocem naturaliter Christianam*, having recourse to a god whom they invoke almost without knowing him. *Ignoto Deo*.[44]

Deep in the forests of Wisconsin Allouez found the Fox Indians acknowledging a great spirit who had created heaven and earth. One of those with whom the priest conversed "told me in private

43. "Relation . . . 1635," VIII, 116–118; "Relation . . . 1636," X, 124–138, 158–160.

44. "Relation . . . 1647 & 1648," XXXIII, 224–226.

that his ancestor had come from heaven, and he had preached the unity and the sovereignty of a god who had made all the other gods: who had assured them that he would go to heaven after his death. . . . These are fables which God uses for their salvation." [45] But Allouez could find no such providence working among the nearby Ottawas. They believed in many spirits, whom they invoked when they went to war or on journeys. But they recognized no sovereign master; nor, because they were people of such gross natures, could they perceive a purely spiritual divinity of any sort.[46] Without doubt Allouez agreed with Le Mercier, the Ottawas were almost entirely abandoned.

"The gift of prayer" constituted the fourth major evidence of religious sentiment. Although it was difficult for them to memorize Latin, which had no meaning for them, they prayed in their own way, privately and without ceremony, before the missionaries taught them Christian prayers. Of the Montagnais, for instance, Le Jeune once wrote:

Other times I have heard them pray for spring or for deliverance from evil and other similar things; and all that is done by means of the desires that they express, crying as loudly as they can, "I would be very happy if this day continued or the wind changed," etc. To say to whom these wishes are addressed I could not, for they do not know themselves, at least those whom I have asked have not been able to tell me.

Another time he met an old man who had vowed to save the tail of every beaver he caught in order to be sure of a larger catch; but "to whom he made this vow, neither he nor I could say." [47] Le Jeune called such prayer superstitious and shook his head; yet had he, like Ragueneau, known Tertullian, this patent ignorance of God need not have troubled him. On the other hand, Brébeuf rejoiced simply that the Hurons prayed, even if they prayed now only to demons. He prayed in turn: "My God, listen to them and make Yourself known to them, for they wish to address themselves to You." At a great council the leader first thanked the village chiefs for attending; then "thanks were rendered, I know not to whom, that everyone arrived without mishap." [48] Superstition,

45. "Relation . . . 1666 & 1667," LI, 45; "Relation . . . 1669 & 1670," LIV, 220–222.
46. "Relation . . . 1666 & 1667," L, 285, 289.
47. "Relation . . . 1634," VI, 202–204, 214.
48. "Relation . . . 1636," X, 166, 255.

then, was not incorrigible. Its mere presence among these simple people revealed a salutary awareness of the unknown; and while it was important that they learn to pray to the Christian God, their very praying gratified the missionaries. The priests might have experienced much more difficulty in converting heathens who knew to whom they prayed. Indeed, any supernatural knowledge to which the savages in their natural state laid claim was, according to the Jesuits, inevitably wrong. The vaguer their sense of the spiritual the better, lest ignorance seduce them to diabolical worship.

Where natural tendencies toward religion did not appear, the missionaries found cause for hope in the absence of false religious sentiments. When Le Jeune tried to convince the Hurons of the errors in their ideas, he was pleased to hear them admit they were not very certain about them and not much attached to them anyway.[49] Similarly Father Nouvel was encouraged when he discovered that "there is no false religion to combat" among the Algonquins; and, since they were intelligent and gentle, they grasped Christian principles all the more quickly.[50] But the missionaries were deluded either by Indian complacence or their own expectations. Closer acquaintance gave them a more correct view of their prospects. Thus in 1642 Jérôme Lallemant wrote as follows:

Before we had the knowledge of these tribes which time has given us: seeing no worship which they rendered to any false divinity, we concluded that their conversion would be so much easier; because, as on a bare slate, there being nothing to erase, we could without opposition impress the ideas of a true God and guide them to the respect and the adoration which is due him from all the earth. But experience has made us see that they are full of diabolical superstitions, taking their dreams for their divinities, upon whom the happiness of their lives depends. Besides that, we see that they acknowledge more puissant genii who dispose of public affairs, who cause famines, who conduct wars and give victory to those who render themselves most pliant to their wishes.[51]

It became clear that the Jesuits faced the same enemies in New France as in Europe: not ignorance alone but, in addition, the

49. "Relation . . . 1637," XII, 149.
50. "Relation . . . 1663 & 1664," XLIX, 54.
51. "Relation . . . 1642," XXIII, 150–152.

forces of evil, which craftily abused the natural instincts of men. Yet here, because necessity banished luxury, the triumph over evil might be speedier. Le Jeune argued with steady optimism that the Canadians would become Christian more easily than the South Americans, who were so fondly attached to their luxuries and superstitions. "In New France there are only sins to destroy, and even those in small number: for these poor people, so far from all luxury, have not abandoned themselves to many offenses. There is very little superstition or false religion, if they do exist in some places." Seven more years in the wilderness made superstitions more apparent to him. But he could still write with dogged hope that these were "not very deeply rooted in their minds," and that, being dissipated by the rays of reasonable truth, they "fall of themselves." Ragueneau ridiculed the Indians bitterly for attributing great power to charms and totems, and the western missionaries sternly reproached the Ottawas for their idolatry.[52] Nevertheless, whether the Jesuits scolded or pleaded, the vicious ignorance of the Indians rebuffed them; the number of conversions, although gradually increasing, always remained meager.

"Grace is more powerful than nature," Father Vimont wrote. He was convinced not only that the Word would bring order to the chaos of America but also that grace alone could give the human nature of the Indians its proper direction.[53] The most enlightened savage, upon whom nature shed some dim diffuse rays, stood only on the threshold of the road to salvation; he needed the Word and the water of baptism to be able to cross it and commence a spiral life. Therefore, while the missionaries rejoiced to find some Indians naturally predisposed to Christianity, they were happy simply to baptize mute dying infants. But of course they reached the peak of pious joy in converting those who seemed naturally predisposed and watching them exceed all their fellows in devotion.

For example, Membertou as a Christian was "beyond all others, so wondrously moved within that he understood much more of our faith than he could have learned from our instruction." [54] Baptism alone was necessary to awaken all the potentialities lying dormant

---

52. "Relation . . . 1632," V, 34; "Relation . . . 1639," XVI, 198; "Relation . . . 1647 & 1648," XXXIII, 211–215.
53. "Relation . . . 1642," XXII, 68.
54. Biard, "Missio Canadensis," *Jesuit Relations,* II, 96.

in such happy persons as long as they remained heathen. Le Jeune, too, knew many neophytes who enjoyed similar favors. In one man's conduct he found nothing lacking: he was gentle, courteous, compliant, industrious, heroic, wise, and prudent; and of course "he admired the beauty of our faith." [55] Le Mercier once devoted an entire chapter to a captain "whose heart God has touched, who is in no respect inferior to the most zealous Catholic in France." This man, declaring that "I am neither French nor savage, but I wish to be a child of God," changed his whole life in order to conform to his new Christianity. In closing his chapter, Le Mercier wrote joyously:

Sometimes he would say to the father who instructed him more particularly: mortify me in public before the others, so that those who wish to be baptized may persuade themselves that you must practice virtue when you are a child of God. Behold the grand effects of grace. Blessed be God forever by men and by angels, by Scythians and by barbarians, as well as by Greeks. Amen.[56]

When the Huron fugitives near Quebec became Christian, Le Mercier saw their conduct as "an index that the hearts of the savages are not insensible to the movements of God and that faith lifts them, as well as us, above the sentiments of nature." [57] Of such transformations was Ragueneau thinking when he wrote in imitation of Vimont: "I must confess that grace has more power than all nature over a heart animated by God." [58]

Christian Indians showed by their efforts to win their pagan brothers for the faith as great a capacity for spiritual perfection as Europeans. Moreover, by the law of charity they were obligated to set what examples of virtue and faith their primitive condition permitted.[59] A missionary to the Iroquois in 1656 presented the following evidence of their "dispositions . . . toward the faith":

These murderers of the preachers of the gospel, these flesh-eating wolves who had vented their rage on the flock of Jesus Christ with more fury and with more atrocious torments than the Neros and Diocletians, embrace our holy religion with more fervor than those whom they exterminated, and take up the yoke of this same faith of which

55. "Relation . . . 1639," XVI, 172–174.
56. "Relation . . . 1638," XV, 76; "Relation . . . 1639," XVI, 112–132.
57. "Relation . . . 1653 & 1654," XLI, 164.
58. "Relation . . . 1645 & 1646," XXX, 78.
59. Cf. "Relation . . . 1643 & 1644," XXVI, 119.

they were the oppressors a few years ago. . . . The providence of God makes them take the place of the poor Christians whom they have exterminated; and the exhortations of our martyrs, more ardent than the flames and the coals from the midst of which they preached, have now such marvelous effects among their executioners that more Iroquois have been made Christian in two months than there were Hurons converted in several years: they ask with as much fervor and veneration for the waters of baptism as they had scorned them with insolence, pouring boiling water on the heads of the preachers in derision of this sacrament. . . . Their zeal would make this infant church be taken for a church formed and established for several years or several centuries: indeed it would be very difficult to find in the old churches so great an eagerness to be at the public prayers and instructions, joined to such a great modesty and such a perfect submission to all the duties of a Christian.[60]

But apparently the Word fell upon rock; their sudden zeal as suddenly withered. Twelve years later, when Father Jacques Frémin visited the Senecas, he saw the faith cherished only by the Huron captives. These, ardent for salvation and innocent in their morals, resembled the first Christians, "although all deprived as they were of the presence of their pastors, without having either preachers to fortify them in the faith or confessors to reconcile them with God or any of the external aids with which Europe is so powerfully assisted. . . ." And, Frémin speculated, "Will not a fidelity and a constancy in the faith as invincible as that of the Hurons in this country serve on the day of judgment to damn the laxity and corruption of the Christians of Europe?"[61]

Even if the missionaries failed in their primary task, the good examples that they recorded cast a harsh light on the imperfect condition of the church at home. The contrast between the primitive and the older churches, although seldom phrased as explicitly as in the foregoing passage, hovered constantly in the background of the Relations and revealed their didactic purpose. When the Indians stated the contrast, the moral was even more obvious; then the priests did not hesitate to labor the point. In 1646, for instance, Ragueneau wrote that the Christian Hurons

say, "it is not here as in France, where those whom we would meet would speak to us only of God." These good people imagine that in France everybody breathes nothing but holiness, that in gatherings

60. "Relation . . . 1656 & 1657," XLIII, 282–284.
61. "Relation . . . 1669 & 1670," LIV, 84.

the conversation is solely about God, that vice keeps itself hidden there and would not dare to appear, and that it is as difficult to find a debauched person there, everyone being Christian, as it is here in an infidel world to meet people who have their affections only for the good.[62]

Dequen reported similarly naïve opinions that could have shamed the French: "The Christian savages ask why those who are baptized, beyond the sea, that is in Europe, make war on each other, instead of coming to help them against those who prevent them from being instructed and from believing in God peacefully, and who make the faithful die." [63] In 1655, when these lines were written, many missionaries and colonists were undoubtedly vexed with the same question.

It was Charlevoix who exploited every aspect of Indian life; for his particular interest lay in reforming European morals, and he bluntly sought to improve his countrymen by showing them the higher virtue of a lower culture. Thus, he concluded that while religion alone could perfect the Indians and correct their vices, yet, for religion to have its full effect, all professing Catholics had to set good examples to the savages in their own lives.[64]

As with the private conduct of the savages, so did the missionaries applaud what was naturally good in the savage intellect and religious propensities. What was bad they deplored; but for long they persisted in regarding the evil as temporary and contingent upon paganism. The missionary goal drew only imperceptibly nearer with the passage of time, and as a result the missionaries turned ever more earnestly to consider the means to their end. In the process they emphasized the civilizing aspects of Christianity. At the same time, along with the body, mind, and soul of the individual Indian they gave much attention to the outstanding aspects of his community life.

62. "Relation . . . 1645 & 1646," XXX, 52.
63. "Relation . . . 1655 & 1656," XLII, 222.
64. *Journal,* VI, 62.

IX

POLITICAL CONDUCT OF THE INDIANS

IN ONE of the letters of the *Journal* Charlevoix asserted that he saw little of interest in the political customs of the Indians. But on the next page he contradicted himself: their political principles had "almost nothing about them that smacks of barbarism"; and he launched into a long discussion of the subject.[1] In fact, everything Indian attracted Charlevoix. He was simply warning his readers not to be disappointed; after a century of Relations and journals about New France, they would find no startling novelties in his book. Charlevoix's poised criticism contrasted sharply with the gaping curiosity of Biard or Le Jeune and their readers, to whom the Americans seemed utterly outlandish.

When the first missionaries landed in Canada, they knew no form of government but the French monarchy—hereditary, proprietary, and authoritarian. The organization of a society in New France seemed so simple as to lack political elements altogether. Their rapid transition from the dazzling Capetian absolutism to the pitch-black American anarchy at first blinded the Jesuits. But with time familiarity restored their vision. They came to see that basic political institutions did exist among the Indians, albeit in forms simpler and more natural than those of Europe; and they evolved standards for comparison with European regimes. While differences stood out as clearly as before, under the influence of relativism American novelties turned to banalities. Barbarisms became accepted as natural, commonplace, and therefore of little interest.

Furthermore, during the seventeenth century in France such diverse theorists as Bossuet, Jurieu, and Bayle were stressing the moral responsibility that the possession of absolute political power involved. Earlier, necessity had justified the consolidation of absolutism, which the religious turmoil of the sixteenth century had intensified. Yet both Calvinism and Catholicism de-

1. *Journal*, V, 390–391.

manded a moral sanction for the perpetuation of absolutism. The new emphasis on political morality, although springing from religion, gave an added impetus to the study of society. Now the missionaries in the early part of the century were gathering much information about Indian customs, conduct, and public opinion —but only as incidental to conversion. It remained for later writers, aware of the growing secular interest of their readers, to spell out the connection between such subjects and political activity.

In glaring contrast to the hoary old French monarchy with its intricate, overlapping, and often obsolete institutions, the missionaries saw in New France a very simple form of government. The framework was supplied by the families and clans, whose only complication was geneological. Beyond the jurisdiction of the household, chiefs and councils directed affairs that pertained to the clan, tribe, or federation. But high public posts were not many, nor did the incumbents fulfill all the functions that the missionaries customarily associated with governing. Where public power apparently existed, its limits seemed ill defined. The Jesuits soon came to see that private rights supplemented public powers, and found it extremely difficult to distinguish between the two, either in essence or in effect. Whether exercised officially or privately, the realm of individual action was great.

It was natural, then, for the missionaries to be struck by the extreme individualism of the Indians and to call the basic condition of their government variously anarchy, license, or liberty. Biard first called attention to the looseness of their social organization when he wrote about the Etchemins that "loving justice, they also hate violence and robbery. Which is truly wonderful in men who have neither laws nor magistrates. For each man is his own master and protector. They have certain sagamos, that is leaders in war, but their authority is extremely precarious, if it is indeed to be called authority, where there is no necessity of obedience." [2] Without doubt some such necessity—the same that decreed the very conditions of life—did exist; but it was hard to discern a civil sanction within the limits that instinct prescribed. So Le Jeune discovered after he opened his first school for Indian boys in Quebec: "There is nothing so difficult as to control the tribes of America. All these barbarians have the law of wild asses, they are born, live, and die in a liberty without restraint, they do not know what a bridle or a cavesson is: it is a

2. "Missio Canadensis," *Jesuit Relations,* II, 72.

great joke among them to check their passions and high philosophy to grant to the senses all that they desire." [3] The observation applied to spheres of activity far from the classroom, and generally the Jesuits corroborated it: "free and independent to the last degree," these people cherished liberty, "the greatest of all their goods," more than life itself. "They hate utterly all things which check liberty, no matter how slightly"; therefore they refused to obey any laws but remained absolute masters over themselves.[4] Father Charlevoix concurred, albeit somewhat sententiously: ". . . these Americans are perfectly convinced that man was born free, that no power on earth has a right to infringe his liberty, and that nothing could repay him for the loss of it." [5]

Children learned a horror of control early in life; confident of parental love, they lived without fear of reprimand or chastisement.[6] The strong family affection, so praiseworthy on other grounds, made the task of teaching children doubly difficult. But the nuns at Quebec, for instance, did not excuse their pupils' slow progress by blaming sinful pagan obstinacy. The cause was much more evident:

Little chickens fear the kite, little lambs flee the wolf, and little savages abhor restraint. All that comes from the selfsame principle, that is to say, from nature. The savages spend almost their entire life either hunting or on short trips or long journeys, very often taking their wives and children with them; so that being conceived in this passion [which is] fortified by long practice, their children love liberty almost as naturally as ducklings love brooks and rivers.[7]

As elsewhere with customs, so here environment helped to explain a fundamental attitude of the Indians. But once again, the Jesuits resorted to environment only to explain the natural aspects of life; they refrained from considering supernatural matters in the same light.

In general the missionaries attributed a sort of liberty to the Indians. Their religious principles precluded them from defining liberty in the juridical terms of the political theorist. On the

3. "Relation . . . 1637," XII, 60.
4. "Relation . . . 1647 & 1648," XXXII, 248; "Relation . . . 1651 & 1652," XXXVII, 154–156; "Relation . . . 1670 & 1671," LV, 88; "Relation . . . 1642 & 1643," XXV, 246; Marest, "Lettre au Père Germon," Jesuit Relations, LXVI, 220.
5. Journal, V, 401–402.
6. "Relation . . . 1656 & 1657," XLIII, 271.
7. "Relation . . . 1657 & 1658," XLIV, 258.

other hand, they found that they could not define it in theological terms; they could not have admitted that true liberty existed among people who wandered in the outer darkness of heathendom. Father Le Jeune touched upon this point when he wrote that "The law of our Lord is far removed from this dissoluteness, it gives us boundaries and prescribes to us limits outside of which we cannot go without offending God and reason." [8] When Charlevoix illustrated his idea of Indian liberty, he enlarged on Le Jeune's line of reasoning. It was hard, he felt, to disabuse the new converts of their extremely libertarian ideas and to teach them that, in view of the corruption of human nature and our habitual tendency toward evil, a liberty that was freed from doing evil was not far different from a sort of necessity to commit evil. The law, in restraining us, brought us nearer to our original liberty, while appearing to deprive us of it.[9]

The two foregoing opinions were typical of the missionaries; no Jesuit could conceive of true liberty without its accompaniment of grace. This broadest kind of liberty, which Molina had called freedom, was supernatural. It involved the will and all man's faculties. In its very essence it differed from the natural liberty that the Indians knew; the missionaries did not confuse the two. Liberty among the heathens, then, merely meant freedom from external restraint, the negative connotation implicit in the distinction of Le Jeune and Charlevoix. This definition was permitted by the extreme individualism that the Indians practiced and was also reconcilable with the traces of primitive innocence or of the Old Dispensation that many Jesuits professed to discern in the American wilderness.

Because freedom from external restraint apparently led to vice almost by necessity, many priests equated it with license. But even they preferred to pity for their ignorance rather than condemn for their liberty these people to whom the grace of the redemption had not come. On the other hand, they did not deny that ignorance, operating upon the natural liberty of the savages, produced vice; for such liberty was essentially negative. A well-intentioned Huron convert told Father Brébeuf he did not wish to go back to his own people, because "there is great difficulty in saving oneself; the occasions for sin are frequent in our villages; liberty is great there." [10] The effects of liberty upon the Illinois,

8. "Relation . . . 1637," XII, 60.
9. *Journal*, V, 402.
10. "Relation . . . 1642 & 1643," XXIV, 108.

who boasted they were absolute masters of themselves, Father
Marest more roundly condemned:

. . . the independence in which they live enslaves them to the most
brutal passions.

It is from this independence that are born all sorts of vice which
dominate them. They are lazy, treacherous, fickle and inconstant,
knavish, naturally thievish, even to the point of boasting of their skill
at stealing; brutal, without honor; oath-breakers. . . .[11]

More temperate, Charlevoix observed that the corollaries of liberty
—which he designated as tolerance, impunity, and insubordination—occasioned great disorder and destroyed the hierarchies
of society and the family. But happily the corollaries were not
present in America; civilization had not yet reached the point
at which liberty could seduce the Indians into crime. Here, like
Biard, Charlevoix saw a benign providence at work, trimming the
desires of the Indians to suit their material means. Thus did liberty
compensate the Indians for their privations and make them content in the bosom of poverty. It was only in wealthier, more cultivated lands (like France) that the insidious corollaries of liberty
drowned out the voice of nature and upset the divine order.[12] But
there, too, providence provided a remedy, through a knowledge
of God and the redemption. Consequently ignorance there was
inexcusable; license was really vice.

Along with natural liberty the fathers observed that equality
also permeated Indian society. When the Jesuits wrote that men
were men everywhere, they were looking at men in their spiritual
aspect. If they preached tolerance it was for religious, not political,
purposes; indeed, when Charlevoix condemned tolerance as a dis-
ruptive corollary of liberty, he was thinking narrowly of the
political order. But the Indians themselves went much further.
They had no conception of supernatural values; yet "in this
country all men believe themselves equally men, and what they
esteem most in man is man." [13]

The harsh American wilderness made inevitable a large measure
of equality. In fact, the further the missionaries went into the
sparse lands of the north, the more egalitarian tribal life became.
Generally the struggle for life was hard. Most families lived
from hand to mouth. The fortunate few who were rich, like Bré-

11. "Lettre au Père Germon," *Jesuit Relations*, LXVI, 220.
12. *Journal*, VI, 31–32.
13. *Ibid.*, p. 62.

beuf's Huron host of 1635, shared their surplus, motivated either by sympathy or fear of their poorer neighbors. Indian liberality, which sprang from a simple, intimate society, led many priests to repeat about other tribes what Jérôme Lallemant wrote about the Algonquins: ". . . they do not know what avarice is, their goods are held almost in common." [14] Charlevoix was similarly struck by their mutual sympathy and the real charity with which they cared for the sick and the destitute. He attributed such conduct to their idea that all things should be common among men; "those cold words, mine and thine," were absent from Indian language. Of course the maxim that no man should be under obligation to another was bad, and Charlevoix deplored the insubordination that resulted from its practice. But on the other hand, its corollary—that no man should wrong one who has not offended him—worked strongly for civil peace among the Indians and so counterbalanced the evil. [15]

Within the area of Indian activity that can be called political, the sentiment of equality manifested itself clearly. The natural necessity that decreed equality at the same time fostered self-reliance and retarded social organization; hence it allowed wide scope for individual action. The Indians were equal in their independence and their necessity; they conducted themselves accordingly. "The savages," Le Jeune remarked, "cannot tolerate in any way those who wish to assume superiority over others"; instead they preferred a gentle apathy more in harmony with their individual self-respect. [16] While class distinctions existed, Charlevoix noted, they did not set the Indians apart from each other or make some haughty; all acknowledged their fellows as equals—a true insight they had gained by studying themselves. Of course, prerogatives of rank, ancillary to the functions of paterfamilias, clan leader, or chief, existed; but they never prejudiced individual rights. Nor did any pre-eminence derived from merit injure pride or start a feeling of inferiority in less eminent men. To judge from these remarks, then, Indian equality depended on nature and was natural. Consequently there was room for natural inequalities as well, in physical, mental, or moral traits of individuals. As long as such a natural dualism prevailed, the most politically conservative Jesuit could find little to condemn

14. "Relation . . . 1663 & 1664," XLIX, 54.
15. *Journal*, VI, 11–13.
16. "Relation . . . 1639," XVI, 164.

in Indian society. In fact, some sort of equality was necessary for any society calling itself Christian, and Charlevoix found this communion among the Indians: "... to enter into men's hearts, you must somehow equal them." [17]

The social cohesion that individual liberty did not stifle and that a sense of equality facilitated did not generally extend beyond the limits of the separate tribes. When Biard angrily reported that the Indians were stupid because they did not acknowledge the great virtue and power of the king of France, he was indulging in a natural feeling of group loyalty. But at the same time he was ignoring the possibility that Americans cherished a similar loyalty. Later missionaries willingly recognized the tribal spirit of the Indians as their highest expression of group consciousness. Many priests deplored tribalism, in which they saw a hindrance to conversion. For instance, Bressani failed to convert the Iroquois because "their sins and especially pride are a great impediment to the grace of God, *Qui humilia respicit, et alta a longe cognoscit.* They account themselves all champions, like Mars, they despise the Europeans as vile and cowardly people and think they were born to conquer the world." [18]

Bressani's observation applied to other tribes as well. The Hurons, Ragueneau found, "naturally have less love and respect for those who are not of their nation. They are fond of one another; but they have only importunity for all strangers." [19] Rasles came across tribes who cherished their independence as fiercely as individuals did, "for there is not one savage nation that patiently endures to be regarded as subjugated to any power whatsoever." [20] The Illinois were the most extreme in this respect: they insisted that "Illinois" alone meant "man" and called all their neighbors beasts.[21]

This narrow tribal sentiment was not surprising: the ordinary life of the Indian revolved around his household or clan, and it was only matters of moment that precipitated him into the public activity of the tribe. Outside the accustomed boundaries set by tribal life there was nothing. Exception must be made with regard to such intertribal federations as the Iroquois and the Ottawa;

17. *Journal,* VI, 61.
18. "Breve relazione," XXXIX, 82.
19. "Relation . . . 1651 & 1652," XXXVII, 148.
20. "Lettre à M. son neveu," *Jesuit Relations,* LXVII, 102.
21. Marquette, *Voyages et découvertes,* p. 20.

yet even here awareness of relations transcending the tribe came only with unusual pressure. Generally the tribe circumscribed their lives; beyond its close confines gaped a void as deep and obscure as the forests that hemmed in every village. The tribe was society; no standards of intertribal activity were to be found, except as the federations operated. It was the tribe, therefore, to which the missionaries looked for standards of conduct and upon which the Indians relied when dealing with other tribes. They considered generosity to persons not of their tribe exceptional and proffered it either for some ulterior purpose or with a studious disregard of the tribe to which the recipients belonged. Indeed, the appearance of a stranger who advertised his tribal allegiance intensified the tribalism of other savages; and it was in embassies and in war, when each person was most closely identified with his tribe, that hatred of the outsider reached its height.

In their writings the Jesuits showed little comprehension of the economic causes of tribal warfare. They saw that Dutch and English pressure from the south agitated the Iroquois, and regretted the diversion of the fur trade from the St. Lawrence to the Hudson. But they persisted in ascribing war chiefly to personal motives of which the first was vengeance. Biard stated that "they wage war as a tribe, on account of wrongs done to individuals. The whole race is avid of vengeance, and like barbarians, insolent in victory; they parade the heads of their captives around very jubilantly, as well as sumptuous trophies and necklaces." Charlevoix concurred.[22] The Indians, keenly sensitive to their personal rights, were themselves barely aware of deeper-lying reasons for war. Thus it became natural for the Jesuits, who concentrated upon the individuals as future converts, to think along the same lines and interpret group action in terms of individual motives.

When the Jesuits looked for concrete evidence of political organization, they seldom saw more than the chief and council, who were common to all tribes. The amount of respect paid to the chiefs and council was inversely proportionate to the value that the various tribes placed on individual rights, and demonstrated plainly how such rights retarded the growth of a more intense tribal loyalty. But the Jesuits still found it difficult to clarify the powers and functions that belonged to these two governmental agencies.

22. "Missio Canadenis," *Jesuit Relations*, II, 74; *Journal*, V, 317.

For example, the government that Bressani saw among the Hurons differed radically from government as he knew it; to explain it, he resorted to an analogy drawn from family life. He found the government

admirable in this, that being very different from ours and to that extent unknown to many, it is nevertheless quite as effective as our own, since very few disorders appear in the midst of extreme liberty. . . .

These people have neither king nor absolute prince, but certain as it were heads of a republic, whom we call captains, but different from those in war. . . . These captains have not *vim coactivam*, which even the fathers do not exercise toward the sons to correct them, using words alone; and the sons thus brought up, the more they increase in age, the more they respect and love their fathers; the former as well as the latter thus obtaining everything *precario* with eloquence, exhortation, and prayer. . . .[23]

The tentative definition of captains as "certain as it were heads" illustrated the confusion that embroiled many relators when they attempted to discuss bizarre Indian institutions. But in fact, with regard to the office of captain the Jesuits knew much and fully described its functions and attributes.

Usually the office was quasi-paternal in character. The right of succession, as Le Jeune wrote, was determined either by heredity or election, depending on tribal custom. "These people are not so barbarous that they do not show some respect to the descendants of the chiefs, so that if the son of a captain is something of a leader, especially if he has some natural eloquence, he will hold his father's place without opposition." [24] Yet by itself blood did not confer title. Sons succeeded their fathers, at least among the Hurons, "only so far as they have the proper qualifications, and if they accept and are accepted by the whole country. There are some who refuse these honors, either because they are not apt in discourse or have not enough discretion or patience or because they love repose; for these positions are more servitudes than anything else." Thus ability was an essential requisite, as Brébeuf revealed in his account of "the authority of commanding":

In the large villages there will sometimes be several captains, as much of civil affairs as of war, who divide among themselves the families of

23. "Breve relazione," XXXVIII, 264.
24. "Relation . . . 1639," XVI, 134.

the village, as into so many captaincies; sometimes one even sees captains, to whom all these governmental matters are brought because of their intelligence, popularity, wealth, or other qualities that make them influential in the country. There is none who by virtue of his election is more powerful than others. Those hold the first rank who have acquired it by their intelligence, eloquence, magnificence, courage, and wise conduct.[25]

Where blood and ability coincided, it was possible for the Jesuits to construe popular assent to hereditary succession as election.

Unlike many public positions that the Jesuits had known in Europe, the Indian captaincies were truly functional. The prerogatives of the office did not compensate fully for its burdensome duties. When a Huron died his name was passed on to his successor, and "He who takes a new name assumes also the duties which are attached to it, and thus he is a captain, if the defunct was." [26] Indeed, many captains sought to withdraw from their offices when they became too laborious, like the Nipissing who explained himself to Father Dequen in the following terms:

I would like . . . to be able to resign from my charge of captain in favor of Philippe Sakapwam; it belongs to him by right of birth being the son of a captain, so if I have received and retained it until the present, it is because he was too young to be able to exercise it after the death of his father; but since at present he is of age, and his strength suffices him to acquit himself of this office and to fulfill all its duties, I think it is reasonable that he should enjoy it: I do not wish to retain what is not mine; besides we need captains here who are vigorous, who can discourse in favor of the faith, and who have authority with the young people, and all these qualities show to better advantage in him than in me, who has no wit, no words, nor anything to give me credit and authority; and since I am not proud to have these honors, I scorn them in my heart, I fear also to be responsible for the actions and conduct of my people, I should be very glad if someone else should be responsible for them.[27]

Here, incidentally, was further support for Le Jeune's contention that "the two tyrants who provide Gehenna and torture for

25. "Relation . . . 1636," X, 230–232; cf. "Relation . . . 1670 & 1671," LV, 37.
26. "Relation . . . 1642," XXIII, 166.
27. "Relation . . . 1642 & 1643," XXV, 154–156.

a large number of our Europeans do not reign in their great forests, I mean ambition and avarice." [28]

After the Indians had chosen a new captain they installed him. Vimont described a typical installation in a chapter of the Relation of 1643–44, entitled "Of the Creation of a Captain at Tadoussac." After the heads of the neighboring villages had assembled, a herald introduced the captain-elect. Then his people enthroned him, dressed him in rich garments, and gravely presented him with a pipe and tobacco.

The captain being clothed according to his dignity, a third officer . . . rises and . . . declares the object of all the ceremony. "Let everyone remain quiet," he cries, "open your ears and shut your mouths, what I have to say is important. We are here to resuscitate a dead man and to make a great captain live again"; thereupon he names him and all his posterity, he tells the place and manner of his death, then turning toward him who is to succeed, he raises his voice: "There he is," says he, "covered with that fine robe. It is no longer he whom you saw in past days calling himself Nehap. He has given his name to another savage, he calls himself Etouait (that was the name of the dead man), consider him as the true captain of this tribe, it is to him that you owe obedience, it is he to whom you must listen and whom you must honor." . . . this new captain maintains a gravity that indicates nothing of his barbarism.

Next, the herald showed off the gifts of Etouait to each of the villages and distributed them.

This done, the herald resumes his discourse, "let us rejoice, the first action of our captain is to invite us all to a feast. . . ." They began to sing and dance, each according to the custom of his people, the captains, finishing their songs, speak briefly in praise of him whom they have just resuscitated; one cries, "let us take courage, this brave man will save the country"; another adds that his liberality will banish poverty and will make those who are under his direction live a long time.

During the feast the captain modestly disclaimed his merit for the high office and promised to carry on as well as he could.

When this harangue was ended, each retires to his quarters, and this resuscitated captain wishing to begin his duties, sends for the principal men of his nation and some poor widows and straightway gives the

28. "Relation . . . 1634," VI, 230.

best of what he had in his cabin. To one he gives a blanket, to another a beaver robe, to this one a calumet, to those others a sack of Indian corn, to the poor women some beaver skins to make robes of. He gave to some warriors his sword, his poignard, and his pistol, and then dismissed them with these three words: "While I live I will assist you and aid you with all my power." Those are the revenues of the offices of the lords and principalities of the savages.[29]

It would have been difficult to state more exactly the correspondence between the privileges and duties of a captain. As Jérôme Lallemant remarked elsewhere, gifts were the "symbols of his authority." He was the "custodian of the public presents," only because his elevation had converted his private goods into public property.[30]

The powers of the office were less apparent than the obligations. As Bressani indicated, authority was, literally, precarious rather than coercive. Biard also said as much, when he described the war chiefs: "sagamores, that is leaders in war, whose rule is entirely in persuasion, if indeed that may be called rule where there is no necessity of obeying." The levy that an Acadian chief assessed against his villages did not testify to a more powerful captaincy, because the levy went to a common war chest. In effect, the considerable power that Etchemin chiefs "no doubt" wielded they secured by means of example, custom, kinship, and family alliance.[31] Montagnais chiefs exercised an equally tenuous authority. Le Jeune counted as one of their virtues their indifference to office; in addition, "they have neither policy nor offices nor dignities nor any rule, for they obey their captain simply out of friendliness." Yet the ignorance that caused this happy state was the first "of their vices and imperfections":

The savages being filled with errors are also haughty and proud. Humility is born from truth, vanity from error and falsehood; they are devoid of the knowledge of truth and consequently very full of themselves. They imagine that by right of birth they ought to enjoy the liberty of young savage asses, rendering no account to anyone, except when it pleases them: they have reproached me a hundred times that we fear our captains, but as for them they mock and make sport of theirs; the entire authority of their chief is in the tip of his tongue,

29. "Relation . . . 1643 & 1644," XXVI, 154–162; cf. "Relation . . . 1642," XXIII, 216.
30. "Relation . . . 1644 & 1645," XXVIII, 86.
31. "Missio Canadensis," *Jesuit Relations*, II, 72–74.

he is as powerful as he is eloquent; and although he killed himself with talking and haranguing, he will not be obeyed unless he pleases the savages.[32]

Brébeuf found a similar insubordination among the Hurons, where the chiefs could not compel the people to do their duty. "Their government is merely civil; they set forth only what is to be done for the good of the village or the whole country. After that, he who will takes action." [33] The Tadoussac captains likewise refrained from using force and as a result received slight obedience, although the people acknowledged a moral obligation to obey, heed, and honor every new captain. Here again the savages refused to subject their wills to any power whatsoever. "Fathers here have no control over their children, captains over their subjects, or the laws of the country over any of them, except as each one pleases to submit." [34] The Sillery Indians, although Christian, were equally wild.[35] Marest found the Illinois so independent that they would desert any chief who sought to impose his will by force. One man among them, desiring "to be chief in reality," would not take the office without a previous promise of obedience. But once he had secured the promise, this man did not assume exceptional power. On the contrary, his first act was to discharge a duty and provide meat for destitute widows and orphans.[36]

Obedience, then, while obligatory, was rarely compelled. According to Jérôme Lallemant, the chiefs generally carried natural taciturnity so far as to ignore the misdeeds of their people, although occasionally they reproved the conduct of the young men —in a paternal fashion.[37] Lallemant also told how a chief had once been able to recover a stolen crucifix for him; but apparently the thief obeyed rather out of superstitious fear than respect for legal authority.[38]

Slight as the authority of the chief was, it nevertheless sufficed for the conduct of ordinary affairs; more would have irked the people without real effect. In time the Jesuits came to accept weak

32. "Relation . . . 1634," VI, 242.
33. "Relation . . . 1636," X, 234.
34. "Relation . . . 1643 & 1644," XXVI, 116; "Relation . . . 1644 & 1645," XXVIII, 48.
35. "Relation . . . 1645 & 1646," XXIX, 81.
36. "Lettre au Père Germon," *Jesuit Relations*, LXVI, 220; Louis Vivier, "Lettre du Père Vivier," *Jesuit Relations*, LXIX, 226.
37. "Relation . . . 1645 & 1646," XXIX, 99.
38. "Relation . . . 1640," XIX, 215.

tribal leadership as normal, and exceptions amazed them. Le Jeune, for instance, met one chief possessed of "great vanity and insupportable pride," who addressed him in these words:

Perhaps you do not know that I have commanded since my youth, that I was born to command, as soon as I open my mouth, everyone listens to me; it is also true that I support and preserve the whole country during the life of my grandchildren and of my nephews—it is thus he calls his people—the Hurons even heed me, and I command among them as if I were captain; I say not a word over there, the others talk, but nothing is done that I do not intend; I am like a tree, men are its branches, to which I give strength: To see a man completely naked, who has neither shoes on his feet nor any clothing but a miserable scrap of skin, which protects only half his body; disgraced by nature having but half his eyes, for he is blind in one; dried up like an old tree without leaves; to see, I say, a skeleton, or rather a beggar, parading like a president and speaking like a king, that is to see vanity and pride under rags: This Thraso . . .[39]

The most conspicuous exception occurred not in New France but in the lower Mississippi Valley. There the Natchez regarded their chief as the "absolute master, not only of their property but even of their lives." He ruled despotically, with a hierarchy of dependent officials who acted as his alter egos and enjoyed his privileges and immunities. The succession passed by inheritance through the oldest sister of the incumbent chief. The elaborate ritual surrounding the chief reminded Charlevoix, who devoted many pages to the Natchez, of the Egyptians.[40]

But Charlevoix was interested in the Natchez simply as one curious extreme of Indian society, which he contrasted with the customs of the Canadian tribes. Although the wild insubordination of the northern Indians repelled him, his general impression of them was favorable, and he found much that counterbalanced their excessive equality. The chief never needed to abuse what little authority he possessed, for in the woods it was reason that governed. Thus the rule of the chief was efficacious in proportion as the people were free to obey him. Reason allayed the fear that authority would degenerate into tyranny. Moreover the war chief enjoyed no more authority in theory than the civil captain. Since

39. "Relation . . . 1641," XX, 156.
40. Le Petit, "Lettre au Père d'Avaugour," *Jesuit Relations*, LXVIII, 130–136; Charlevoix, *Journal*, VI, 177–183.

he was brave, disinterested, and guided by reason, reason also counseled his independent tribesmen to obey him.[41]

In view of the indefinite nature of the captaincy as well as the inordinate amount of individualism, Charlevoix concluded that in most tribes government was actually aristocratic. He reported that the council of each tribe made the final decisions, which the tribesmen then executed as they wished, under the chief's leadership. Each family elected a representative to the council to safeguard its interests. The council was usually divided into three parts: the assistants to the captain; the elders, all those who had attained mature years; and the warriors, all men capable of bearing arms. With such an organization, "anyone who enjoyed any esteem in his village was occupied only with the general welfare"; conversely, few transactions remained strictly private in character. It was in the council sessions that the Indians displayed to best advantage their intellectual powers, dignity, and eloquence. To top what had already been written about these traits, Charlevoix felt the obligation to

admit that they proceed in these assemblies with a wisdom, a maturity, a skill, I shall say normally a probity, which would have done honor to the Areopagus of Athens, or the Senate of Rome, in the sunniest days of those republics. Nothing is concluded in them with precipitation, and the grand passions, which have affected politics so strongly even among Christians, have not yet had any influence upon the public welfare among these savages.[42]

The functions of the council were many and more obvious than the functions of the captain. As a rule the appropriate corps of the council met before every occasion of consequence for the group it represented—with, of course, the amplest feast possible. The ranking captain summoned the assembly; he also presided and often steered the discussion. With regard to intratribal affairs, the councilors mainly advised and directed the captain. The elders determined the succession, whether elective or hereditary, ratified and published it, and installed the new man in his dignity.[43] Thenceforward they consulted with him constantly, either individually or in formal convocations, and lent to his actions the weight of

41. *Journal*, V, 395–397.
42. *Ibid.*, p. 392–400.
43. "Relation . . . 1642," XXIII, 217; "Relation . . . 1643 & 1644," XXVI, 161; "Relation . . . 1645 & 1646," XXX, 58–61.

their years and experience. Where a public treasury existed distinct from the captain's own goods, the councilors supervised its use. Men who had fallen from public esteem reinstated themselves with gifts to the elders, who deposited them in the treasury.[44] Sometimes the council even levied a tax upon the cabins, in the event of famine or war; but payment was voluntary, for the council could enforce its wishes with no weapons but public opinion and persuasion.[45] When famine stripped the villages of their reserve supplies and forced whole tribes to go out hunting or migrate to richer regions, it was the collective wisdom of the elders that determined the time, direction, and order of march. Finally, the councils met to perform the elaborate funeral rites that the tribes practiced.

In dealing with foreigners, the council played an equally decisive role. It negotiated alliances of confederation, neutrality, and military cooperation and concluded peace treaties with other tribes or Europeans.[46] The council also deliberated upon the question of conversion, which it not unreasonably considered a kind of alliance. Although Membertou made a whole village follow him into the faith, most captains were not so powerful. When missionaries first appeared in a tribe, a council usually convened to consider the business of religion. In one such assembly, which Vimont described, the acceptance of Christianity was proposed, and the leading men spoke for and against it. Then the people thought over the question whether they should permit the priests to build a chapel and preach among them; at the end of three days they cast their votes, to the accompaniment of further long speeches.[47]

The council reserved to itself the ultimate decision to declare war, after seriously considering all the relevant matters. But, once they determined upon war, the council did not dictate its conduct; that business they turned over to the war captains. If the war parties returned victorious, the council assumed jurisdiction over the captives and decided their fate: how many and who should be adopted into the tribe, tortured, or killed.[48] They did not ordain the manner of torture or death, which was largely customary and carried out by the women and children.

44. "Relation . . . 1636," X, 235; Charlevoix, *Journal*, V, 395.
45. "Relation . . . 1637," XIV, 45.
46. "Relation . . . 1641," XXI, 29.
47. "Relation . . . 1640," XVIII, 90–105.
48. "Relation . . . 1652 & 1653," XL, 199.

Once the council reached a momentous decision, the task of executing it fell to the captains. But, as the missionaries pointed out, the theoretical power of the latter depended for its effectiveness upon custom, eloquence, and moral suasion. Ultimately, "he who will takes action." [49] Men owed no more obedience to the council than to the chief. This freedom prevailed even among the more civil Iroquois, of whom Milet wrote, "there is no government here as in France, to make individuals subject to the resolutions of the council." [50]

A few priests, going further than Milet, concluded that, because government did not exist "here as in France," law was altogether absent. But most priests saw that the Indians possessed a kind of law, although one not clearly distinct from its matrix of popular custom and opinion. Brébeuf well expressed the general view when he wrote:

Furthermore, if laws are like the governing wheel which regulates communities, or to be more exact, the soul of republics : it seems to me that I am right, considering that understanding which is so perfect among them, in maintaining that they are not without laws. They punish murderers, thieves, traitors, and sorcerers ; and as to the murderers, although they do not preserve the severity which their ancestors exercised in olden days, nevertheless the little disorder that there is in this respect makes me conclude that their procedure is hardly less effective than the punishment of death is elsewhere . . .[51]

The myriad barbarisms of the Indians did not disturb Jérôme Lallemant. Even though the savages punished crimes only by public shame, "we see here incomparably less disorder by far than there is in France." [52] Where justice involved a more personal pain or a harsher deprivation, the shame was still the crowning humiliation; any other penalty merely symbolized public disapproval. Sometimes an appeal to the tribunal of opinion was also made in intertribal disputes. A Huron captain once rebuked the Iroquois for their treachery:

Your mind is furnished with seven linings, when one is taken away, six more remain. . . . You have forgotten the mutual oaths, which

49. "Relation . . . 1636," X, 234.
50. "Relation . . . 1669 & 1670," LIII, 282.
51. "Relation . . . 1636," X, 214.
52. "Relation . . . 1644 & 1645," XXVIII, 62.

our ancestors exchanged, when they took up arms against each other. . . . you have trampled under foot the orders and the oath of your ancestors. They blush for shame in the country of souls, seeing that you violate, with an intolerable perfidy, the laws of nature, the right of nations, and all human society.[53]

Charlevoix praised public opinion as a deterrent to crime, but he considered it a poor substitute for law. Yet Indian lawlessness did not upset him:

The greatest weakness of this government is that there is almost no criminal justice among these people; in truth, this fault does not have in this country the same consequences that it would have with us; the great violence of our passions and the principal source of the disorders that most disturb civil society, that is to say, interest, having almost no effect upon nations who give no thought to amassing treasure and bother themselves very little about the morrow.[54]

In government, then, as in other fields, innocence compensated the Indians for their barbarism.

Of the four classes of criminals that Brébeuf mentioned, thieves were by far the most common; against them the Indians found their best remedy in self-help.

Although the country is full of them, they are nevertheless not tolerated; if you find someone possessed of something that belongs to you, you can in good conscience play the despoiled king and take what is yours and thus leave him naked as your hand; if he is fishing, take his canoe, his nets, his fish, his robe, all that he has: it is true that on such an occasion the strongest prevails; still, that is the custom of the country, which does not fail to keep many to their obligations.[55]

Charlevoix went further: in earlier times men punished thieves with beating or even death; it was still lawful to strip thieves of all their goods, including the clothing of their women and children.[56] Among the Iroquois, people could keep whatever they found. But if the former owner had merely misplaced the property or intended to recover it later, the finder was very liable to be accused of theft himself and to suffer accordingly.[57] The majority of thefts that the

---

53. "Relation . . . 1652 & 1653," XL, 178–180.
54. *Journal,* V, 401.
55. "Relation . . . 1636," X, 222.
56. *Journal,* V, 405–406.
57. "Breve relazione," XXXVIII, 268–270.

Relations recorded were committed against Frenchmen. Naturally the Jesuits would be more likely to notice such crimes; and the French possessed more valuable property than the Indians. But in addition the French were outsiders, to whom custom did not give the legal protection it gave to the native tribesmen.

"These people are extremely suspicious, particularly when life is at stake," wrote Le Mercier.[58] But as Biard hinted when he wrote about polygamy, life was a kind of property. Thus, while the Indians considered murder a serious crime they did not value life so highly as to demand another in expiation. Among the Hurons, wrote Brébeuf, "the relatives of the deceased do not pursue only him who has committed the murder but address themselves to the whole village, which is to do satisfaction for it and furnish as soon as possible for this purpose up to sixty presents, the least of which must have the value of a new beaver robe." The village captain gives the presents to the family of the dead man and the guilty person "signifies the regret which he has for having killed him and that he would be quite ready to restore life to him if it were possible." Then other presents are made to restore the peaceful unity of the village and erase the evil fame of murder. "For it is not here as it is in France and other places, where the public and an entire town does not generally take up the quarrel of an individual. . . . In this way wars are born." [59] On the other hand, justice did not always follow such a pattern. If the relatives of the deceased found the murderer before composition was offered, sometimes, according to Vimont, "he is put to death on the spot, without any other form of justice." [60]

Jérôme Lallemant protested against punishing murder by composition: it was not the guilty man alone who suffered the consequences of his crime, but "it is the public that must make satisfaction for the faults of individuals." Since all contributions were voluntary, Lallemant was not complaining out of concern for the poor who might otherwise be imposed upon. His reasons were far different, and thoroughly consistent with his vocation:

Now while this form of justice restrains all these people and, it seems, prevents disorders more effectually than the personal punishment of criminals does in France; it is nonetheless a proceeding full of nothing

58. "Relation . . . 1637," XIII, 156.
59. "Relation . . . 1636," X, 214–218.
60. "Relation . . . 1642," XXII, 290.

but mildness, which leaves individuals in that spirit of liberty that they never see themselves as subject to any laws and follow no other impulse but that of their will, which without doubt is a disposition absolutely contrary to the spirit of the faith.[61]

Ragueneau, who concurred, added:

It would be to attempt the impossible, and even to make matters worse rather than to remedy them, to try to proceed with the savages according to the justice of France, which condemns to death him who is convicted of murder. Each country has its own customs, conforming to the diverse natures of each nation. Now in view of the character of the savages, their justice is undoubtedly very efficacious to check evil, although in France it would appear an injustice: for it is the public that makes satisfaction for the crimes of individuals, whether the criminal be known or remain hidden. In a word it is the crime that is punished.[62]

Charlevoix felt that composition did not "satisfy justice" or insure the public tranquility; but he saw in it one virtue that made it more effective than the severest laws, "since these satisfactions cost much to men whose pride surpasses description, the criminal is more sensible to the pain to which he sees the public go on his account than he would be to his own [pain], and zeal for the honor of the nation restrains these barbarians much more potently than could the fear of death and punishments." [63]

The punishment meted out to sorcerers was the most harsh and summary justice that the Jesuits reported. Murder was a black crime. But sorcery was even blacker, owing to its occult aspect. To the Jesuits, sorcery, the epitome of diabolical heathenism, was their worst enemy. Brébeuf defined sorcerers as "those who concern themselves with poisoning and causing death by charms." He went on to tell about their severe punishment, which "is authorized by the consent of the whole [Huron] country; so that whoever takes them in the act, has the right to split their skulls and rid the world of them, without fear of being called to account or obliged to make any satisfaction." [64] But it was not always necessary to catch a sorcerer red-handed in order to kill him immediately. Le Mercier cited instances in which clear evidence of sorcery was

61. "Relation . . . 1644 & 1645," XXVIII, 48–50.
62. "Relation . . . 1647 & 1648," XXXIII, 232–234.
63. *Journal*, V, 404, 407–408.
64. "Relation . . . 1636," X, 222.

necessary to doom a man to death; yet he also saw a woman sentenced to death as a witch on the bare accusation of her alleged victims.[65] Here superstition crowned ignorance, and barbarian law furnished an urgent argument for conversion.

In fact, all the traits of the Indians made them appear as ideal subjects for missionary activity. They loved liberty and embraced it as far as necessity and heathen ignorance permitted. They were devoid of false ideas about inheritance and property and lived in communal peace within the confines of tribal society. While necessity dictated submission to authority, their passionate hatred of restraint held political organization to a minimum. Only when external forces exerted pressure on the tribe did it harden into a self-conscious and exclusive unit. Now when the missionaries observed the Indians, they usually saw them withdrawn into the tribal unit. Indeed, the very presence of outsiders in New France connoted change, however slight, and made the natives restless beyond their true nature. The more ominous the threat of change, the more brutal did the savages become. Yet to the end the Jesuits, while recognizing and deploring their faults, remained ardent advocates of the Indians. For a composite picture of what the missionaries saw, in the light of their peculiar motives and preconceptions, few passages surpassed two paragraphs that Charlevoix penned as he prepared to depart from New France.

Finally, to draw for you briefly the portrait of these peoples with a savage exterior and manners and habits which appear to belong completely to barbarism: one notices in them a society exempt from almost all the defects which so often mar the charms of our own. They appear to lack passion, but they are self-controlled and sometimes by a principle which the most violent and unrestrained passion can inspire in those who no longer listen to reason. They seem to lead the most miserable lives in the world, and perhaps they were the only happy people on the earth before the knowledge of the things which motivate and seduce us had aroused in them a cupidity which ignorance retained in subjection and which has nevertheless not yet made great ravages among them. One perceives in them a mixture of the most ferocious and the softest manners, the vices of carnivorous beasts, and the virtues and qualities of the heart and head which do the greatest honor to humanity. At first one would believe that they have no form of government, that they know neither laws nor subordination, and that living in

65. "Relation . . . 1637," XIII, 157, XIV, 36.

utter independence they let themselves be directed solely by the most untamed hazard and caprice; but they enjoy almost all the advantages which a well-regulated authority can procure for the most civilized nations. Born free and independent, they hold even the shadow of despotic power in horror, but they rarely avoid certain principles and usages, founded on good sense, that for them take the place of laws and that supply in some fashion a legitimate authority. All constraint revolts them, but reason alone keeps them in a sort of subordination which, although voluntary, nonetheless attains the end that they have set for themselves.

A man whom they could admire greatly would find them docile enough and would make them do almost everything that he would wish; but in this respect it is not easy to gain their esteem. They surrender it only to merit, and to a superior merit, of which they are as good judges as those who among us pride themselves the more for their judgment. Above all they are attracted by demeanor, and it is not perhaps men of the world who know most about that; it is a fact that they do not have for everyone that deference which seduces us, and that studying nature only, they know it well. Since they are not slaves of ambition and interest and since there hardly exist among them these two passions that have enfeebled in us the sentiment of humanity which the Author of nature has engraved in our hearts, the inequality of conditions is not necessary to them for the maintenance of society.[66]

66. *Journal,* VI, 59–61.

X

THE SAVAGE IN FRANCE

RECORDS show that the first savages came to France in the year 1534, with Cartier. At the same time Las Casas, pleading for a more humane treatment of the Caribs, introduced the American natives to a broader public. When Montaigne presented his "Cannibals" to French readers in 1580, the savage may be said to have taken his place, albeit then a minor one, among French literary personages. But throughout the century the Indian remained a curious creature of fancy. He appeared only in fiction and then with all the attributes of classical primitivism. Except for a few superficial traits, he might as easily have been a citizen of Pliny's Pandoria as of Cartier's *ysles de Canada*.

After 1607 the writings of the French in Canada gave the savage the flesh and gestures of a real person. *Mémoires, journals,* and *découvertes* of artless laymen supplemented the Relations of the missionaries. Assiduous readers of these accounts could not only see the naked men and women in their villages but also smell the fetid air of their cabins in winter, hear their war cries, and perhaps even feel burning torture. As he became more real, the savage took on larger proportions. He entered into the consciousness of many, winning the compassion of the devout and the studious attention of the curious. In the seventeenth century, which Catholicism dominated, those who described the savage could not avoid placing him in the framework of their own orthodox conceptions. Thus, while his portrait was taking shape, the savage played a primarily spiritual role as an increment to the zeal of the faithful. In the eighteenth century, as Cartesian rationalism overwhelmed the spirit of the Counter Reformation, the savage seemed to offer living proof for many of the arguments of the enemies of the church.

The Catholic church revived under the menace of Protestantism and set out to win the world. She found one outlet for her crusading energy in America, where heathenism made the Indian a prize. Catholic missionaries, at first meeting no competition in America, undertook the spiritual conquest with high optimism. In France, by consenting to support the Acadian mission, Henry IV brought his government into closer harmony not only with the papacy but also with those of his Catholic subjects who had already welcomed other projects of the Counter Reformation. The faithful lavished their bounty on the overseas missions as eagerly as upon church institutions at home. Some donors simply hoped to save heathens from a perpetual life in outer darkness. But many more anticipated a personal reward as well: the religious, expiation of past sins; the worldly, profits; still others, the pleasure of helping to extend French culture and empire.

Members of the high aristocracy patronized the missions in the most spectacular and unselfish manner. Indeed, it was one of them, the Marquise de Guercheville, who made the first Acadian venture possible. With her money and her position at court that lady compensated the Jesuits for the loss caused them by the assassination of Henry IV. Other noblewomen imitated her example, whispering sympathetic pleas to Richelieu or Anne of Austria, sending off chests full of altar cloths and cassocks, depositing funds with their bankers for the college at Quebec or the Hôtel-Dieu at Montreal. Charlotte de Montmorency, Princesse de Condé, seconded the claims of Champlain upon the three successive governors of New France who were her husband, brother, and nephew. The cardinal's niece, the Duchesse d'Aiguillon, made Charles Lallemant her almoner, and he gave her alms to Quebec. The Duchesse de Bouillon, like the parliamentarian Ragois de Bretonvilliers two generations later, made a special charity of Sulpician Montreal.

Two men best typified the piety abroad at court in the seventeenth century: Henri de Lévis de Ventadour, a duke and peer, and Noel Brulart, Chevalier de Sillery. Ventadour, nephew of the Princesse de Condé, was perhaps the most generous individual patron of the missions. He subsidized the second expedition (1625) of the Jesuits and the next year procured them extensive holdings in Quebec. In 1629 Ventadour renounced the world to become a lowly canon of Notre Dame in Paris. But he reserved the right to dispose of his property and continued to aid the missions until he died in 1680. Sillery, a soldier and diplomat from a distinguished parliamentary family, took minor orders in 1625 and nine years later became a priest. He too retained control over his property, which he devoted to charity. In 1639 he richly endowed the mission of St. Joseph, which the Jesuits renamed Sillery in his honor.

The Canadian savage certainly counted as an object of that charity so fervently enjoined by Vincent de Paul and his followers.

Although few members of the first estate could be so munificent as Ventadour or Sillery, many clerics made substantial donations, like the canon of the royal chapel in Paris who gave the Jesuits two seignories or the priest who created an endowment for a college among the Hurons. Indeed, some missionaries signed over their own rights of inheritance for use in New France. Their mere presence in the field, moreover, often led their relatives to make modest gifts.

Naturally, the bourgeoisie, who stood to gain as much as the other estates spiritually and more financially, contributed freely. Colonists like Robert Griffard donated sections of their own lands. In France, for the good of their souls or in memory of their beloved dead, merchants and lawyers gave seignories to the missions instead of chapels to the local churches. Aside from twelve hundred thousand livres, the Company of New France (managed by businessmen, if financed also by nobles and crown) itself granted much land. It ratified alienations made by others and directly gave the Jesuits many acres at Quebec, Three Rivers, and Tadoussac. But of course the company's most notable gift was the island of Montreal, which two of the Hundred Associates purchased for the ultimate enjoyment of the Sulpicians.

Besides the policy of official patronage that the Bourbon dynasty adopted, then, the generosity of members of all three estates furnished a dramatic proof of the progress of the Counter Reformation. Such benevolence also attested to the vividness with which people in France envisaged the Indians.

It was chiefly through the Jesuits that the French learned about their savage beneficiary. The Jesuits far outnumbered the Recollets and Sulpicians; they ranged farther afield, for a longer period of time; and they had the advantage of regular publication. But other firsthand accounts of the Indians cannot be ignored. Most of the published works of laymen and other missionaries simply corroborated or qualified the Jesuit descriptions. Yet they gave a broader currency to the French conception of the savage.

Of the other missionaries, the Recollets alone published their writings at the time. The Sulpician accounts remained in manuscript until the nineteenth century. The first Recollet historian, Gabriel Sagard-Théodat, was by far the most significant. He wrote with a genuine missionary purpose: to edify his readers about the patience and modesty of the savages, their truly noble hearts, and the admirable peace and union in which they lived. And, he submitted, if he favored the savages, it was in God's interest and out of a dutiful desire to combat their detractors.[1] But Sagard, who spent a year in New France, did not recount simply his own experiences and impressions; his books represented compilations of all that his brethren had learned from 1615 to 1629. Furthermore, he did not write for edification alone: he also defended his order, to explain their failure as missionaries. The other important Recollet author, Chrétien le Clercq, worked in the very successful Acadian field at the height of the second Recollet mission. His books depicted the Micmacs and Etchemins in transition to the settled Christian life and thus differed considerably from those of Sagard.[2] Yet his pages rang even louder with the justification and defense of the order, which was then struggling to retain a foothold in the country.

Two other Franciscans produced books of lively interest—but books that, while devoid of sectarian contention, were also quite innocent of concern for the Indians. Louis Hennepin's travel accounts, although full of falsehoods, revealed many new things about the geography and wild life of the upper Mississippi Valley.[3] In 1742 Emmanuel Crespel published an account of his adventures with an exploring party in the west.[4] Crespel was writing for a public that demanded entertainment, not instruction; therefore he rarely commented objectively on the Indians or their ways. That subject had long ago lost its savor. Indeed, by 1742 several missionaries were overlooking the importance of New France as a hunting ground for souls, in favor of its more material aspects.

On the other hand, the shift to worldly considerations served to emphasize the interests that laymen had always had in the country. With little reticence or literary style, explorers, soldiers, merchants, and public officials set down their observations of the savages. These men pursued a less ethereal goal than the priests; but each group used the same methods to achieve its goal: con-

1. *Histoire du Canada et voyages que les Frères Mineurs Recollects y ont faictes,* I, 11–12; *Le Grand voyage au pays des Hurons* (Paris, 1632).

2. *Nouvelle Relation de la Gaspésie* (Paris, 1691); *First Establishment of the Faith in New France.*

3. *Description de la Louisiane* (Paris, 1683); *Nouvelles découvertes d'un très grand pays; Nouveau voyage d'un païs plus grand que l'Europe* (Utrecht, 1698).

4. *Voiages du R. P. Emmanuel Crespel dans le Canada et son naufrage en revenant en France mis au jour par le Sr. Louis Crespel* (Francfort-sur-le-Meyn, 1742).

version, civilization, colonization, and conquest. Like the missionaries, too, the laymen who stressed the first two methods depicted Indian life in more detail than those more narrowly concerned with trade or politics.

The explorers, who were all soldiers as well, generally paid particular attention to the land itself. Thus Cartier mentioned some Indian traits—but incuriously: they were striking, perhaps, but not very relevant to his primary task.[5] Henri Joutel, the only companion of La Salle to publish his memoirs at the time, also gave merely sidelong glances at the savages.[6] He wished to glorify the feats of his martyred leader. The Flemish adventurer Le Page du Pratz, who followed La Salle up the Mississippi forty years later, brought the west again to the notice of French readers at an opportune moment.[7] But while he revealed much about the Natchez, among whom he lived, his chief contribution was to describe the routes to the Pacific.

On the other hand, Champlain, whose aspirations and work have already been discussed, gave the fullest and most objective documentation of the Americans ever to come from the pen of a layman.[8] One other man, Bacqueville de la Potherie, who served with the French forces in Hudson Bay and Quebec (1697–1702), also presented a factual account of the savages.[9] Potherie's book enjoyed a wide sale and went through four editions (owing perhaps to its illustrations and its fashionable note of skepticism). But the author lifted many of his facts from earlier accounts, to which his brief residence in the country lent a spurious air of authenticity.

As New France became more settled, a small class of merchants and petty officials came to prominence. These men, anxious to see the colony grow, advertised its benefits. Their "true and natural" histories often included chapters on "the manners, customs,

5. *Bref récit et succincte narration de la navigation faite en 1535 et 1536; Brief récit et succincte narration de la navigation faicte es ysles de Canada* (Paris, 1865); *Discours du voyage fait par le capitaine Iacques Cartier aux Terres-Neufves de Canadas, Norembegue, Hochelage, Labrador et pays adiacens, dite Nouvelle France* (Paris, 1865).

6. *Journal historique du dernier voyage que feu M. de la Sale fit dans le golfe de Mexique pour trouver l'embouchure et le cours de la rivière de Missisipi* (Paris, 1713).

7. *Histoire de la Louisiane* (Paris, 1758).

8. *Oeuvres* (5 vols., Québec, 1870).

9. Claude C. le Roy Bacqueville de la Potherie, *Nouveau voyage du Canada et de la Nouvelle France, et les guerres des français avec les anglais et les originaires du pays* (4 vols., Paris, 1716).

and religion" of the natives. Pierre Boucher started the vogue with a methodical description of the geographical features, vegetation, and animals of the land and a brief general treatment of the Indians.[10] Being a trader at Three Rivers, after a youth spent among the Hurons, Boucher knew his subject well. He presented nothing new, but he provided prospective colonists with a handy catalogue of information. Nicolas Denys, a merchant and provincial governor in Acadia, published a similar book a few years later.[11] While Denys did not know the Indians so intimately and his book had a more commercial tone, his final chapter sympathetically contrasted the present corruption of the savages with their former natural innocence. Soon afterward Nicolas Perrot, who had interpreted and negotiated for the French with the western tribes, devoted a book entirely to the Indians, which he based upon his own experiences.[12] The last factual account to issue from French Canada (published, ironically, in London) came from the pen of Thomas Pichon.[13] Pichon served as secretary to the governor of Cape Breton and turned spy for the English in 1759. He knew the Indians well and described them with some art. He argued strongly that they were reasonable human beings, and therefore they deserved from the white men a rational, tolerant rule. As at the beginning of French rule in Canada, so at the end: the firsthand observers—whether lay or religious—presented their facts with reference to the intellectual mood that dominated France. In 1610 orthodoxy reigned; in 1760 rationalism. The savage served the uses of both.

Four Jesuit treatments merit brief mention, before a consideration of how the savage served the philosophes. Two of these represented editions of the Relations; the remaining two combined historical or didactic speculation with direct observation. In 1664 François du Creux culled from the Relations examples of Indian atrocity, wove them into a narrative of the growth of the missions, and issued the whole as a history of Canada.[14] As he admitted, Du

10. *Histoire véritable et naturelle des moeurs et productions du pays de la Nouvelle France* (Paris, 1663).

11. *Description géographique et historique des costes de l'Amerique Septentrionale* (Paris, 1671).

12. *Mémoire sur les moeurs, coustumes, et relligion des sauvages de l'Amérique Septentrionale* (Paris, 1864).

13. *Lettres et mémoires pour servir à l'histoire naturelle, civile, et politique de Cap Breton* (Londres, 1760).

14. Franciscus Creuxius, *Historia Canadensis* (Parisis, 1664).

Creux was pleading for adequate military defense of the colony. He presented no new facts, but he did give old ones a wider currency. The other abridgment made a less special case. Joseph Jouvency, writing a general history of the order, produced a generalized account of the Indians, which he distilled from the writings of Biard and various Relations.[15] In the larger work the chapters dealing with New France could not have made much sense to people not already conversant with the American mission field. But undoubtedly Jouvency too brought the savage to the attention of many new readers.

Unlike Du Creux and Jouvency, Joseph Lafitau and Pierre Charlevoix spent several years in New France. Both priests interlarded their knowledge of the savages with classical erudition and literary pretension. Neither sought simply to inform; both, with pedantry, to edify. The scholarly Lafitau produced much more than a compendium of American customs. Fully conscious of the threats to orthodoxy in his day, he tried to prove the universality of divine revelation and thus conquer atheism and deism.[16] He attacked the opinion that the savages were beasts simply because they were pagans. He scanned Indian legends and customs for intimations of God, compared his findings with similar aspects of ancient primitive societies, and offered the fruits of his study as historical corroboration of the validity of Christianity. Lafitau saw in revelation a source of religion common to all men. On that religious basis, he argued, despite the alterations of ritual and custom that various peoples have undergone, common legal and moral codes should also prevail throughout the world. For this attempt to relate culture to the influence of religion among primitive societies Meinicke has compared Lafitau to his illustrious Italian contemporary Vico.[17] Lafitau also opened broad vistas for the embryonic social sciences; and he convincingly demonstrated that the method of empirical rationalism was no monopoly of Cartesians and skeptics; the church could use it legitimately in self-defense.

Beside the bold originality of Lafitau, Charlevoix seems a pedes-

15. *De regione et moribus Canadensium seu barbarorum Novae Franciae* (Romae, 1710); *Canadicae missionis relatio ab anno 1611 usque ad annum 1613, cum statu eiusdem missionis annis 1703 et 1710* (Romae, 1710).

16. *Moeurs des sauvages américquains,* I, 5–16.

17. Friedrich Meinicke, *Die Entstehung des Historismus* (2 vols., Berlin, 1936), I, 74–77.

trian compiler of facts.[18] But what Charlevoix lacked in scholarship he made up in his didactic fervor. He particularly brought out two points that earlier missionaries had merely mentioned: for all their faults, the Americans seemed naturally more virtuous than Europeans; and what would happen when they added to their natural virtue the supernatural aids of the faith? In an effort to elevate the personal morality and stimulate the devotion of his readers, Charlevoix harped on these two themes again and again. He used his experiences and the writings of his predecessors as texts for sermons. His books achieved a widespread commercial success and have left an apparently indelible stamp on the European concept of the American savage.

By 1722, when Charlevoix completed his journal, the savage must have already grown used to being the subject of discussion, whether of a homiletic or a more worldly variety. During his formative years the savage remained almost exclusively the property of devout Catholics. But the firsthand accounts were propagating his fame. At the same time dissent from the established codes of religion, philosophy, and social theory was spreading, Sensationalism, grafted upon Cartesian logic, led to natural or empirical rationalism. Scientific discovery was making the world more anthropocentric, and rationalizing a revived classical pantheism into a new deism. Travel and exploration stimulated rather than dispelled curiosity about the primitive and the exotic.

Voltaire, in L' Ingénu, brought his Huron to France in 1689—a more significant date for his arrival than either 1534 or 1607. At that time, during what Paul Hazard has called a crise de conscience, the orthodox began to yield the intellectual leadership of France to the freethinkers. They also surrendered many of their former monopolies. The savage, whom orthodox men, in large measure, had created on orthodox principles, came into the public domain. The Cartesians and skeptics seized upon the savage as a vehicle for their own ideas—often to destroy those very men and principles.

Nevertheless, the savage leaped neither suddenly nor wholly into the arms of the critics of official doctrines. Whenever the missionaries praised an aspect of Indian life that had a counterpart in France, they certainly implied criticism. Yet they contemplated reform within the existing framework of absolutism and orthodoxy,

18. Journal; Histoire et description générale de la Nouvelle France (4 vols., Paris, 1744).

consonant with the Counter Reformation. Likewise the lay observers, except for a few comments from Bacqueville de la Potherie and Pichon (both late), left their criticism implicit. On the other hand, the freethinkers who visited New France leavened their observations with a conspicuous amount of pointed reference to institutions at home. Those critics who stayed in France cavalierly assumed a thorough knowledge of the facts of Indian life in themselves and their readers and used those facts to annotate their theories.

In the seventeenth century one writer had already taken advantage of his personal contact with the Indians to criticize institutions in France explicitly. Marc Lescarbot stood apart from his plainer contemporaries, Champlain and Biard, by reason of his conscious artistry and his fundamental escapism. In 1606, "to flee a corrupt world," Lescarbot gave up his law practice in Paris and sailed for Port Royal, which Poutrincourt had just founded. He remained in Acadia over a year and then returned home, to resume his career and win high repute as the first historian of New France.[19] During the regency Lescarbot's works probably overshadowed those of Biard and Champlain in sustaining interest in America. Generally Lescarbot shared the hopes of his contemporaries for the country. He prayed fervently for the conversion of the heathens.[20] He begged the queen mother to support the infant colony, told his compatriots it was their duty to help civilize the barbarians, and counted up the riches that the land offered to settlers.[21] Such aims might have labeled Lescarbot as one more lay narrator who gave his work a literary fillip.

But two personal factors distinguished his treatment. In the first place, Lescarbot escaped to New France from injustice at home. His heart still remained in his career. While Biard made New France a duty, and Champlain a life work, Lescarbot made it a mere enthusiasm—genuine but transitory. In the second place, he saw a fellow victim of society in Poutrincourt. As he avowed,

19. *Histoire de la Nouvelle France* (3e ed., Paris, 1618), p. 502–503; *La Défaite des sauvages armouchiquois par le sagamos, Membertou et ses alliez sauvages* (Boston, 1927); "La Conversion des sauvages," *Jesuit Relations,* I, 49–113; "Relation dernière de ce qui s'est passé au voyage du Sieur Poutrincourt," *Jesuit Relations,* II, 119–191; *Les Muses de la Nouvelle France* (Paris, 1618).

20. "La Conversion des sauvages," *Jesuit Relations,* I, 63, 80, 83–85; *Histoire de la Nouvelle France,* p. 7, 605–608, 712–713.

21. "La Conversion des sauvages," *Jesuit Relations,* I, 55–69, 89, 91, 101; *La Défaite des sauvages armouchiquois,* p. 105; *Histoire de la Nouvelle France,* p. 6, 708–921 *passim.*

the desire to champion that hapless man motivated all his writings; and he heaped scorn on the court, the Jesuits, and rival traders for their shabby treatment of his hero.[22] Thus Lescarbot's concern for New France grew out of personal quarrels, not harmonious cooperation, with the established order. Finding a temporary haven from less congenial conditions at home, he often lapsed into extravagant praise of the people who had welcomed him. His last work, a lyric masque, nearly portrayed the country as another Arcadia.

No one else in the seventeenth century put his American experience to the same critical use as Lescarbot. When later critical observers appeared, they found the description of the savage already quite complete. Accordingly, they made less mention of the specific physical aspects of Indian life. Instead, anxious above all to secure wide audiences for their views, they put a heavier emphasis upon the novelty of their presentation.

Louis-Armand de Lom d'Arce, Baron de Lahontan (1666–1715?), vividly demonstrated the new tendency among critics. When Lahontan was eight his father died, and the son's inheritance was swallowed up by debts. Until 1693 the landless baron sued in the courts and at Versailles to recover his estates and prerogatives, but in vain. In the meantime he served as a valiant if fractious officer in New France. In 1693, fearing exile or imprisonment, Lahontan fled French soil and began a vagabondage that lasted presumably to his death. His books about New France were published ten years after he left America, to earn money and win patronage in "enlightened" circles.[23] He succeeded, and his modernism brought him sudden if fleeting fame.

Like Lescarbot, Lahontan regarded New France in the light of his personal problems; but the former's troubles had lasted only a year, while Lahontan's vitiated his entire life. It is not surprising, then, that he venomously indicted the whole complex of European society. He despised religion and monarchy, law courts and ministers, and would replace them all with the ideals of equality and anarchy he found in America. People who kneeled to such demigods as ministers of state he called more savage than

22. "La Conversion des sauvages," *Jesuit Relations,* I, 63–65, 80–82; "Relation dernière," *Jesuit Relations,* II, 127, 129, 137, 147.

23. *Nouveaux voyages de M. le baron de Lahontan* (La Haye, 1703); *Mémoires de l'Amérique Septentrionale, ou la suite des voyages de M. le baron de Lahontan* (La Haye, 1703); *Supplement aux voyages de M. le baron de Lahontan* (La Haye, 1703).

the Indians. Property, which the Americans lacked, seemed to him "the sole source of all the disorders that trouble the society of Europeans." [24] Yet Lahontan himself had bent the knee before royal secretaries and scrambled panting after his inheritance. Not simply an escapist, he was also a malcontent.

Nevertheless, Lahontan released the American savage from the spiritual atmosphere that had hitherto surrounded him. In the *Supplement aux voyages* Adario, "a savage of good sense who has traveled," in his own right as a creature of natural reason criticized French civilization. Now, in 1703, as M. Chinard has written, the battle between the philosophes and the orthodox was joined—before the *Lettres persanes* or the *Lettres philosophiques*. In addition, Lahontan "definitively fixed the character of the 'good savage,' of the 'man of nature' whose figure was to dominate the entire literature of the coming century." [25] The savage lost the stamp of classical primitivism that he had retained down through Fénelon's account of the natives of Bétique (1699). He emerged as the missionaries knew him: with red skin, lank black hair, normal intelligence, natural morals, and barbarous manners. But Lahontan did more than determine the character of the savage. He also determined the roles he would play in secular literature: passively, the model of conduct, and actively, the critic.

Yet before he could play either role effectively, the savage needed introduction to people outside his former claque of the devout and the curious—to the vulgar, the sophisticated, and the frivolous. The widespread success of Lahontan's books began the process. Another popularization, gayer but less penetrating, was the rhymed account of Diéreville, a commercial agent who spent less than a year in Acadia.[26] Indian manners amused Diéreville. He praised the savages for their natural morality and especially for their lack of hypocrisy. He agreed with the missionaries that men were men everywhere, but couched his proof in far more flippant language. Thus, with regard to sexual promiscuity:

> Women are always pleased by size and strength,
> No need to search so far, we find such near;

24. Gilbert Chinard, ed., *Dialogues curieux entre l'auteur et un sauvage de bon sens qui a voyagé et mémoires de l'Amérique Septentrionale* (Baltimore, 1931), p. 75–78, 82–84.

25. *Ibid.*, Introd., p. 70–72.

26. *Relation du voyage du Port Royal de l'Acadie, ou de la Nouvelle France* . . . (Rouen, 1708).

How many ladies here prefer
To their own husbands slim and small,
A lackey, vigorous and tall? [27]

Such wit made the savage welcome to many who could not stomach
the ponderous pieties or crudities of more earnest commentators.
Other observers catered to more genteel tastes, like the traveler
Bonrepos. He dedicated his book "to Mademoiselle D————," that
she might shine in the salons and be both clever and wise when
she talked of Louisiana.[28] Bonrepos did not criticize French society any more seriously than Diéreville. Rather, in the urbane
manner of Fontenelle, he spread new knowledge among people of
fashion.

The last critical writer in New France, Claude Lebeau, also
wrote primarily to spread information. A rake and a wastrel,
Lebeau had been deported to the colony at the instigation of his
father. Like Lescarbot and Lahontan, he came to America because he could not conform at home. But Lebeau was no sour escapist; he made no attempt to justify himself. Instead, he determined to enjoy his punishment and promptly launched into a
liaison with an Iroquois woman. If Lebeau spiced his book with
romantic adventures, he produced no mere fictional tale. He
sketched Indian customs with a keen and faithful eye. Knowing
the savages well, he liked them and wrote that he wished to correct the false impression of them that Lahontan had created. He
accused the angry baron of distorting the truth and putting his
own ideas into the mouths of the Indians. Enough of a freethinker
to scorn the Jesuits as "slaves of a vile interest," Lebeau yet
found the priests generally told the truth about the Indians.[29]
Admittedly, the savages combined horrifying vices with eminent
virtues; still, the French should respect them because they lived
by the laws of nature alone.

As a model, the savage served the lay critics even better than
he did the missionaries. In fact, the missionaries (except Charlevoix and Lafitau) focused their attention on the savage himself;
only tacitly and incidentally did they draw a contrast with the
Indians unfavorable to the French. On the other hand, the free-

27. *Relation of the Voyage to Port Royal in Acadia or New France*, p. 186.

28. Chevalier de Bonrepos, *Description du Mississippi* (Paris, 1720).

29. *Avantures du Sr. C. Lebeau ou voyage curieux et nouveau, parmi les sauvages de l'Amérique Septentrionale* (2 vols., Amsterdam, 1738), I, "Epître dédi-
catoire," "Préface," 264–265, 268; II, 2.

thinkers, searching for ideal criteria of conduct, were pleased to find them among the savages.

Rousseau raised the savage to his highest eminence as a model of human perfection and praised him particularly for his freedom and equality. The savage for him owed his virtue to instinct unspoiled by corroding reason. In the *Discourse on Inequality* Rousseau drew heavily on the accounts from New France for his conception of the savage, who, he imagined, simply existed, like an animal. A benevolent providence, depriving him of the power of abstraction, limited his wants to the physical order; he satisfied the desires of his robust and healthy body: he was happy. "There was neither education nor progress; the generations multiplied without purpose; and, each one always starting from the same place, the centuries rolled on in all the rudeness of the first ages, the species was already old, and man still remained a child." [30] Such conditions were conducive to anarchic individualism and self-reliance; therefore, Rousseau concluded, "inequality is hardly noticeable in the state of nature." [31]

With respect to freedom and equality, other philosophes agreed with Rousseau. In its definition of *Sauvage*, for instance, the *Encyclopédie* made freedom the mark of distinction:

All the Indian people who are not subject to the yoke of the country and who live apart are called savage. There is this difference between the savages and the barbarians, that the first are made up of little, dispersed nations who do not wish to unite, while the barbarians often unite, and that happens when one chief has conquered others. Natural freedom is the only object of the polity of the savages; with this freedom do nature and climate rule almost alone among them. . . . Withdrawn to the forests and mountains, they maintain their freedom and find there abundant nourishment. . . . barbarous people who live without laws, without police, without religion, and who have no fixed dwelling.[32]

Voltaire's deism led him to concede a sort of equality, as well, to the savages. After calling "those who inhabit the forests of America innumerable subjects of invincible error," he added the follow-

---

30. Jean Jacques Rousseau, *Discours sur l'origine et les fondements de l'inégalité parmi les hommes* (Cambridge, 1941), p. 61.
31. *Ibid.*, p. 64.
32. *Encyclopédie ou dictionnaire raisonné des sciences, des arts et des métiers* (3e ed., 36 vols., Genève, 1778–79).

ing lines: "God has created us, God would save us all: everywhere he instructs us, everywhere he speaks to us; he engraves in every heart the law of nature, alone the same forever, and alone always pure. By this law, without doubt, he judges the pagans, and if their hearts have been true, they have been Christian." [33]

But over savage reason most philosophes quarreled violently with Rousseau. As the baleful offspring of civilized society, the Genevan hated reason. He dreaded the advance of civilization upon a state of nature just because it destroyed the virtue that grew out of man's animal instincts. His contemporaries, on the contrary, prided themselves on their rationalism and valued the savage the more highly because he enjoyed his reason in a free and natural condition. It was reason that gave Indian freedom and equality their real significance. If the savage suffered now from "invincible error," that was the fault of ignorance. Reason, if corruptible, was not inherently corrupt—as the orthodox had also thought. Voltaire scolded Rousseau for debasing man to the level of an animal.[34] Yet, whether rationalist or antirationalist, the philosophes agreed that the savage furnished examples of conduct which reformers could advocate with profit.

In 1703 Adario, Lahontan's friend, turned the tables on the French: he became the critic, they the subject. But Adario had been content to remain in America. Twenty-five years later the savage took the final step of his progress in France. Following the fashion set by the Persians, Rica and Usbek, he came to see France for himself. In the same year that Lebeau's *Avantures* appeared, the "expatriate savage" Zakaro published the letters he was writing to "his correspondent in America." Zakaro probably borrowed his epistolary skill from one Joubert de la Rue and from the Marquis d'Argens, another of those disinherited aristocrats who found life under the French Catholic monarchy intolerable. "A philosophical savage," Zakaro judged the French according to his "poor savage reason"; he found both their manners unreasonable and their morals corrupt.[35] He named as the root of their evils Catholicism, a fraud that a grasping priesthood—led by the Jesuits—had organized for the sake of power.

33. Louis Moland, ed., *Oeuvres complètes de Voltaire* (52 vols., Paris, 1877–85), VIII, 171–172.

34. *Ibid.*, XXXVIII, 447.

35. J. Joubert de la Rue and Jean Baptiste de Boyer, marquis d'Argens, *Lettres d'un sauvage dépaysé, contenant une critique des moeurs du siècle, et des réflexions sur les matières de religion et de politique* (Amsterdam, 1738), p. 13, 38.

Zakaro did not reject Christian morality; but he accused the church of perverting it, and castigated all Europeans for their religious intolerance. He himself would always be happy to offer "the respectful worship due to the supreme being alone, the sovereign of the heavens and the earth." And he concluded that "they would be very happy in these countries if they enjoyed here that freedom of conscience that people in America enjoy." [36]

If, with typical Indian courage, Zakaro had crossed the ocean, yet with equal modesty he refrained from injecting himself into his letters. Igli, a later American critic, whom Maubert de Gouvest conjured up, had all the attributes of a real person.[37] More at home in France and more conversant with French ways, he contrasted them quite specifically with the customs of his homeland. Where the French amused Zakaro, they provoked in Igli nothing but scorn. He despised the Jesuits and the hierarchy and dogmas of the church and mercilessly ridiculed justice, administration, and the caprices of the aristocracy. But he admired "the people" and carefully avoided direct attacks on the king himself.

When Voltaire's *L'Ingénu* appeared in 1767, the characterization of the savage in France was complete.

On the evening of the fifteenth of July, in the year 1689, the Abbé de Kerkabon, prior of Notre Dame de la Montagne, was taking the air along the seashore with his sister, Mlle. de Kerkabon. . . .

As he looked out to sea, the prior said to his sister, "Alas, here it is that our poor brother embarked with his dear wife, our dear sister-in-law Mme. de Kerkabon, on the frigate *Hirondelle* in 1669, to go to serve his king in Canada. If he had not been killed we might hope to see him again."

"Do you think," asked Mlle. de Kerkabon, "that our sister-in-law has been eaten by the Iroquois, as we were told? If she had not been eaten, surely she would have come home. . . ."

As they were both growing sentimental over these memories, they saw a little ship come into the Bay of Rence on the tide; it was manned by Englishmen coming to sell things from their country. They jumped ashore without noticing M. the prior or Mlle. his sister, who was most offended at the scant attention they paid her.

Not so with a very handsome youth who leaped with one bound over

36. *Ibid.,* p. 38, 61.
37. J. H. Maubert de Gouvest, *Lettres iroquoises* (Irocopolis, 1752); cf. J. J. Rufus, *Lettres chérakéesiennes* (Rome, 1769), a reprinting of 36 of the 43 *Lettres iroquoises.*

the heads of his comrades and pulled up face to face with Mlle. He nodded to her, not being accustomed to bow. His face and dress attracted the brother and sister. He was bareheaded and barelegged; his feet were shod in light sandals; his head was graced with long braids; a short jacket enclosed a lithe and agile figure; his bearing was martial and gentle. He held in one hand a small bottle of Barbados water and in the other a sort of pouch in which were a goblet and very good sea biscuit. He spoke French most intelligibly. He offered his Barbados water to Mlle. de Kerkabon and to M. her brother. He drank with them. He made them drink again and all with such a simple and natural air that the brother and sister were entranced with him. They offered him their services and asked him who he was and where he was going. The youth answered that he did not know, he was curious, and had wanted to see how the coasts of France looked; he had come and now he was going to go home.

M. the prior, guessing that he was not English by his accent, took the liberty of asking him where his home was. "I am Huron," the youth replied.[38]

L'Ingénu—he had no other name, speaking always as he thought and doing as he wished—played both the roles in which the philosophes cast the savage. His conduct showed him a model of what a man should be; and he criticized the weaknesses of French society with reason and candor. The conduct, moreover, sharpened the criticism, which in turn made the conduct reasonable. As the Huron made his way through the tangle of French life, he demonstrated the virtues for which his people had become famed. His innocence embroiled him in absurdities and hardships, from which reason could not extricate him, so averse were the French to natural ways of thinking and acting. But Hercules—as he was baptized, after seeing the reasonableness of that rite—always displayed a savage's dignity and manliness. When, for artistic purposes, Hercules turned out to be the nephew of the Kerkabons, he simply proved the superiority of environment over innate ideas in forming a man. To Voltaire L'Ingénu was a savage drawn from life: a natural man. If he closely resembled the philosophical savages Adario and Igli, that too was only natural. His kind was well known.

The savage in France possessed all the traits that the missionaries, explorers, and colonists had claimed for him. At least the

38. Moland, ed., *Oeuvres complètes de Voltaire*, XXI, p. 247-249.

French, and Europeans generally, accepted their version of his character; and so they thought of him until the scientific re-examination of Indian culture in the nineteenth century. The orthodox men of the seventeenth century had introduced him—but not to use him. They regarded him as an end in himself, a soul to be saved for his own sake, and only secondarily for their own spiritual benefit and for the triumph of the church. They lost him, when the Counter Reformation stood on the defensive, to the enemies of their church. The philosophes and their fore-runners did not regard the savage primarily as an end in himself but rather as a weapon, for the benefit of natural men in their struggle against the enemies of rational reform.

"It is," wrote Raynal, who always echoed current common-places, "among these people that philosophers can study natural man. . . . Without doubt it is important to future generations not to lose the picture of the life and customs of the savages. It is perhaps to this knowledge that we owe all the progress that moral philosophy has made among us." [39] Rather than to any knowledge, it was to men of orthodoxy—above all the Jesuits in New France—who supplied "this knowledge" that Frenchmen truly owed their debt.

39. Guillaume T. F. Raynal, *Histoire philosophique des Indes* (7 vols., Amsterdam, 1773), VI, 19, 45.

BIBLIOGRAPHICAL NOTE

Guides

BESIDE the basic historical bibliographies dealing with France, some specialized works concerning the missionary orders, Canada, and the literature of travel and exploration have also been used.

Among the religious orders exhaustive aids exist for the writings of the Jesuits alone. These are: Augustin de Backer and Carlos Sommervogel, *Bibliothèque de la Compagnie de Jésus* (11 vols., Bruxelles, Paris, 1890–1932); and Ernest M. Rivière, *Corrections et additions à la Bibliothèque de la Compagnie de Jésus. Supplément au "De Backer-Sommervogel"* (Toulouse, 1911–30). The other orders have been less adequately treated; but two general works should be cited: Louis Bertrand, *Bibliothèque sulpicienne* (3 vols., Paris, 1900); and René de Nantes, *Bibliothèque d'histoire franciscaine* (Couvin, 1909). Reuben G. Thwaites, ed., *The Jesuit Relations and Allied Documents* (73 vols., Cleveland, 1896–1901), gives most comprehensive bibliographical information concerning the Jesuit writings that issued from New France, and renders all previous work on that subject obsolete. Nevertheless, for related American aspects the studies of Henry Harrisse, Edmund B. O'Callaghan, Justin Winsor, John G. Shea, and others remain essential. Since 1901 the chief contribution to Canadian Jesuitica has been James C. McCoy, *Jesuit Relations of Canada, 1632–1673* (Paris, 1937). R. P. Hugolin, *Notes bibliographiques pour servir à l'histoire des Récollets du Canada* (4 vols., Montréal, 1932–33) alone covers the writings of that order.

For Canada the most helpful single volume has been Henry Harrisse, *Notes pour servir à l'histoire, à la bibliographie et à la cartographie de la Nouvelle France et des pays adjacents* (Paris, 1872). A handy, more modern work is Frances M. Staton and Marie Tremaine, *A Bibliography of Canadiana* (Toronto, 1934).

Travel and exploration have nowhere received definitive treatment, although several of the *Authorities* below contain good partial lists. Among older works, the most profitable have proved to be: Boucher de la Richarderie, *Bibliothèque universelle des voyages* (6 vols., Paris, 1808); and John Pinkerton, *A General Collection of the Best and most Interesting Voyages and Travels* (17 vols., London, 1814), with particular reference to Vol. XVII. Séraphin Marion, *Relations de voyageurs français en Nouvelle France au XVIIe siècle* (Paris, 1923), presents critical comment on a highly selective list.

Sources

It has not seemed necessary to list all the materials studied or used. Full bibliographical information for material specifically cited has been given in the footnotes. Where not otherwise indicated, editions are original or facsimilies thereof.

Since Chapters VI–IX have aimed to epitomize the picture of the savages that the Jesuits presented to the French reading public, care has been taken to draw only upon sources published reasonably soon after they were written. To this rule there have been three exceptions—two of inclusion and one of omission. Antoine Silvy, *Relation par lettres de l'Amérique Septentrionale* (Paris, 1904); and Nicolas Perrot, *Mémoire sur les moeurs, coustumes, et relligion des sauvages de l'Amérique Septentrionale* (Paris, 1864), were both composed before 1700 and circulated in manuscript at that time. Because they exerted such a strong influence on Pierre F. X. Charlevoix, *Histoire et déscription générale de la Nouvelle France* (4 vols., Paris, 1744), they have been included with contemporary publications. For that same reason Charlevoix's *Histoire* has not been cited specifically; it revealed no facts that Silvy, Perrot, or other earlier writers had not already given. Charlevoix's chief contribution, his didacticism, came out more clearly in the *Journal d'un voyage fait par l'ordre du roi dans l'Amérique Septentrionale* (2 vols., Paris, 1744), which appeared in a uniform set with the *Histoire*.

Reuben G. Thwaites, ed., *The Jesuit Relations and Allied Documents,* contains almost the entire body of Canadian Jesuitica. It also lists Jesuit and related material known to exist that was not included in the series. Its chief faults are neither serious nor frequent: needlessly intricate indexes, some inaccurate historical annotation, and overgentility of translation which the present writer has tried to remedy. Otherwise the series is a model of editing and textual reproduction.

The following noncontemporary publications merit special mention here:

Jean Delanglez, ed., *Journal of Jean Cavelier* (Chicago, 1938); La Salle's last expedition recorded by his Sulpician brother.

François Dollier de Casson, *Histoire du Montréal, Mémoires de la Société Historique de Montréal,* Vol. IV (Montréal, 1869); by a Sulpician.

Sixte le Tac, *Histoire chronologique de la Nouvelle France* (Paris, 1888); by a Recollet.

Pierre Margry, ed., *Découvertes et établissements des français dans l'ouest et dans le sud de l'Amérique Septentrionale, 1614–1698* (6 vols., Paris, 1879–88); particularly valuable concerning La Salle, but also publishing many missionary documents.

François Vachon de Belmont, "Histoire du Canada," *Collection de mémoires et de relations sur l'histoire ancienne du Canada. Société Lit-*

téraire et Historique de Québec, Vol. I, Pt. 2 (Québec, 1840); by a Sulpician.

Authorities

No attempt is made to give full lists of the published literature on any phase of the subject of this book.

I. The Jesuits

Unfortunately the order has not yet found its Ranke. A comprehensive and impartial history must wait on the completion and monographic digestion of the *Monumenta Historica Societatis Jesu* (70 vols., Matriti, 1894–   ). Almost without exception, the extant general studies are controversial and prejudiced to a degree that makes them thoroughly unreliable. The most satisfactory is Joseph Brucker, *La Compagnie de Jésus* (Paris, 1919). James Brodrick has begun to use the material in the *Monumenta* in *The Origin of the Jesuits* (London, 1940), and *The Progress of the Jesuits* (London, 1947). But his approach so far is too biographical for a broad perspective; and he has not got beyond 1579. Brodrick's earlier work, *The Life and Works of Blessed Robert Francis Cardinal Bellarmine, S. J., 1542–1621* (2 vols., London, 1928), aside from being broader, brilliantly sets forth Bellarmine's career and is especially helpful with regard to Baianism and Molinism.

Concerning their educational contributions, the Jesuits have fared better. Gabriel Compayré, *Histoire critique des doctrines de l'éducation en France depuis le seizième siècle* (2 vols., Paris, 1911), very anti-Jesuit; and André Schimberg, *L'Education morale dans les collèges de la Compagnie de Jésus en France* (Paris, 1913), equally pro-Jesuit, are still good general treatments. But their prestige is being undermined by more recent special works, notably: Edward A. Fitzpatrick, *St. Ignatius and the Ratio Studiorum* (New York, 1933); Allan P. Farrell, *The Jesuit Code of Liberal Education* (Milwaukee, 1938); and two excellent critiques by François de Dainville, *La Géographie des humanistes* (Paris, 1940), and *La Naissance de l'humanisme moderne* (Paris, 1940).

While there are scores of accounts of separate Jesuit colleges, three stand out: Aristide Douarche, *L'Université de Paris et les Jésuites* (Paris, 1888); Gustave Dupont-Ferrier, *Du collège de Clermont au lycée Louis-le-Grand, 1563–1920* (3 vols., Paris, 1921–25); and Camille de Rochemonteix, *Un collège de Jésuites aux XVIIᵉ et XVIIIᵉ siècles. Le Collège Henri IV de la Flèche* (4 vols., Le Mans, 1889).

François Rousseau, *L'Idée missionaire aux XVIᵉ et XVIIᵉ siècles* (Paris, 1930), presents briefly "the doctrines, methods, and conceptions of organization" of the missions of that period. Joseph Schmidlin, *Catholic Mission Theory* (Techny, Illinois, 1933), analyzes the subject much more thoroughly and systematically.

II. New France

The best general treatment of this subject is still Francis Parkman, *Works* (11 vols., Boston, 1912). The pertinent sections of Justin Winsor, ed., *Narrative and Critical History of North America* (8 vols., Boston, 1884–89), are also indispensable. Gabriel L. Jaray, *L'Empire française d'Amérique (1534–1803)* (Paris, 1938), carries out the thesis of the *mission civilisatrice* but is guilty of frequent factual inaccuracies.

A. Exploration and Settlement

Justin Winsor, *Cartier to Frontenac: Geographical Discovery in the Interior of North America in Its Historical Relations, 1534–1700* (Boston, New York, 1894), furnishes the most competent introduction to Canadian exploration. The following have been especially useful: Narcisse E. Dionne, *La Nouvelle France de Cartier à Champlain, 1540–1603* (Québec, 1891); Henry P. Biggar, *The Precursors of Jacques Cartier, 1497–1534* (Ottawa, 1911); and Benjamin Sulte, "Poutrincourt en Acadie—1604–1623," *Mémoires et comptes rendus de la Société Royale du Canada pour l'année 1884* (Montreal, 1885), II, Sec. I, 31–50.

Champlain's life and work has been accorded full and competent treatment in Gabriel Gravier, *Vie de Samuel Champlain* (Paris, 1900); Narcisse E. Dionne, *Samuel Champlain* (2 vols., Québec, 1906); and Morris Bishop, *Champlain: The Life of Fortitude* (New York, 1948). The last is the most sympathetic and personal study, but it does not supersede the earlier works.

La Salle has not fared so well. Gabriel Gravier, *Découvertes et établissements de Cavelier de la Salle* (Paris, 1870), antedates the revelations of Margry. For more modern books the reader must be satisfied with Charles G. M. B. de la Roncière, *Le Père de la Louisiane, Cavelier de la Salle* (Tours, 1936).

The opening of the country to trade is well covered in Henry P. Biggar, *The Early Trading Companies of New France* (Toronto, 1901). Harold A. Innis, *The Fur Trade in Canada* (New Haven, 1930), is a definitive historical treatment. A precise, adequate account of colonists, companies, and commerce may be found in Ivanhoe Caron, *La Colonisation du Canada sous la domination française* (Québec, 1916).

B. Missionaries

Many books have dealt with the missionaries in New France, but most are either superficial or eulogies or condemnations. Exceptions are: Georges Goyau, *Une épopée mystique, les origines religieuses du Canada* (Paris, 1924), a very general introduction; Auguste H. Gosselin, *La Mission du Canada avant Monseigneur de Laval (1615–1659)* (Evreux, 1909), and *L'Eglise du Canada depuis Monseigneur de Laval jusqu'à la conquête* (3 vols., Québec, 1911–14).

With regard to the Jesuits several books supplement their own writings: Thomas A. Hughes, *History of the Society of Jesus in North America* (3 vols., London, 1907–17), Vol. II; Camille de Rochemonteix, *Les Jésuites et la Nouvelle France au XVII*ᵉ *siècle* (3 vols., Paris, 1895–96), and *Les Jésuites et la Nouvelle France au XVIII*ᵉ *siècle* (2 vols., Paris, 1906); Jean Delanglez, *Frontenac and the Jesuits* (Chicago, 1939), and *The French Jesuits in Lower Louisiana, 1700–1763* (Washington, 1935). Among a horde of biographies only two are worthy of notice: Francis X. Talbot, *Saint among Savages—the Life of Isaac Jogues* (New York, 1935), and *Saint among the Hurons—the Life of Jean de Brébeuf* (New York, 1949).

For the other orders the following have been helpful: H. R. Casgrain, *Les Sulpiciens et les prêtres des missions-étrangères en Acadie (1676–1762)* (Québec, 1897); and O. M. Jouve, *Les Franciscains et le Canada* (2 vols., Québec, 1915–34).

The following have given indispensable reference aid:

Jean B. A. Allaire, *Dictionnaire biographique du clergé canadien-français* (6 vols., Montréal, 1908–34).

Mgr. Alfred Baudrillart, ed., *Dictionnaire d'histoire et de géographie écclesiastique* (11 vols., Paris, 1912–   ).

Arthur Melançon, *Liste des missionaires-jésuites, Nouvelle-France et Louisiane, 1611–1800* (Montréal, 1929).

Cyprien Tanguay, *Repertoire général du clergé canadien, par ordre chronologique* (Québec, 1868).

C. Indians

Clark Wissler, *The American Indian* (New York, 1917), provides an excellent introduction. Lewis H. Morgan, *Ancient Society* (New York, 1878), while obsolescent, demonstrates the far-reaching influence of the missionary writings and proved most provocative. More special treatments include: Alfred G. Bailey, *Conflict of European and Eastern Algonkian Cultures, 1504–1700* (St. John, 1937); Horatio E. Hale, *The Iroquois Book of Rites* (Philadelphia, 1883), a linguistic study; Arthur E. Jones, *"Thendake Ehen" or Old Huronia* (Toronto, 1909), a painstaking geographical investigation; and William C. MacLeod, *The Origin of the State* (Philadelphia, 1924), a very thoughtful revaluation of tribal government.

III. *Orthodox and* philosophique *Thought*

Orthodox opinion is exhaustively presented in Henri Brémond, *Histoire littéraire du sentiment religieux en France, depuis la fin des guerres de la religion jusqu'à nos jours* (11 vols., Paris, 1916–33), for seventeenth-century churchmen; and in Henri Busson, *La Pensée religieuse française de Charron à Pascal* (Paris, 1933); and Albert Monod, *De Pascal à Chateaubriand* (Paris, 1916), for the contemporary laity. Gustave Lanson,

"Origines et premières manifestations de l'ésprit philosophique dans la littérature française de 1675 à 1748," and "Formation et développement de l'ésprit philosophique au XVIIIᵉ siècle," *Révue hebdomadaire des cours et conférences,* XVI–XVIII (1907–10), *passim;* have presented *philosophique* tendencies with equal mastery. Paul Hazard, *La Crise de la conscience européenne (1680–1715)* (3 vols., Paris, 1935), has interpreted the opinion of both groups at the crucial period of their rivalry. R. R. Palmer, *Catholics and Unbelievers in Eighteenth-century France* (Princeton, 1939), has, by re-examining the attitude of both parties toward nature, rendered Hazard somewhat obsolete. Palmer has also, in the process, contributed heavily to a revision of studies about the period that would retain the distinctions yet diminish the antipathies that historians have seen between the ideas, if not the basic premises, held by the two groups.

Scores of titles exist criticizing the literature of travel and the savage. Here only those most closely related need be mentioned:

Geoffroy Atkinson, *Relations de voyages de XVIIᵉ siècle et l'évolution des idées* (Paris, 1924).

———, *The Extraordinary Voyage in French Literature before 1700* (New York, 1920).

———, *The Extraordinary Voyage in French Literature from 1700 to 1720* (Paris, 1922).

Gilbert Chinard, *L'Amérique et le rêve exotique dans la littérature française au XVIIᵉ et XVIIIᵉ siècle* (Paris, 1913); a search for pre-romantic tendencies, including considerations of the missionary writings.

Hoxie N. Fairchild, *The Noble Savage: A Study in Romantic Naturalism* (New York, 1928); literary manifestations of the subject in England.

Arthur O. Lovejoy, "The Supposed Primitivism of Rousseau's *Discourse on Inequality,*" *Modern Philology,* XXI (1923), 165–186.

INDEX